A Brief History of Neoliberalism

A Brief History of Neoliberalism

David Harvey

OXFORD
UNIVERSITY PRESS

OXFORD

UNIVERSITY PRESS

Great Clarendon Street, Oxford OX2 6DP

Oxford University Press is a department of the University of Oxford.
It furthers the University's objective of excellence in research, scholarship,
and education by publishing worldwide in

Oxford New York

Auckland Cape Town Dar es Salaam Hong Kong Karachi
Kuala Lumpur Madrid Melbourne Mexico City Nairobi
New Delhi Shanghai Taipei Toronto

With offices in

Argentina Austria Brazil Chile Czech Republic France Greece
Guatemala Hungary Italy Japan Poland Portugal Singapore
South Korea Switzerland Thailand Turkey Ukraine Vietnam

Oxford is a registered trade mark of Oxford University Press
in the UK and in certain other countries

Published in the United States
by Oxford University Press Inc., New York

© David Harvey 2005

The moral rights of the author have been asserted
Database right Oxford University Press (maker)

First published 2005
First published in paperback 2007
Reprinted 2009 (thrice)

British Library Cataloguing in Publication Data

Data available

Library of Congress Cataloging in Publication Data

Data to follow

Typeset by RefineCatch Limited, Bungay, Suffolk
Printed in Great Britain
on acid-free paper by
Clays Ltd, St Ives plc

ISBN 978–0–19–928326–2
ISBN 978–0–19–928327–9 (Pbk.)

Contents

Figures and Tables

Figures and Tables

Tables

Acknowledgements

Figures 4.1, 4.3, 4.4 and 5.1 are reproduced by kind permission of the Guilford Press from P. Dicken, *Global Shift: Reshaping the Global Economic Map in the 21st Century*. 4th Edition, 2003.

Figure 1.3 is reproduced courtesy of MIT Press Journals from Thomas Piketty and Emmanuel Saez, 'Income Inequality in the United States, 1913–1988,' *The Quarterly Journal of Economics*, 118:1 (February, 2003).

Figure 5.2 is reproduced courtesy of J. Perloff from Wu, X and Perloff, J, *China's Income Distribution over Time: Reasons for Rising Inequality*. CUDARE Working Papers 977.

Figure 1.6 is reproduced courtesy of Verso Press from R. Pollin, *Contours of Descent*, 2003.

Figures 1.4, 1.7, 1.8, 1.9 and 7.1 are reproduced by kind permission of Gérard Duménil and are available on the website http://www.cebremap.ens.fr/levy.

Figures 1.2, 1.5 and 6.2 reprinted by permission of the publisher from *Capital Resurgent: Roots of the Neoliberal Revolution* by Gérard Duménil and Dominique Lévy, translated by Derek Jeffers, Cambridge, Mass.: Harvard University Press, Copyright © 2004 by the President and Fellows of Harvard College.

Figure 4.2 is reproduced courtesy Blackwell Publishing from S. Corbridge, *Debt and Development*, 1993.

Introduction

Future historians may well look upon the years 1978–80 as a revolutionary turning-point in the world's social and economic history. In 1978, Deng Xiaoping took the first momentous steps towards the liberalization of a communist-ruled economy in a country that accounted for a fifth of the world's population. The path that Deng defined was to transform China in two decades from a closed backwater to an open centre of capitalist dynamism with sustained growth rates unparalleled in human history. On the other side of the Pacific, and in quite different circumstances, a relatively obscure (but now renowned) figure named Paul Volcker took command at the US Federal Reserve in July 1979, and within a few months dramatically changed monetary policy. The Fed thereafter took the lead in the fight against inflation no matter what its consequences (particularly as concerned unemployment). Across the Atlantic, Margaret Thatcher had already been elected Prime Minister of Britain in May 1979, with a mandate to curb trade union power and put an end to the miserable inflationary stagnation that had enveloped the country for the preceding decade. Then, in 1980, Ronald Reagan was elected President of the United States and, armed with geniality and personal charisma, set the US on course to revitalize its economy by supporting Volcker's moves at the Fed and adding his own particular blend of policies to curb the power of labour, deregulate industry, agriculture, and resource extraction, and liberate the powers of finance both internally and on the world stage. From these several epicentres, revolutionary impulses seemingly spread and reverberated to remake the world around us in a totally different image.

Transformations of this scope and depth do not occur by accident. So it is pertinent to enquire by what means and paths the new economic configuration—often subsumed under the term 'globalization'—was plucked from the entrails of the old. Volcker, Reagan, Thatcher, and Deng Xaioping all took minority arguments that had long been in circulation and made them majoritarian (though in no case without a protracted struggle). Reagan brought to life the minority tradition that stretched back within the Republican Party to Barry Goldwater in the early 1960s. Deng saw the rising tide of wealth and influence in Japan, Taiwan, Hong Kong, Singapore, and South Korea and sought to mobilize market socialism instead of central planning to protect and advance the interests of the Chinese state. Volcker and Thatcher both plucked from the shadows of relative obscurity a particular doctrine that went under the name of 'neoliberalism' and transformed it into the central guiding principle of economic thought and management. And it is with this doctrine—its origins, rise, and implications—that I am here primarily concerned.[1]

Neoliberalism is in the first instance a theory of political economic practices that proposes that human well-being can best be advanced by liberating individual entrepreneurial freedoms and skills within an institutional framework characterized by strong private property rights, free markets, and free trade. The role of the state is to create and preserve an institutional framework appropriate to such practices. The state has to guarantee, for example, the quality and integrity of money. It must also set up those military, defence, police, and legal structures and functions required to secure private property rights and to guarantee, by force if need be, the proper functioning of markets. Furthermore, if markets do not exist (in areas such as land, water, education, health care, social security, or environmental pollution) then they must be created, by state action if necessary. But beyond these tasks the state should not venture. State interventions in markets (once created) must be kept to a bare minimum because, according to the theory, the state cannot possibly possess enough information to second-guess market signals (prices) and because powerful interest groups will inevitably distort and bias state interventions (particularly in democracies) for their own benefit.

There has everywhere been an emphatic turn towards neoliberalism in political-economic practices and thinking since the 1970s.

Introduction

Deregulation, privatization, and withdrawal of the state from many areas of social provision have been all too common. Almost all states, from those newly minted after the collapse of the Soviet Union to old-style social democracies and welfare states such as New Zealand and Sweden, have embraced, sometimes voluntarily and in other instances in response to coercive pressures, some version of neoliberal theory and adjusted at least some policies and practices accordingly. Post-apartheid South Africa quickly embraced neoliberalism, and even contemporary China, as we shall see, appears to be headed in this direction. Furthermore, the advocates of the neoliberal way now occupy positions of considerable influence in education (the universities and many 'think tanks'), in the media, in corporate boardrooms and financial institutions, in key state institutions (treasury departments, the central banks), and also in those international institutions such as the International Monetary Fund (IMF), the World Bank, and the World Trade Organization (WTO) that regulate global finance and trade. Neoliberalism has, in short, become hegemonic as a mode of discourse. It has pervasive effects on ways of thought to the point where it has become incorporated into the common-sense way many of us interpret, live in, and understand the world.

The process of neoliberalization has, however, entailed much 'creative destruction', not only of prior institutional frameworks and powers (even challenging traditional forms of state sovereignty) but also of divisions of labour, social relations, welfare provisions, technological mixes, ways of life and thought, reproductive activities, attachments to the land and habits of the heart. In so far as neoliberalism values market exchange as 'an ethic in itself, capable of acting as a guide to all human action, and substituting for all previously held ethical beliefs', it emphasizes the significance of contractual relations in the marketplace.[2] It holds that the social good will be maximized by maximizing the reach and frequency of market transactions, and it seeks to bring all human action into the domain of the market. This requires technologies of information creation and capacities to accumulate, store, transfer, analyse, and use massive databases to guide decisions in the global marketplace. Hence neoliberalism's intense interest in and pursuit of information technologies (leading some to proclaim the emergence of a new kind of 'information society'). These technologies have compressed the rising density of market transactions in both space and time. They have produced a particularly intensive burst of what I have elsewhere called 'time-space compression'. The greater the geographical range (hence the emphasis on 'globalization') and the shorter the term of market contracts the better. This latter preference parallels Lyotard's famous description of the postmodern condition as one where 'the temporary contract' supplants 'permanent institutions in the professional, emotional, sexual, cultural, family and international domains, as well as in political affairs'. The cultural consequences of the dominance of such a market ethic are legion, as I earlier showed in *The Condition of Postmodernity*.[3]

While many general accounts of global transformations and their effects are now available, what is generally missing—and this is the gap this book aims to fill—is the political-economic story of where neoliberalization came from and how it proliferated so comprehensively on the world stage. Critical engagement with that story suggests, furthermore, a framework for identifying and constructing alternative political and economic arrangements.

I have benefited in recent times from conversations with Gerard Duménil, Sam Gindin, and Leo Panitch. I have more long-standing debts to Masao Miyoshi, Giovanni Arrighi, Patrick Bond, Cindi Katz, Neil Smith, Bertell Ollman, Maria Kaika, and Erik Swyngedouw. A conference on neoliberalism sponsored by the Rosa Luxemburg Foundation in Berlin in November 2001 first sparked my interest in this topic. I thank the Provost at the CUNY Graduate Center, Bill Kelly, and my colleagues and students primarily but not exclusively in the Anthropology Program for their interest and support. I absolve everyone, of course, from any responsibility for the results.

1

Freedom's Just Another Word . . .

For any way of thought to become dominant, a conceptual apparatus has to be advanced that appeals to our intuitions and instincts, to our values and our desires, as well as to the possibilities inherent in the social world we inhabit. If successful, this conceptual apparatus becomes so embedded in common sense as to be taken for granted and not open to question. The founding figures of neoliberal thought took political ideals of human dignity and individual freedom as fundamental, as 'the central values of civilization'. In so doing they chose wisely, for these are indeed compelling and seductive ideals. These values, they held, were threatened not only by fascism, dictatorships, and communism, but by all forms of state intervention that substituted collective judgements for those of individuals free to choose.

Concepts of dignity and individual freedom are powerful and appealing in their own right. Such ideals empowered the dissident movements in eastern Europe and the Soviet Union before the end of the Cold War as well as the students in Tiananmen Square. The student movements that swept the world in 1968—from Paris and Chicago to Bangkok and Mexico City—were in part animated by the quest for greater freedoms of speech and of personal choice. More generally, these ideals appeal to anyone who values the ability to make decisions for themselves.

The idea of freedom, long embedded in the US tradition, has played a conspicuous role in the US in recent years. '9/11' was immediately interpreted by many as an attack on it. 'A peaceful world of growing freedom', wrote President Bush on the first anniversary of that awful day, 'serves American long-term interests, reflects enduring American ideals and unites America's allies.' 'Humanity', he concluded, 'holds in its hands the opportunity to offer freedom's triumph over all its age-old foes', and 'the United States welcomes its responsibilities to lead in this great mission'. This language was incorporated into the US National Defense Strategy document issued shortly thereafter. 'Freedom is the Almighty's gift to every man and woman in this world', he later said, adding that 'as the greatest power on earth we have an obligation to help the spread of freedom'.[1]

When all of the other reasons for engaging in a pre-emptive war against Iraq were proven wanting, the president appealed to the idea that the freedom conferred on Iraq was in and of itself an adequate justification for the war. The Iraqis were free, and that was all that really mattered. But what sort of 'freedom' is envisaged here, since, as the cultural critic Matthew Arnold long ago thoughtfully observed, 'freedom is a very good horse to ride, but to ride somewhere'.[2] To what destination, then, are the Iraqi people expected to ride the horse of freedom donated to them by force of arms?

The Bush administration's answer to this question was spelled out on 19 September 2003, when Paul Bremer, head of the Coalition Provisional Authority, promulgated four orders that included 'the full privatization of public enterprises, full ownership rights by foreign firms of Iraqi businesses, full repatriation of foreign profits . . . the opening of Iraq's banks to foreign control, national treatment for foreign companies and . . . the elimination of nearly all trade barriers'.[3] The orders were to apply to all areas of the economy, including public services, the media, manufacturing, services, transportation, finance, and construction. Only oil was exempt (presumably because of its special status as revenue producer to pay for the war and its geopolitical significance). The labour market, on the other hand, was to be strictly regulated. Strikes were effectively forbidden in key sectors and the right to unionize restricted. A highly regressive 'flat tax' (an ambitious tax-reform plan long advocated for implementation by conservatives in the US) was also imposed.

These orders were, some argued, in violation of the Geneva and Hague Conventions, since an occupying power is mandated to guard the assets of an occupied country and not sell them off.[4] Some Iraqis resisted the imposition of what the London *Economist* called a 'capitalist dream' regime upon Iraq. A member of the US-appointed Coalition Provisional Authority forcefully criticized the imposition of 'free market fundamentalism', calling it 'a flawed logic that ignores history'.[5] Though Bremer's rules may have been illegal when imposed by an occupying power, they would become legal if confirmed by a 'sovereign' government. The interim government, appointed by the US, that took over at the end of June 2004 was declared 'sovereign'. But it only had the power to confirm existing laws. Before the handover, Bremer multiplied the number of laws to specify free-market and free-trade rules in minute detail (on detailed matters such as copyright laws and intellectual property rights), expressing the hope that these institutional arrangements would 'take on a life and momentum of their own' such that they would prove very difficult to reverse.[6]

According to neoliberal theory, the sorts of measures that Bremer outlined were both necessary and sufficient for the creation of wealth and therefore for the improved well-being of the population at large. The assumption that individual freedoms are guaranteed by freedom of the market and of trade is a cardinal feature of neoliberal thinking, and it has long dominated the US stance towards the rest of the world.[7] What the US evidently sought to impose by main force on Iraq was a state apparatus whose fundamental mission was to facilitate conditions for profitable capital accumulation on the part of both domestic and foreign capital. I call this kind of state apparatus a *neoliberal state*. The freedoms it embodies reflect the interests of private property owners, businesses, multinational corporations, and financial capital. Bremer invited the Iraqis, in short, to ride their horse of freedom straight into the neoliberal corral.

The first experiment with neoliberal state formation, it is worth recalling, occurred in Chile after Pinochet's coup on the 'little September 11th' of 1973 (almost thirty years to the day before Bremer's announcement of the regime to be installed in Iraq). The coup, against the democratically elected government of Salvador Allende, was promoted by domestic business elites threatened by Allende's drive towards socialism. It was backed by US corporations, the CIA, and US Secretary of State Henry Kissinger. It violently repressed all the social movements and political organizations of the left and dismantled all forms of popular organization (such as the community health centres in poorer neighbourhoods). The labour market was 'freed' from regulatory or institutional restraints (trade union power, for example). But how was the stalled economy to be revived? The policies of import substitution (fostering national industries by subsidies or tariff protections) that had dominated Latin American attempts at economic development had fallen into disrepute, particularly in Chile, where they had never worked that well. With the whole world in economic recession, a new approach was called for.

A group of economists known as 'the Chicago boys' because of their attachment to the neoliberal theories of Milton Friedman, then teaching at the University of Chicago, was summoned to help reconstruct the Chilean economy. The story of how they were chosen is an interesting one. The US had funded training of Chilean economists at the University of Chicago since the 1950s as part of a Cold War programme to counteract left-wing tendencies in Latin America. Chicago-trained economists came to dominate at the private Catholic University in Santiago. During the early 1970s, business elites organized their opposition to Allende through a group called 'the Monday Club' and developed a working relationship with these economists, funding their work through research institutes. After General Gustavo Leigh, Pinochet's rival for power and a Keynesian, was sidelined in 1975, Pinochet brought these economists into the government, where their first job was to negotiate loans with the International Monetary Fund. Working alongside the IMF, they restructured the economy according to their theories. They reversed the nationalizations and privatized public assets, opened up natural resources (fisheries, timber, etc.) to private and unregulated exploitation (in many cases riding roughshod over the claims of indigenous inhabitants), privatized social security, and facilitated foreign direct investment and freer trade. The right of foreign companies to repatriate profits from their Chilean operations was guaranteed. Export-led growth was favoured over import substitution. The only sector reserved for the state was the key resource of copper (rather like oil in Iraq). This proved crucial to the budgetary viability of the state since copper revenues flowed exclusively into its coffers. The immediate

8

revival of the Chilean economy in terms of growth rates, capital accumulation, and high rates of return on foreign investments was short-lived. It all went sour in the Latin American debt crisis of 1982. The result was a much more pragmatic and less ideologically driven application of neoliberal policies in the years that followed. All of this, including the pragmatism, provided helpful evidence to support the subsequent turn to neoliberalism in both Britain (under Thatcher) and the US (under Reagan) in the 1980s. Not for the first time, a brutal experiment carried out in the periphery became a model for the formulation of policies in the centre (much as experimentation with the flat tax in Iraq has been proposed under Bremer's decrees).[8]

The fact that two such obviously similar restructurings of the state apparatus occurred at such different times in quite different parts of the world under the coercive influence of the United States suggests that the grim reach of US imperial power might lie behind the rapid proliferation of neoliberal state forms throughout the world from the mid-1970s onwards. While this has undoubtedly occurred over the last thirty years, it by no means constitutes the whole story, as the domestic component of the neoliberal turn in Chile shows. It was not the US, furthermore, that forced Margaret Thatcher to take the pioneering neoliberal path she took in 1979. Nor was it the US that forced China in 1978 to set out on a path of liberalization. The partial moves towards neoliberalization in India in the 1980s and Sweden in the early 1990s cannot easily be attributed to the imperial reach of US power. The uneven geographical development of neoliberalism on the world stage has evidently been a very complex process entailing multiple determinations and not a little chaos and confusion. Why, then, did the neoliberal turn occur, and what were the forces that made it so hegemonic within global capitalism?

Why the Neoliberal Turn?

The restructuring of state forms and of international relations after the Second World War was designed to prevent a return to the catastrophic conditions that had so threatened the capitalist order in the great slump of the 1930s. It was also supposed to prevent the re-emergence of inter-state geopolitical rivalries that had led to the war. To ensure domestic peace and tranquillity, some sort of class compromise between capital and labour had to be constructed. The thinking at the time is perhaps best represented by an influential text by two eminent social scientists, Robert Dahl and Charles Lindblom, published in 1953. Both capitalism and communism in their raw forms had failed, they argued. The only way ahead was to construct the right blend of state, market, and democratic institutions to guarantee peace, inclusion, well-being, and stability.[9] Internationally, a new world order was constructed through the Bretton Woods agreements, and various institutions, such as the United Nations, the World Bank, the IMF, and the Bank of International Settlements in Basle, were set up to help stabilize international relations. Free trade in goods was encouraged under a system of fixed exchange rates anchored by the US dollar's convertibility into gold at a fixed price. Fixed exchange rates were incompatible with free flows of capital that had to be controlled, but the US had to allow the free flow of the dollar beyond its borders if the dollar was to function as the global reserve currency. This system existed under the umbrella protection of US military power. Only the Soviet Union and the Cold War placed limits on its global reach.

A variety of social democratic, Christian democratic and dirigiste states emerged in Europe after the Second World War. The US itself turned towards a liberal democratic state form, and Japan, under the close supervision of the US, built a nominally democratic but in practice highly bureaucratic state apparatus empowered to oversee the reconstruction of that country. What all of these various state forms had in common was an acceptance that the state should focus on full employment, economic growth, and the welfare of its citizens, and that state power should be freely deployed, alongside of or, if necessary, intervening in or even substituting for market processes to achieve these ends. Fiscal and monetary policies usually dubbed 'Keynesian' were widely deployed to dampen business cycles and to ensure reasonably full employment. A 'class compromise' between capital and labour was generally advocated as the key guarantor of domestic peace and tranquillity. States actively intervened in industrial policy and moved to set standards for the social wage by constructing a variety of welfare systems (health care, education, and the like).

This form of political-economic organization is now usually referred to as 'embedded liberalism' to signal how market processes and entrepreneurial and corporate activities were surrounded by a web of social and political constraints and a regulatory environment that sometimes restrained but in other instances led the way in economic and industrial strategy.[10] State-led planning and in some instances state ownership of key sectors (coal, steel, automobiles) were not uncommon (for example in Britain, France, and Italy). The neoliberal project is to disembed capital from these constraints.

Embedded liberalism delivered high rates of economic growth in the advanced capitalist countries during the 1950s and 1960s.[11] In part this depended on the largesse of the US in being prepared to run deficits with the rest of the world and to absorb any excess product within its borders. This system conferred benefits such as expanding export markets (most obviously for Japan but also unevenly across South America and to some other countries of South-East Asia), but attempts to export 'development' to much of the rest of the world largely stalled. For much of the Third World, particularly Africa, embedded liberalism remained a pipe dream. The subsequent drive towards neoliberalization after 1980 entailed little material change in their impoverished condition. In the advanced capitalist countries, redistributive politics (including some degree of political integration of working-class trade union power and support for collective bargaining), controls over the free mobility of capital (some degree of financial repression through capital controls in particular), expanded public expenditures and welfare state-building, active state interventions in the economy, and some degree of planning of development went hand in hand with relatively high rates of growth. The business cycle was successfully controlled through the application of Keynesian fiscal and monetary policies. A social and moral economy (sometimes supported by a strong sense of national identity) was fostered through the activities of an interventionist state. The state in effect became a force field that internalized class relations. Working-class institutions such as labour unions and political

11

parties of the left had a very real influence within the state apparatus.

By the end of the 1960s embedded liberalism began to break down, both internationally and within domestic economies. Signs of a serious crisis of capital accumulation were everywhere apparent. Unemployment and inflation were both surging everywhere, ushering in a global phase of 'stagflation' that lasted throughout much of the 1970s. Fiscal crises of various states (Britain, for example, had to be bailed out by the IMF in 1975–6) resulted as tax revenues plunged and social expenditures soared. Keynesian policies were no longer working. Even before the Arab-Israeli War and the OPEC oil embargo of 1973, the Bretton Woods system of fixed exchange rates backed by gold reserves had fallen into disarray. The porosity of state boundaries with respect to capital flows put stress on the system of fixed exchange rates. US dollars had flooded the world and escaped US controls by being deposited in European banks. Fixed exchange rates were therefore abandoned in 1971. Gold could no longer function as the metallic base of international money; exchange rates were allowed to float, and attempts to control the float were soon abandoned. The embedded liberalism that had delivered high rates of growth to at least the advanced capitalist countries after 1945 was clearly exhausted and was no longer working. Some alternative was called for if the crisis was to be overcome.

One answer was to deepen state control and regulation of the economy through corporatist strategies (including, if necessary, curbing the aspirations of labour and popular movements through austerity measures, incomes policies, and even wage and price controls). This answer was advanced by socialist and communist parties in Europe, with hopes pinned on innovative experiments in governance in places such as communist-controlled 'Red Bologna' in Italy, on the revolutionary transformation of Portugal in the wake of the collapse of fascism, on the turn towards a more open market socialism and ideas of 'Eurocommunism', particularly in Italy (under the leadership of Berlinguer) and in Spain (under the influence of Carrillo), or on the expansion of the strong social democratic welfare state tradition in Scandinavia. The left assembled considerable popular power behind such programmes, coming close to power in

Italy and actually acquiring state power in Portugal, France, Spain, and Britain, while retaining power in Scandinavia. Even in the United States, a Congress controlled by the Democratic Party legislated a huge wave of regulatory reform in the early 1970s (signed into law by Richard Nixon, a Republican president, who in the process even went so far as to remark that 'we are all Keynesians now'), governing everything from environmental protection to occupational safety and health, civil rights, and consumer protection.[12] But the left failed to go much beyond traditional social democratic and corporatist solutions and these had by the mid-1970s proven inconsistent with the requirements of capital accumulation. The effect was to polarize debate between those ranged behind social democracy and central planning on the one hand (who, when in power, as in the case of the British Labour Party, often ended up trying to curb, usually for pragmatic reasons, the aspirations of their own constituencies), and the interests of all those concerned with liberating corporate and business power and re-establishing market freedoms on the other. By the mid-1970s, the interests of the latter group came to the fore. But how were the conditions for the resumption of active capital accumulation to be restored?

How and why neoliberalism emerged victorious as the single answer to this question is the crux of the problem we have to solve. In retrospect it may seem as if the answer was both inevitable and obvious, but at the time, I think it is fair to say, no one really knew or understood with any certainty what kind of answer would work and how. The capitalist world stumbled towards neoliberalization as the answer through a series of gyrations and chaotic experiments that really only converged as a new orthodoxy with the articulation of what became known as the 'Washington Consensus' in the 1990s. By then, both Clinton and Blair could easily have reversed Nixon's earlier statement and simply said 'We are all neoliberals now.' The uneven geographical development of neoliberalism, its frequently partial and lop-sided application from one state and social formation to another, testifies to the tentativeness of neoliberal solutions and the complex ways in which political forces, historical traditions, and existing institutional arrangements all shaped why and how the process of neoliberalization actually occurred.

There is, however, one element within this transition that deserves specific attention. The crisis of capital accumulation in the 1970s affected everyone through the combination of rising unemployment and accelerating inflation (Figure 1.1). Discontent

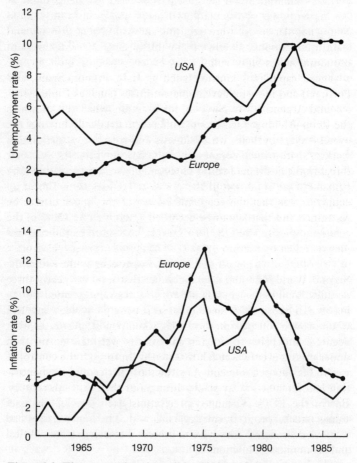

Figure 1.1 The economic crisis of the 1970s: inflation and unemployment in the US and Europe, 1960–1987
Source: Harvey, *The Condition of Postmodernity*.

was widespread and the conjoining of labour and urban social movements throughout much of the advanced capitalist world appeared to point towards the emergence of a socialist alternative to the social compromise between capital and labour that had grounded capital accumulation so successfully in the post-war period. Communist and socialist parties were gaining ground, if not taking power, across much of Europe and even in the United States popular forces were agitating for widespread reforms and state interventions. There was, in this, a clear *political* threat to economic elites and ruling classes everywhere, both in the advanced capitalist countries (such as Italy, France, Spain, and Portugal) and in many developing countries (such as Chile, Mexico, and Argentina). In Sweden, for example, what was known as the Rehn–Meidner plan literally offered to gradually buy out the owners' share in their own businesses and turn the country into a worker/share-owner democracy. But, beyond this, the *economic* threat to the position of ruling elites and classes was now becoming palpable. One condition of the post-war settlement in almost all countries was that the economic power of the upper classes be restrained and that labour be accorded a much larger share of the economic pie. In the US, for example, the share of the national income taken by the top 1 per cent of income earners fell from a pre-war high of 16 per cent to less than 8 per cent by the end of the Second World War, and stayed close to that level for nearly three decades. While growth was strong this restraint seemed not to matter. To have a stable share of an increasing pie is one thing. But when growth collapsed in the 1970s, when real interest rates went negative and paltry dividends and profits were the norm, then upper classes everywhere felt threatened. In the US the control of wealth (as opposed to income) by the top 1 per cent of the population had remained fairly stable throughout the twentieth century. But in the 1970s it plunged precipitously (Figure 1.2) as asset values (stocks, property, savings) collapsed. The upper classes had to move decisively if they were to protect themselves from political and economic annihilation.

The coup in Chile and the military takeover in Argentina, promoted internally by the upper classes with US support, provided one kind of solution. The subsequent Chilean experiment with

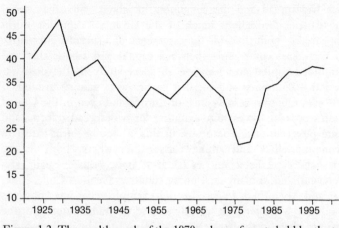

Figure 1.2 The wealth crash of the 1970s: share of assets held by the top
1% of the US population, 1922–1998
Source: Duménil and Lévy, *Capital Resurgent*.

neoliberalism demonstrated that the benefits of revived capital
accumulation were highly skewed under forced privatization. The
country and its ruling elites, along with foreign investors, did
extremely well in the early stages. Redistributive effects and
increasing social inequality have in fact been such a persistent
feature of neoliberalization as to be regarded as structural to the
whole project. Gérard Duménil and Dominique Lévy, after careful
reconstruction of the data, have concluded that neoliberalization
was from the very beginning a project to achieve the restoration of
class power. After the implementation of neoliberal policies in the
late 1970s, the share of national income of the top 1 per cent of
income earners in the US soared, to reach 15 per cent (very close
to its pre–Second World War share) by the end of the century. The
top 0.1 per cent of income earners in the US increased their share
of the national income from 2 per cent in 1978 to over 6 per cent by
1999, while the ratio of the median compensation of workers to the
salaries of CEOs increased from just over 30 to 1 in 1970 to nearly
500 to 1 by 2000 (Figures 1.3 and 1.4). Almost certainly, with the
Bush administration's tax reforms now taking effect, the concentration of income and wealth in the upper echelons of society is

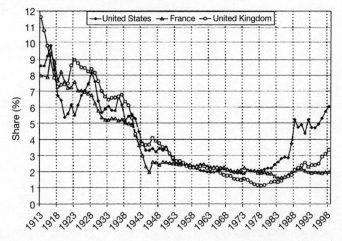

Figure 1.3 The restoration of class power: share in national income of the top 0.1% of the population, US, Britain, and France, 1913–1998

Source: Task Force on Inequality and American Democracy, *American Democracy in an Age of Rising Inequality*.

continuing apace because the estate tax (a tax on wealth) is being phased out and taxation on income from investments and capital gains is being diminished, while taxation on wages and salaries is maintained.[13]

The US is not alone in this: the top 1 per cent of income earners in Britain have doubled their share of the national income from 6.5 per cent to 13 per cent since 1982. And when we look further afield we see extraordinary concentrations of wealth and power emerging all over the place. A small and powerful oligarchy arose in Russia after neoliberal 'shock therapy' had been administered there in the 1990s. Extraordinary surges in income inequalities and wealth have occurred in China as it has adopted free-market-oriented practices. The wave of privatization in Mexico after 1992 catapulted a few individuals (such as Carlos Slim) almost overnight into Fortune's list of the world's wealthiest people. Globally, 'the countries of Eastern Europe and the CIS have registered some of the largest increases ever . . . in social inequality. OECD countries also

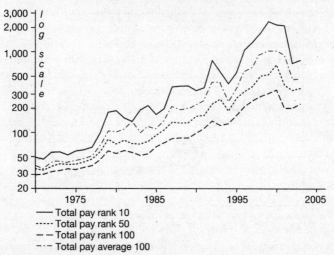

Total pay rank 10
Total pay rank 50
Total pay rank 100
Total pay average 100

The first three curves show the rise of the pay of CEOs according to their rank in the hierarchy of remunerations: 10th, 50th, and 100th. The other curve (·—·—) corresponds to the average pay of the 100 CEOs with higher remunerations. Note that 1,000 means 1,000 times the average salary.

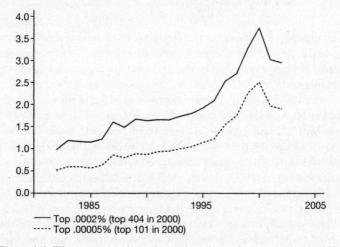

Top .0002% (top 404 in 2000)
Top .00005% (top 101 in 2000)

Figure 1.4 The concentration of wealth and earning power in the US: CEO remuneration in relation to average US salaries, 1970–2003, and wealth shares of the richest families, 1982–2002

Source: Duménil and Lévy, 'Neoliberal Income Trends'.

registered big increases in inequality after the 1980s', while 'the income gap between the fifth of the world's people living in the richest countries and the fifth in the poorest was 74 to 1 in 1997, up from 60 to 1 in 1990 and 30 to 1 in 1960'.[14] While there are exceptions to this trend (several East and South-East Asian countries have so far contained income inequalities within reasonable bounds, as has France—see Figure 1.3), the evidence strongly suggests that the neoliberal turn is in some way and to some degree associated with the restoration or reconstruction of the power of economic elites.

We can, therefore, interpret neoliberalization either as a *utopian* project to realize a theoretical design for the reorganization of international capitalism or as a *political* project to re-establish the conditions for capital accumulation and to restore the power of economic elites. In what follows I shall argue that the second of these objectives has in practice dominated. Neoliberalization has not been very effective in revitalizing global capital accumulation, but it has succeeded remarkably well in restoring, or in some instances (as in Russia and China) creating, the power of an economic elite. The theoretical utopianism of neoliberal argument has, I conclude, primarily worked as a system of justification and legitimation for whatever needed to be done to achieve this goal. The evidence suggests, moreover, that when neoliberal principles clash with the need to restore or sustain elite power, then the principles are either abandoned or become so twisted as to be unrecognizable. This in no way denies the power of ideas to act as a force for historical-geographical change. But it does point to a creative tension between the power of neoliberal ideas and the actual practices of neoliberalization that have transformed how global capitalism has been working over the last three decades.

The Rise of Neoliberal Theory

Neoliberalism as a potential antidote to threats to the capitalist social order and as a solution to capitalism's ills had long been lurking in the wings of public policy. A small and exclusive group of passionate advocates—mainly academic economists, historians, and philosophers—had gathered together around the renowned

Austrian political philosopher Friedrich von Hayek to create the Mont Pelerin Society (named after the Swiss spa where they first met) in 1947 (the notables included Ludvig von Mises, the economist Milton Friedman, and even, for a time, the noted philosopher Karl Popper). The founding statement of the society read as follows:

The central values of civilization are in danger. Over large stretches of the earth's surface the essential conditions of human dignity and freedom have already disappeared. In others they are under constant menace from the development of current tendencies of policy. The position of the individual and the voluntary group are progressively undermined by extensions of arbitrary power. Even that most precious possession of Western Man, freedom of thought and expression, is threatened by the spread of creeds which, claiming the privilege of tolerance when in the position of a minority, seek only to establish a position of power in which they can suppress and obliterate all views but their own.

The group holds that these developments have been fostered by the growth of a view of history which denies all absolute moral standards and by the growth of theories which question the desirability of the rule of law. It holds further that they have been fostered by a decline of belief in private property and the competitive market; for without the diffused power and initiative associated with these institutions it is difficult to imagine a society in which freedom may be effectively preserved.[15]

The group's members depicted themselves as 'liberals' (in the traditional European sense) because of their fundamental commitment to ideals of personal freedom. The neoliberal label signalled their adherence to those free market principles of neoclassical economics that had emerged in the second half of the nineteenth century (thanks to the work of Alfred Marshall, William Stanley Jevons, and Leon Walras) to displace the classical theories of Adam Smith, David Ricardo, and, of course, Karl Marx. Yet they also held to Adam Smith's view that the hidden hand of the market was the best device for mobilizing even the basest of human instincts such as gluttony, greed, and the desire for wealth and power for the benefit of all. Neoliberal doctrine was therefore deeply opposed to state interventionist theories, such as those of John Maynard Keynes, which rose to prominence in the 1930s in response to the Great Depression. Many policy-makers after the Second World War looked to Keynesian theory to guide them as they sought to keep the business cycle and recessions under control. The neoliberals were even more fiercely opposed to theories of centralized state planning, such as those advanced by Oscar Lange working close to the Marxist tradition. State decisions, they argued, were bound to be politically biased depending upon the strength of the interest groups involved (such as unions, environmentalists, or trade lobbies). State decisions on matters of investment and capital accumulation were bound to be wrong because the information available to the state could not rival that contained in market signals.

This theoretical framework is not, as several commentators have pointed out, entirely coherent.[16] The scientific rigour of its neoclassical economics does not sit easily with its political commitment to ideals of individual freedom, nor does its supposed distrust of all state power fit with the need for a strong and if necessary coercive state that will defend the rights of private property, individual liberties, and entrepreneurial freedoms. The juridical trick of defining corporations as individuals before the law introduces its own biases, rendering ironic John D. Rockefeller's personal credo etched in stone in the Rockefeller Center in New York City, where he places 'the supreme worth of the individual' above all else. And there are, as we shall see, enough contradictions in the neoliberal position to render evolving neoliberal practices (vis-à-vis issues such as monopoly power and market failures) unrecognizable in relation to the seeming purity of neoliberal doctrine. We have to pay careful attention, therefore, to the tension between the theory of neoliberalism and the actual pragmatics of neoliberalization.

Hayek, author of key texts such as *The Constitution of Liberty*, presciently argued that the battle for ideas was key, and that it would probably take at least a generation for that battle to be won, not only against Marxism but against socialism, state planning, and Keynesian interventionism. The Mont Pelerin group garnered financial and political support. In the US in particular, a powerful group of wealthy individuals and corporate leaders who were viscerally opposed to all forms of state intervention and

regulation, and even to internationalism sought to organize opposition to what they saw as an emerging consensus for pursuing a
mixed economy. Fearful of how the alliance with the Soviet Union
and the command economy constructed within the US during the
Second World War might play out politically in a post-war setting,
they were ready to embrace anything from McCarthyism to neoliberal think-tanks to protect and enhance their power. Yet this
movement remained on the margins of both policy and academic
influence until the troubled years of the 1970s. At that point it
began to move centre-stage, particularly in the US and Britain,
nurtured in various well-financed think-tanks (offshoots of the
Mont Pelerin Society, such as the Institute of Economic Affairs in
London and the Heritage Foundation in Washington), as well as
through its growing influence within the academy, particularly at
the University of Chicago, where Milton Friedman dominated.
Neoliberal theory gained in academic respectability by the award
of the Nobel Prize in economics to Hayek in 1974 and Friedman in
1976. This particular prize, though it assumed the aura of Nobel,
had nothing to do with the other prizes and was under the tight
control of Sweden's banking elite. Neoliberal theory, particularly
in its monetarist guise, began to exert practical influence in a variety of policy fields. During the Carter presidency, for example,
deregulation of the economy emerged as one of the answers to the
chronic state of stagflation that had prevailed in the US throughout the 1970s. But the dramatic consolidation of neoliberalism as a
new economic orthodoxy regulating public policy at the state level
in the advanced capitalist world occurred in the United States and
Britain in 1979.

In May of that year Margaret Thatcher was elected in Britain
with a strong mandate to reform the economy. Under the influence
of Keith Joseph, a very active and committed publicist and polemicist with strong connections to the neoliberal Institute of
Economic Affairs, she accepted that Keynesianism had to be abandoned and that monetarist 'supply-side' solutions were essential to
cure the stagflation that had characterized the British economy
during the 1970s. She recognized that this meant nothing short of
a revolution in fiscal and social policies, and immediately signalled
a fierce determination to have done with the institutions and

political ways of the social democratic state that had been consolidated in Britain after 1945. This entailed confronting trade union power, attacking all forms of social solidarity that hindered competitive flexibility (such as those expressed through municipal governance, and including the power of many professionals and their associations), dismantling or rolling back the commitments of the welfare state, the privatization of public enterprises (including social housing), reducing taxes, encouraging entrepreneurial initiative, and creating a favourable business climate to induce a strong inflow of foreign investment (particularly from Japan). There was, she famously declared, 'no such thing as society, only individual men and women'—and, she subsequently added, their families. All forms of social solidarity were to be dissolved in favour of individualism, private property, personal responsibility, and family values. The ideological assault along these lines that flowed from Thatcher's rhetoric was relentless.[17] 'Economics are the method', she said, 'but the object is to change the soul.' And change it she did, though in ways that were by no means comprehensive and complete, let alone free of political costs.

In October 1979 Paul Volcker, chairman of the US Federal Reserve Bank under President Carter, engineered a draconian shift in US monetary policy.[18] The long-standing commitment in the US liberal democratic state to the principles of the New Deal, which meant broadly Keynesian fiscal and monetary policies with full employment as the key objective, was abandoned in favour of a policy designed to quell inflation no matter what the consequences might be for employment. The real rate of interest, which had often been negative during the double-digit inflationary surge of the 1970s, was rendered positive by fiat of the Federal Reserve (Figure 1.5). The nominal rate of interest was raised overnight and, after a few ups and downs, by July 1981 stood close to 20 per cent. Thus began 'a long deep recession that would empty factories and break unions in the US and drive debtor countries to the brink of insolvency, beginning the long era of structural adjustment'.[19] This, Volcker argued, was the only way out of the grumbling crisis of stagflation that had characterized the US and much of the global economy throughout the 1970s.

The Volcker shock, as it has since come to be known, has to be

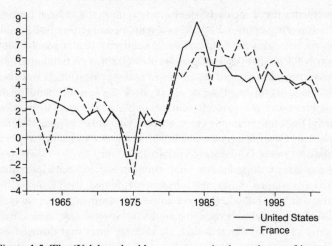

Figure 1.5 The 'Volcker shock': movements in the real rate of interest, US and France, 1960–2001
Source: Duménil and Lévy, *Capital Resurgent*.

interpreted as a necessary but not sufficient condition for neo-liberalization. Some central banks had long emphasized anti-inflationary fiscal responsibility and adopted policies that were closer to monetarism than to Keynesian orthodoxy. In the West German case this derived from historical memories of the runaway inflation that had destroyed the Weimar Republic in the 1920s (setting the stage for the rise of fascism) and the equally dangerous inflation that occurred at the end of the Second World War. The IMF had long set itself against excessive debt creation and urged, if not mandated, fiscal restraints and budgetary austerity on client states. But in all these cases this monetarism was paralleled by acceptance of strong union power and a political commitment to build a strong welfare state. The turn to neoliberalism thus depended not only on adopting monetarism but on the unfolding of government policies in many other arenas.

Ronald Reagan's victory over Carter in 1980 proved crucial, even though Carter had shifted uneasily towards deregulation (of airlines and trucking) as a partial solution to the crisis of stagfla-tion. Reagan's advisers were convinced that Volcker's monetarist 'medicine' for a sick and stagnant economy was right on target. Volcker was supported in and reappointed to his position as chair of the Federal Reserve. The Reagan administration then provided the requisite political backing through further deregulation, tax cuts, budget cuts, and attacks on trade union and professional power. Reagan faced down PATCO, the air traffic controllers' union, in a lengthy and bitter strike in 1981. This signalled an all-out assault on the powers of organized labour at the very moment when the Volcker-inspired recession was generating high levels of unemployment (10 per cent or more). But PATCO was more than an ordinary union: it was a white-collar union which had the character of a skilled professional association. It was, therefore, an icon of middle-class rather than working-class unionism. The effect on the condition of labour across the board was dramatic—perhaps best captured by the fact that the Federal minimum wage, which stood on a par with the poverty level in 1980, had fallen to 30 per cent below that level by 1990. The long decline in real wage levels then began in earnest.

Reagan's appointments to positions of power on issues such as environmental regulation, occupational safety, and health, took the

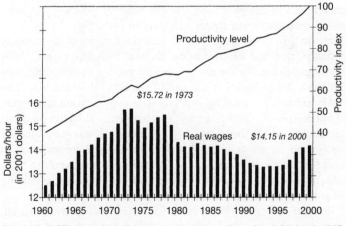

Figure 1.6 The attack on labour: real wages and productivity in the US,
1960–2000
Source: Pollin, *Contours of Descent*.

campaign against big government to ever higher levels. The deregulation of everything from airlines and telecommunications to finance opened up new zones of untrammelled market freedoms for powerful corporate interests. Tax breaks on investment effectively subsidized the movement of capital away from the unionized north-east and midwest and into the non-union and weakly regulated south and west. Finance capital increasingly looked abroad for higher rates of return. Deindustrialization at home and moves to take production abroad became much more common. The market, depicted ideologically as the way to foster competition and innovation, became a vehicle for the consolidation of monopoly power. Corporate taxes were reduced dramatically, and the top personal tax rate was reduced from 70 to 28 per cent in what was billed as 'the largest tax cut in history' (Figure 1.7).

And so began the momentous shift towards greater social inequality and the restoration of economic power to the upper class.

There was, however, one other concomitant shift that also impelled the movement towards neoliberalization during the

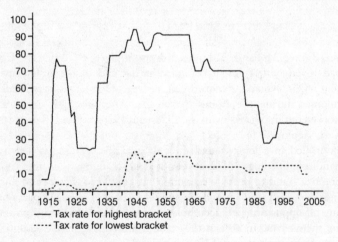

Figure 1.7 The tax revolt of the upper class: US tax rates for higher and lower brackets, 1913–2003
Source: Duménil and Lévy, 'Neoliberal Income Trends'.

1970s. The OPEC oil price hike that came with the oil embargo of 1973 placed vast amounts of financial power at the disposal of the oil-producing states such as Saudi Arabia, Kuwait, and Abu Dhabi. We now know from British intelligence reports that the US was actively preparing to invade these countries in 1973 in order to restore the flow of oil and bring down oil prices. We also know that the Saudis agreed at that time, presumably under military pressure if not open threat from the US, to recycle all of their petrodollars through the New York investment banks.[20] The latter suddenly found themselves in command of massive funds for which they needed to find profitable outlets. The options within the US, given the depressed economic conditions and low rates of return in the mid-1970s, were not good. More profitable opportunities had to be sought out abroad. Governments seemed the safest bet because, as Walter Wriston, head of Citibank, famously put it, governments can't move or disappear. And many governments in the developing world, hitherto starved of funds, were anxious enough to borrow. For this to occur required, however, open entry and reasonably secure conditions for lending. The New York investment banks looked to the US imperial tradition both to prise open new investment opportunities and to protect their foreign operations.

The US imperial tradition had been long in the making, and to great degree defined itself against the imperial traditions of Britain, France, Holland, and other European powers.[21] While the US had toyed with colonial conquest at the end of the nineteenth century, it evolved a more open system of imperialism without colonies during the twentieth century. The paradigm case was worked out in Nicaragua in the 1920s and 1930s, when US marines were deployed to protect US interests but found themselves embroiled in a lengthy and difficult guerrilla insurgency led by Sandino. The answer was to find a local strongman—in this case Somoza—and to provide economic and military assistance to him and his family and immediate allies so that they could repress or buy off opposition and accumulate considerable wealth and power for themselves. In return they would always keep their country open to the operations of US capital and support, and if necessary promote US interests, both in the country and in the region (in the Nicaraguan case, Central America) as a whole. This was the model that was deployed after the Second World War during the phase of global decolonization imposed upon the European powers at US insistence. For example, the CIA engineered the coup that overthrew the democratically elected Mosaddeq government in Iran in 1953 and installed the Shah of Iran, who gave the oil contracts to US companies (and did not return the assets to the British companies that Mossadeq had nationalized). The shah also became one of the key guardians of US interests in the Middle Eastern oil region.

In the post-war period, much of the non-communist world was opened up to US domination by tactics of this sort. This became the method of choice to fight off the threat of communist insurgencies and revolution, entailing an anti-democratic (and even more emphatically anti-populist and anti-socialist/communist) strategy on the part of the US that put the US more and more in alliance with repressive military dictatorships and authoritarian regimes (most spectacularly, of course, throughout Latin America). The stories told in John Perkins's *Confessions of an Economic Hit Man* are full of the ugly and unsavoury details of how this was all too often done. US interests consequently became more rather than less vulnerable in the struggle against international communism. While the consent of local ruling elites could be purchased easily enough, the need to coerce oppositional or social democratic movements (such as Allende's in Chile) associated the US with a long history of largely covert violence against popular movements throughout much of the developing world.

It was in this context that the surplus funds being recycled through the New York investment banks were dispersed throughout the world. Before 1973, most US foreign investment was of the direct sort, mainly concerned with the exploitation of raw material resources (oil, minerals, raw materials, agricultural products) or the cultivation of specific markets (telecommunications, automobiles, etc.) in Europe and Latin America. The New York investment banks had always been active internationally, but after 1973 they became even more so, though now far more focused on lending capital to foreign governments.[22] This required the liberalization of international credit and financial markets, and the US government began actively to promote and support this strategy globally during the 1970s. Hungry for credit, developing countries were encouraged to borrow heavily, though at rates that were advantageous to the New York bankers.[23] Since the loans were designated in US dollars, however, any modest, let alone precipitous, rise in US interest rates could easily push vulnerable countries into default. The New York investment banks would then be exposed to serious losses.

The first major test case of this came in the wake of the Volcker shock that drove Mexico into default in 1982–4. The Reagan administration, which had seriously thought of withdrawing support for the IMF in its first year in office, found a way to put together the powers of the US Treasury and the IMF to resolve the difficulty by rolling over the debt, but did so in return for neoliberal reforms. This treatment became standard after what Stiglitz refers to as a 'purge' of all Keynesian influences from the IMF in 1982. The IMF and the World Bank thereafter became centres for the propagation and enforcement of 'free market fundamentalism' and neoliberal orthodoxy. In return for debt rescheduling, indebted countries were required to implement institutional reforms, such as cuts in welfare expenditures, more flexible labour market laws, and privatization. Thus was 'structural adjustment' invented. Mexico was one of the first states drawn into what was going to become a growing column of neoliberal state apparatuses worldwide.[24]

What the Mexico case demonstrated, however, was a key difference between liberal and neoliberal practice: under the former, lenders take the losses that arise from bad investment decisions, while under the latter the borrowers are forced by state and international powers to take on board the cost of debt repayment no matter what the consequences for the livelihood and well-being of the local population. If this required the surrender of assets to foreign companies at fire-sale prices, then so be it. This, it turns out, is not consistent with neoliberal theory. One effect, as Duménil and Lévy show, was to permit US owners of capital to extract high rates of return from the rest of the world during the 1980s and 1990s (Figures 1.8 and 1.9).[25] The restoration of power to an economic elite or upper class in the US and elsewhere in the advanced capitalist countries drew heavily on surpluses extracted

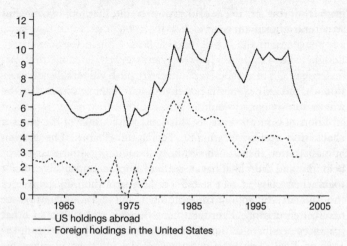

Figure 1.8 Extracting surpluses from abroad: rates of return on foreign and domestic investments in the US, 1960–2002

Source: Duménil and Lévy, 'The Economics of US Imperialism'.

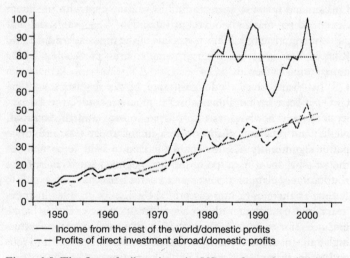

Figure 1.9 The flow of tribute into the US: profits and capital income from the rest of the world in relation to domestic profits

Source: Duménil and Lévy, 'Neoliberal Dynamics: Towards A New Phase?'.

from the rest of the world through international flows and structural adjustment practices.

The Meaning of Class Power

But what exactly is meant here by 'class'? This is always a somewhat shadowy (some would even say dubious) concept. Neoliberalization has, in any case, entailed its redefinition. This poses a problem. If neoliberalization has been a vehicle for the restoration of class power, then we should be able to identify the class forces behind it and those that have benefited from it. But this is difficult to do when 'class' is not a stable social configuration. In some cases 'traditional' strata have managed to hang on to a consistent power base (often organized through family and kinship). But in other instances neoliberalization has been accompanied by a reconfiguration of what constitutes an upper class. Margaret Thatcher, for example, attacked some of the entrenched forms of class power in Britain. She went against the aristocratic tradition that dominated in the military, the judiciary, and the financial elite in the City of London and many segments of industry, and sided with the brash entrepreneurs and the nouveaux riches. She supported, and was usually supported by, this new class of entrepreneurs (such as Richard Branson, Lord Hanson, and George Soros). The traditional wing of her own Conservative Party was appalled. In the US, the rising power and significance of the financiers and the CEOs of large corporations, as well as the immense burst of activity in wholly new sectors (such as computing and the internet, media, and retailing) changed the locus of upper-class economic power significantly. While neoliberalization may have been about the restoration of class power, it has not necessarily meant the restoration of economic power to the same people.

But, as the contrasting cases of the US and Britain illustrate, 'class' means different things in different places, and in some instances (for example in the US) it is often held to have no meaning at all. In addition there have been strong currents of differentiation in terms of class identity formation and re-formation in different parts of the world. In Indonesia, Malaysia, and the Philippines, for example, economic power became strongly concentrated among a few ethnic-minority Chinese, and the mode of acquisition of that economic power was quite different from that in Australia or the US (it was heavily concentrated in trading activities and entailed the cornering of markets[26]). And the rise of the seven oligarchs in Russia derived from the quite unique configuration of circumstances that held in the wake of the collapse of the Soviet Union.

Nevertheless, there are some general trends that can be identified. The first is for the privileges of ownership and management of capitalist enterprises—traditionally separated—to fuse by paying CEOs (managers) in stock options (ownership titles). Stock values rather than production then become the guiding light of economic activity and, as later became apparent with the collapse of companies such as Enron, the speculative temptations that resulted from this could become overwhelming. The second trend has been to dramatically reduce the historical gap between money capital earning dividends and interest, on the one hand, and production, manufacturing, or merchant capital looking to gain profits on the other. This separation had at various times in the past produced conflicts between financiers, producers, and merchants. In Britain, for example, government policy in the 1960s catered primarily to the requirements of the financiers in the City of London, often to the detriment of domestic manufacturing, and in the 1960s conflicts in the US between financiers and manufacturing corporations had often surfaced. During the 1970s much of this conflict either disappeared or took new forms. The large corporations became more and more financial in their orientation, even when, as in the automobile sector, they were engaging in production. Since 1980 or so it has not been uncommon for corporations to report losses in production offset by gains from financial operations (everything from credit and insurance operations to speculating in volatile currency and futures markets). Mergers across sectors conjoined production, merchanting, real estate, and financial interests in new ways to produce diversified conglomerates. When US Steel changed its name to USX (purchasing strong stakes in insurance) the chairman of the board, James Roderick, replied to the question 'What is X?' with the simple answer 'X stands for money.'[27]

All of this connected to the strong burst in activity and power within the world of finance. Increasingly freed from the regulatory constraints and barriers that had hitherto confined its field of action, financial activity could flourish as never before, eventually everywhere. A wave of innovations occurred in financial services to produce not only far more sophisticated global interconnections but also new kinds of financial markets based on securitization, derivatives, and all manner of futures trading. Neoliberalization has meant, in short, the financialization of everything. This deepened the hold of finance over all other areas of the economy, as well as over the state apparatus and, as Randy Martin points out, daily life.[28] It also introduced an accelerating volatility into global exchange relations. There was unquestionably a power shift away from production to the world of finance. Gains in manufacturing capacity no longer necessarily meant rising per capita incomes, but concentration on financial services certainly did. For this reason, the support of financial institutions and the integrity of the financial system became the central concern of the collectivity of neoliberal states (such as the group comprising the world's richest countries known as the G7). In the event of a conflict between Main Street and Wall Street, the latter was to be favoured. The real possibility then arises that while Wall Street does well the rest of the US (as well as the rest of the world) does badly. And for several years, particularly during the 1990s, this is exactly what happened. While the slogan was often advanced in the 1960s that what was good for General Motors was good for the US, this had changed by the 1990s into the slogan that what is good for Wall Street is all that matters.

One substantial core of rising class power under neoliberalism lies, therefore, with the CEOs, the key operators on corporate boards, and the leaders in the financial, legal, and technical apparatuses that surround this inner sanctum of capitalist activity.[29] The power of the actual owners of capital, the stockholders, has, however, been somewhat diminished unless they can gain a sufficiently large voting interest to affect corporate policy. Shareholders have on occasion been bilked of millions by the operations of the CEOs and their financial advisers. Speculative gains have also made it possible to amass enormous fortunes within a very short period of time (examples are Warren Buffett and George Soros).

But it would be wrong to confine the notion of the upper class to this group alone. The opening up of entrepreneurial opportunities, as well as new structures in trading relations, have allowed substantially new processes of class formation to emerge. Fast fortunes were made in new sectors of the economy such as biotechnology and information technologies (for example by Bill Gates and Paul Allen). New market relations opened up all manner of possibilities to buy cheap and sell dear, if not to actually corner markets in such a way as to build fortunes that can either extend horizontally (as in the case of Rupert Murdoch's sprawling global media empire) or be diversified into all manner of businesses, extending backwards into resource extraction and production and forwards from a trading base into financial services, real-estate development, and retailing. In this it frequently happened that a privileged relationship to state power also played a key role. The two businessmen who were closest to Suharto in Indonesia, for example, both fed the Suharto family financial interests but also fed off their connections to that state apparatus to become immensely rich. By 1997 one of them, the Salim Group, was 'reportedly the world's largest Chinese-owned conglomerate, with $20 billion in assets and some five hundred companies'. Starting with a relatively small investment company, Carlos Slim gained control over the newly privatized telecommunications system in Mexico and quickly parlayed that into a huge conglomerate empire that controls not only a huge slice of the Mexican economy but has sprawling interests in US retailing (Circuit City and Barnes and Noble) as well as throughout Latin America.[30] In the US, the Walton family has become immensely rich as Wal-Mart has surged into a dominant position in US retailing but with integration into Chinese production lines as well as retail stores worldwide. While there are obvious links between these sorts of activities and the world of finance, the incredible ability not only to amass large personal fortunes but to exercise a controlling power over large segments of the economy confers on these few individuals immense economic power to influence political processes. Small wonder that the net worth of the 358 richest people in 1996 was 'equal to the combined income of the poorest 45 per cent of the world's population—2.3 billion people'. Worse still, 'the world's 200 richest people more than doubled their net worth in the four years to 1998, to more than $1 trillion. The assets of the top three billionaires [were by then] more than the combined GNP of all least developed countries and their 600 million people.'[31]

There is, however, one further conundrum to be considered in this process of radical reconfiguration of class relations. The question arises, and has been much debated, as to whether this new class configuration should be considered as transnational or whether it can be still understood as something based exclusively within the parameters of the nation-state.[32] My own position is this. The case that the ruling class anywhere has ever confined its operations and defined its loyalties to any one nation-state has historically been much overstated. It never did make much sense to speak of a distinctively US versus British or French or German or Korean capitalist class. The international links were always important, particularly through colonial and neocolonial activities, but also through transnational connections that go back to the nineteenth century if not before. But there has undoubtedly been a deepening as well as a widening of these transnational connections during the phase of neoliberal globalization, and it is vital that these connectivities be acknowledged. This does not mean, however, that the leading individuals within this class do not attach themselves to specific state apparatuses for both the advantages and the protections that this affords them. *Where* they specifically attach themselves is important, but is no more stable than the capitalist activity they pursue. Rupert Murdoch may begin in Australia then concentrate on Britain before finally taking up citizenship (doubtless on an accelerated schedule) in the US. He is not above or outside particular state powers, but by the same token he wields considerable influence via his media interests in politics in Britain, the US, and Australia. All 247 of the supposedly independent editors of his newspapers worldwide supported the US invasion of Iraq. As a form of shorthand, however, it still makes sense to speak about US or British or Korean capitalist class interests because corporate interests like Murdoch's or those of Carlos Slim or the Salim group both feed off and nurture specific state apparatuses. Each can and typically does, however, exert class power in more than one state simultaneously.

While this disparate group of individuals embedded in the corporate, financial, trading, and developer worlds do not necessarily conspire as a class, and while there may be frequent tensions between them, they nevertheless possess a certain accordance of interests that generally recognizes the advantages (and now some of the dangers) to be derived from neoliberalization. They also possess, through organizations like the World Economic Forum at Davos, means of exchanging ideas and of consorting and consulting with political leaders. They exercise immense influence over global affairs and possess a freedom of action that no ordinary citizen possesses.

Freedom's Prospect

This history of neoliberalization and class formation, and the proliferating acceptance of the ideas of the Mont Pelerin Society as the ruling ideas of the time, makes for interesting reading when placed against the background of counter-arguments laid out by Karl Polanyi in 1944 (shortly before the Mont Pelerin Society was established). In a complex society, he pointed out, the meaning of freedom becomes as contradictory and as fraught as its incitements to action are compelling. There are, he noted, two kinds of freedom, one good and the other bad. Among the latter he listed 'the freedom to exploit one's fellows, or the freedom to make inordinate gains without commensurable service to the community, the freedom to keep technological inventions from being used for public benefit, or the freedom to profit from public calamities secretly engineered for private advantage'. But, Polanyi continued, 'the market economy under which these freedoms throve also produced freedoms we prize highly. Freedom of conscience, freedom of speech, freedom of meeting, freedom of association, freedom to choose one's own job'. While we may 'cherish these freedoms for their own sake',—and, surely, many of us still do—they were to a large extent 'by-products of the same economy that was also responsible for the evil freedoms'.[33] Polanyi's answer to this duality makes strange reading given the current hegemony of neoliberal thinking:

The passing of [the] market economy can become the beginning of an era of unprecedented freedom. Juridical and actual freedom can be made wider and more general than ever before; regulation and control can achieve freedom not only for the few, but for all. Freedom not as an appurtenance of privilege, tainted at the source, but as a prescriptive right extending far beyond the narrow confines of the political sphere into the intimate organization of society itself. Thus will old freedoms and civic rights be added to the fund of new freedoms generated by the leisure and security that industrial society offers to all. Such a society can afford to be both just and free.[34]

Unfortunately, Polanyi noted, the passage to such a future is blocked by the 'moral obstacle' of liberal utopianism (and more than once he cites Hayek as an exemplar of that tradition):

Planning and control are being attacked as a denial of freedom. Free enterprise and private ownership are declared to be essentials of freedom. No society built on other foundations is said to deserve to be called free. The freedom that regulation creates is denounced as unfreedom; the justice, liberty and welfare it offers are decried as a camouflage of slavery.[35]

The idea of freedom 'thus degenerates into a mere advocacy of free enterprise', which means 'the fullness of freedom for those whose income, leisure and security need no enhancing, and a mere pittance of liberty for the people, who may in vain attempt to make use of their democratic rights to gain shelter from the power of the owners of property'. But if, as is always the case, 'no society is possible in which power and compulsion are absent, nor a world in which force has no function', then the only way this liberal utopian vision could be sustained is by force, violence, and authoritarianism. Liberal or neoliberal utopianism is doomed, in Polanyi's view, to be frustrated by authoritarianism, or even outright fascism.[36] The good freedoms are lost, the bad ones take over.

Polanyi's diagnosis appears peculiarly appropriate to our contemporary condition. It provides a powerful vantage point from which to understand what President Bush intends when he asserts that 'as the greatest power on earth we [the US] have an obligation to help the spread of freedom'. It helps explain why neoliberalism has turned so authoritarian, forceful, and anti-democratic at the very moment when 'humanity holds in its hands the opportunity to offer freedom's triumph over all its age-old foes'.[37] It makes us focus on how so many corporations have profiteered from withholding the benefits of their technologies (such as AIDS drugs) from the public sphere, as well as from the calamities of war (as in the case of Halliburton), famine, and environmental disaster. It raises the worry as to whether or not many of these calamities or near calamities (arms races and the need to confront both real and imagined enemies) have been secretly engineered for corporate advantage. And it makes it all too clear why those of wealth and power so avidly support certain conceptions of rights and freedoms while seeking to persuade us of their universality and goodness. Thirty years of neoliberal freedoms have, after all, not only restored power to a narrowly defined capitalist class. They have also produced immense concentrations of corporate power in energy, the media, pharmaceuticals, transportation, and even retailing (for example Wal-Mart). The freedom of the market that Bush proclaims as the high point of human aspiration turns out to be nothing more than the convenient means to spread corporate monopoly power and Coca Cola everywhere without constraint. With disproportionate influence over the media and the political process this class (with Rupert Murdoch and Fox News in the lead) has both the incentive and the power to persuade us that we are all better off under a neoliberal regime of freedoms. For the elite, living comfortably in their gilded ghettos, the world must indeed seem a better place. As Polanyi might have put it, neoliberalism confers rights and freedoms on those 'whose income, leisure and security need no enhancing', leaving a pittance for the rest of us. How is it, then, that 'the rest of us' have so easily acquiesced in this state of affairs?

2

The Construction of Consent

How was neoliberalization accomplished, and by whom? The answer in countries such as Chile and Argentina in the 1970s was as simple as it was swift, brutal, and sure: a military coup backed by the traditional upper classes (as well as by the US government), followed by the fierce repression of all solidarities created within the labour and urban social movements which had so threatened their power. But the neoliberal revolution usually attributed to Thatcher and Reagan after 1979 had to be accomplished by democratic means. For a shift of this magnitude to occur required the prior construction of political consent across a sufficiently large spectrum of the population to win elections. What Gramsci calls 'common sense' (defined as 'the sense held in common') typically grounds consent. Common sense is constructed out of long-standing practices of cultural socialization often rooted deep in regional or national traditions. It is not the same as the 'good sense' that can be constructed out of critical engagement with the issues of the day. Common sense can, therefore, be profoundly misleading, obfuscating or disguising real problems under cultural prejudices.[1] Cultural and traditional values (such as belief in God and country or views on the position of women in society) and fears (of communists, immigrants, strangers, or 'others') can be mobilized to mask other realities. Political slogans can be invoked that mask specific strategies beneath vague rhetorical devices. The word 'freedom' resonates so widely within the common-sense understanding of Americans that it becomes 'a button that elites can press to open the door to the masses' to justify almost anything.[2] Thus could Bush retrospectively justify the Iraq war. Gramsci therefore concluded that political questions become 'insoluble' when 'disguised as cultural ones'.[3] In seeking to understand the construction of political consent, we must learn to extract political meanings from their cultural integuments.

So how, then, was sufficient popular consent generated to legitimize the neoliberal turn? The channels through which this was done were diverse. Powerful ideological influences circulated through the corporations, the media, and the numerous institutions that constitute civil society—such as the universities, schools, churches, and professional associations. The 'long march' of neoliberal ideas through these institutions that Hayek had envisaged back in 1947, the organization of think-tanks (with corporate backing and funding), the capture of certain segments of the media, and the conversion of many intellectuals to neoliberal ways of thinking, created a climate of opinion in support of neoliberalism as the exclusive guarantor of freedom. These movements were later consolidated through the capture of political parties and, ultimately, state power.

Appeals to traditions and cultural values bulked large in all of this. An open project around the restoration of economic power to a small elite would probably not gain much popular support. But a programmatic attempt to advance the cause of individual freedoms could appeal to a mass base and so disguise the drive to restore class power. Furthermore, once the state apparatus made the neoliberal turn it could use its powers of persuasion, co-optation, bribery, and threat to maintain the climate of consent necessary to perpetuate its power. This was Thatcher's and Reagan's particular forte, as we shall see.

How, then, did neoliberalism negotiate the turn to so comprehensively displace embedded liberalism? In some instances, the answer largely lies in the use of force (either military, as in Chile, or financial, as through the operations of the IMF in Mozambique or the Philippines). Coercion can produce a fatalistic, even abject, acceptance of the idea that there was and is, as Margaret Thatcher kept insisting, 'no alternative'. The active construction of consent has also varied from place to place. Furthermore, as numerous oppositional movements attest, consent has often wilted or failed in different places. But we must look beyond these infinitely varied ideological and cultural mechanisms—no matter how important they are—to the qualities of everyday experience in order to better identify the material grounding for the construction of consent. And it is at that level—through the experience of daily life under capitalism in the 1970s—that we begin to see how neoliberalism penetrated 'common-sense' understandings. The effect in many parts of the world has increasingly been to see it as a necessary, even wholly 'natural', way for the social order to be regulated.

Any political movement that holds individual freedoms to be sacrosanct is vulnerable to incorporation into the neoliberal fold. The worldwide political upheavals of 1968, for example, were strongly inflected with the desire for greater personal freedoms. This was certainly true for students, such as those animated by the Berkeley 'free speech' movement of the 1960s or who took to the streets in Paris, Berlin, and Bangkok and were so mercilessly shot down in Mexico City shortly before the 1968 Olympic Games. They demanded freedom from parental, educational, corporate, bureaucratic, and state constraints. But the '68 movement also had social justice as a primary political objective.

Values of individual freedom and social justice are not, however, necessarily compatible. Pursuit of social justice presupposes social solidarities and a willingness to submerge individual wants, needs, and desires in the cause of some more general struggle for, say, social equality or environmental justice. The objectives of social justice and individual freedom were uneasily fused in the movement of '68. The tension was most evident in the fraught relationship between the traditional left (organized labour and political parties espousing social solidarities) and the student movement desirous of individual liberties. The suspicion and hostility that separated these two fractions in France (e.g. the Communist Party and the student movement) during the events of 1968 is a case in point. While it is not impossible to bridge such differences, it is not hard to see how a wedge might be driven between them. Neoliberal rhetoric, with its foundational emphasis upon individual freedoms, has the power to split off libertarianism, identity politics, multi-culturalism, and eventually narcissistic consumerism from the social forces ranged in pursuit of social justice through the conquest of state power. It has long proved extremely difficult within the US left, for example, to forge the collective discipline required for political action to achieve social justice without offending the

41

desire of political actors for individual freedom and for full recognition and expression of particular identities. Neoliberalism did not create these distinctions, but it could easily exploit, if not foment, them.

In the early 1970s those seeking individual freedoms and social justice could make common cause in the face of what many saw as a common enemy. Powerful corporations in alliance with an interventionist state were seen to be running the world in individually oppressive and socially unjust ways. The Vietnam War was the most obvious catalyst for discontent, but the destructive activities of corporations and the state in relation to the environment, the push towards mindless consumerism, the failure to address social issues and respond adequately to diversity, as well as intense restrictions on individual possibilities and personal behaviours by state-mandated and 'traditional' controls were also widely resented. Civil rights were an issue, and questions of sexuality and of reproductive rights were very much in play. For almost everyone involved in the movement of '68, the intrusive state was the enemy and it had to be reformed. And on that, the neoliberals could easily agree. But capitalist corporations, business, and the market system were also seen as primary enemies requiring redress if not revolutionary transformation: hence the threat to capitalist class power. By capturing ideals of individual freedom and turning them against the interventionist and regulatory practices of the state, capitalist class interests could hope to protect and even restore their position. Neoliberalism was well suited to this ideological task. But it had to be backed up by a practical strategy that emphasized the liberty of consumer choice, not only with respect to particular products but also with respect to lifestyles, modes of expression, and a wide range of cultural practices. Neoliberalization required both politically and economically the construction of a neoliberal market-based populist culture of differentiated consumerism and individual libertarianism. As such it proved more than a little compatible with that cultural impulse called 'postmodernism' which had long been lurking in the wings but could now emerge full-blown as both a cultural and an intellectual dominant. This was the challenge that corporations and class elites set out to finesse in the 1980s.

None of this was very clear at the time. Left movements failed to recognize or confront, let alone transcend, the inherent tension between the quest for individual freedoms and social justice. But the intuitive sense of the problem was, I suspect, clear enough to many in the upper class, even to those who had never read Hayek or even heard of neoliberal theory. Let me illustrate this idea by comparing the neoliberal turns in the US and Britain in the troubled years of the 1970s.

In the US case I begin with a confidential memo sent by Lewis Powell to the US Chamber of Commerce in August 1971. Powell, about to be elevated to the Supreme Court by Richard Nixon, argued that criticism of and opposition to the US free enterprise system had gone too far and that 'the time had come—indeed it is long overdue—for the wisdom, ingenuity and resources of American business to be marshalled against those who would destroy it'. Powell argued that individual action was insufficient. 'Strength', he wrote, 'lies in organization, in careful long-range planning and implementation, in consistency of action over an indefinite period of years, in the scale of financing available only through joint effort, and in the political power available only through united action and national organizations'. The National Chamber of Commerce, he argued, should lead an assault upon the major institutions—universities, schools, the media, publishing, the courts—in order to change how individuals think 'about the corporation, the law, culture, and the individual'. US businesses did not lack resources for such an effort, particularly when pooled.[4]

How directly influential this appeal to engage in class war was, is hard to tell. But we do know that the American Chamber of Commerce subsequently expanded its base from around 60,000 firms in 1972 to over a quarter of a million ten years later. Jointly with the National Association of Manufacturers (which moved to Washington in 1972) it amassed an immense campaign chest to lobby Congress and engage in research. The Business Roundtable, an organization of CEOs 'committed to the aggressive pursuit of political power for the corporation', was founded in 1972 and thereafter became the centrepiece of collective pro-business action. The corporations involved accounted for 'about one half of the GNP of the United States' during the 1970s, and they spent close to $900 million annually (a huge amount at that time) on political matters. Think-tanks, such as the Heritage Foundation, the Hoover Institute, the Center for the Study of American Business, and the American Enterprise Institute, were formed with corporate backing both to polemicize and, when necessary, as in the case of the National Bureau of Economic Research, to construct serious technical and empirical studies and political-philosophical arguments broadly in support of neoliberal policies. Nearly half the financing for the highly respected NBER came from the leading companies in the Fortune 500 list. Closely integrated with the academic community, the NBER was to have a very significant impact on thinking in the economics departments and business schools of the major research universities. With abundant finance furnished by wealthy individuals (such as the brewer Joseph Coors, who later became a member of Reagan's 'kitchen cabinet') and their foundations (for example Olin, Scaife, Smith Richardson, Pew Charitable Trust), a flood of tracts and books, with Nozick's *Anarchy State and Utopia* perhaps the most widely read and appreciated, emerged espousing neoliberal values. A TV version of Milton Friedman's *Free to Choose* was funded with a grant from Scaife in 1977. 'Business was', Blyth concludes, 'learning to spend as a class.'[5]

In singling out the universities for particular attention, Powell pointed up an opportunity as well as an issue, for these were indeed centres of anti-corporate and anti-state sentiment (the students at Santa Barbara had burned down the Bank of America building there and ceremonially buried a car in the sands). But many students were (and still are) affluent and privileged, or at least middle class, and in the US the values of individual freedom have long been celebrated (in music and popular culture) as primary. Neoliberal themes could here find fertile ground for propagation. Powell did not argue for extending state power. But business should 'assiduously cultivate' the state and when necessary use it 'aggressively and with determination'.[6] But exactly how was state power to be deployed to reshape common-sense understandings?

One line of response to the double crisis of capital accumulation and class power arose in the trenches of the urban struggles of the 1970s. The New York City fiscal crisis was an iconic case.

Capitalist restructuring and deindustrialization had for several years been eroding the economic base of the city, and rapid suburbanization had left much of the central city impoverished. The result was explosive social unrest on the part of marginalized populations during the 1960s, defining what came to be known as 'the urban crisis' (similar problems emerged in many US cities). The expansion of public employment and public provision—facilitated in part by generous federal funding—was seen as the solution. But, faced with fiscal difficulties, President Nixon simply declared the urban crisis over in the early 1970s. While this was news to many city dwellers, it signalled diminished federal aid. As the recession gathered pace, the gap between revenues and outlays in the New York City budget (already large because of profligate borrowing over many years) increased. At first financial institutions were prepared to bridge the gap, but in 1975 a powerful cabal of investment bankers (led by Walter Wriston of Citibank) refused to roll over the debt and pushed the city into technical bankruptcy. The bail-out that followed entailed the construction of new institutions that took over the management of the city budget. They had first claim on city tax revenues in order to first pay off bondholders: whatever was left went for essential services. The effect was to curb the aspirations of the city's powerful municipal unions, to implement wage freezes and cutbacks in public employment and social provision (education, public health, transport services), and to impose user fees (tuition was introduced into the CUNY university system for the first time). The final indignity was the requirement that municipal unions should invest their pension funds in city bonds. Unions then either moderated their demands or faced the prospect of losing their pension funds through city bankruptcy.[7]

This amounted to a coup by the financial institutions against the democratically elected government of New York City, and it was every bit as effective as the military coup that had earlier occurred in Chile. Wealth was redistributed to the upper classes in the midst of a fiscal crisis. The New York crisis was, Zevin argues, symptomatic of 'an emerging strategy of disinflation coupled with a regressive redistribution of income, wealth and power'. It was 'an early, perhaps decisive battle in a new war', the purpose of which was 'to show others that what is happening to New York could and in some cases will happen to them'.[8]

Whether everyone involved in negotiating this fiscal compromise understood it as a strategy to restore class power is an open question. The need to maintain fiscal discipline is a matter of concern in its own right and does not, like monetarism more generally, necessarily entail regressive redistributions. It is unlikely, for example, that Felix Rohatyn, the merchant banker who brokered the deal between the city, the state, and the financial institutions, had the restoration of class power in mind. The only way he could 'save' the city was by satisfying the investment bankers while diminishing the standard of living of most New Yorkers. But the restoration of class power was almost certainly what investment bankers like Walter Wriston had in mind. He had, after all, equated all forms of government intervention in the US and Britain with communism. And it was almost certainly the aim of Ford's Secretary of the Treasury William Simon (later to become head of the ultra-conservative Olin Foundation). Watching the progress of events in Chile with approval, he strongly advised President Ford to refuse aid to the city ('Ford to City: Drop Dead' ran the headline in the *New York Daily News*). The terms of any bail-out, he said, should be 'so punitive, the overall experience so painful, that no city, no political subdivision would ever be tempted to go down the same road'.[9]

While resistance to the austerity measures was widespread, it could only, according to Freeman, slow 'the counterrevolution from above, it could not stop it. Within a few years, many of the historic achievements of working class New York were undone'. Much of the social infrastructure of the city was diminished and the physical infrastructure (for example the subway system) deteriorated markedly for lack of investment or even maintenance. Daily life in New York 'became gruelling and the civic atmosphere turned mean'. The city government, the municipal labour movement, and working-class New Yorkers were effectively stripped 'of much of the power they had accumulated over the previous three decades'.[10] Demoralized, working-class New Yorkers reluctantly assented to the new realities.

But the New York investment bankers did not walk away from

the city. They seized the opportunity to restructure it in ways that suited their agenda. The creation of a 'good business climate' was a priority. This meant using public resources to build appropriate infrastructures for business (particularly in telecommunications) coupled with subsidies and tax incentives for capitalist enterprises. Corporate welfare substituted for people welfare. The city's elite institutions were mobilized to sell the image of the city as a cultural centre and tourist destination (inventing the famous logo 'I Love New York'). The ruling elites moved, often fractiously, to support the opening up of the cultural field to all manner of diverse cosmopolitan currents. The narcissistic exploration of self, sexuality, and identity became the leitmotif of bourgeois urban culture. Artistic freedom and artistic licence, promoted by the city's powerful cultural institutions, led, in effect, to the neoliberalization of culture. 'Delirious New York' (to use Rem Koolhaas's memorable phrase) erased the collective memory of democratic New York.[11] The city's elites acceded, though not without a struggle, to the demand for lifestyle diversification (including those attached to sexual preference and gender) and increasing consumer niche choices (in areas such as cultural production). New York became the epicentre of postmodern cultural and intellectual experimentation. Meanwhile the investment bankers reconstructed the city economy around financial activities, ancillary services such as legal services and the media (much revived by the financialization then occurring), and diversified consumerism (gentrification and neighbourhood 'restoration' playing a prominent and profitable role). City government was more and more construed as an entrepreneurial rather than a social democratic or even managerial entity. Inter-urban competition for investment capital transformed government into urban governance through public–private partnerships. City business was increasingly conducted behind closed doors, and the democratic and representational content of local governance diminished.[12]

Working–class and ethnic–immigrant New York was thrust back into the shadows, to be ravaged by racism and a crack cocaine epidemic of epic proportions in the 1980s that left many young people either dead, incarcerated, or homeless, only to be bludgeoned again by the AIDS epidemic that carried over into the

1990s. Redistribution through criminal violence became one of the few serious options for the poor, and the authorities responded by criminalizing whole communities of impoverished and marginalized populations. The victims were blamed, and Giuliani was to claim fame by taking revenge on behalf of an increasingly affluent Manhattan bourgeoisie tired of having to confront the effects of such devastation on their own doorsteps.

The management of the New York fiscal crisis pioneered the way for neoliberal practices both domestically under Reagan and internationally through the IMF in the 1980s. It established the principle that in the event of a conflict between the integrity of financial institutions and bondholders' returns, on the one hand, and the well-being of the citizens on the other, the former was to be privileged. It emphasized that the role of government was to create a good business climate rather than look to the needs and well-being of the population at large. The politics of the Reagan administration of the 1980s, Tabb concludes, became 'merely the New York scenario' of the 1970s 'writ large'.[13]

The translation of these local conclusions of the mid-1970s to the national level was fast-moving. Thomas Edsall (a journalist who covered Washington affairs for many years) published a prescient account in 1985:

During the 1970s, business refined its ability to act as a class, submerging competitive instincts in favour of joint, cooperative action in the legislative arena. Rather than individual companies seeking only special favours . . . the dominant theme in the political strategy of business became a shared interest in the defeat of bills such as consumer protection and labour law reform, and in the enactment of favourable tax, regulatory and antitrust legislation'.[14]

In order to realize this goal, businesses needed a political class instrument and a popular base. They therefore actively sought to capture the Republican Party as their own instrument. The formation of powerful political action committees to procure, as the old adage had it, 'the best government that money could buy' was an important step. The supposedly 'progressive' campaign finance laws of 1971 in effect legalized the financial corruption of politics. A crucial set of Supreme Court decisions began in 1976 when it was first established that the right of a corporation to make unlimited money contributions to political parties and political action committees was protected under the First Amendment guaranteeing the rights of individuals (in this instance corporations) to freedom of speech.[15] Political action committees (PACs) could thereafter ensure the financial domination of both political parties by corporate, moneyed, and professional association interests. Corporate PACs, which numbered eighty-nine in 1974, had burgeoned to 1,467 by 1982. While these were willing to fund powerful incumbents of both parties provided their interests were served, they also systematically leaned towards supporting right-wing challengers. In the late 1970s Reagan (then Governor of California) and William Simon (whom we have already encountered) went out of their way to urge the PACs to direct their efforts towards funding Republican candidates with right-wing sympathies.[16] The $5,000 limit on each PAC's contribution to any one individual forced PACs from different corporations and industries to work together, and that meant building alliances based on class rather than particular interests.

The willingness of the Republican Party to become the representative of 'its dominant class constituency' during this period contrasted, Edsall notes, with the 'ideologically ambivalent' attitude of the Democrats which grew out of 'the fact that its ties to various groups in society are diffuse, and none of these groups—women, blacks, labour, the elderly, hispanics, urban political organizations—stands clearly larger than the others'. The dependency of Democrats, furthermore, on 'big money' contributions rendered many of them highly vulnerable to direct influence from business interests.[17] While the Democratic Party had a popular base, it could not easily pursue an anti-capitalist or anti-corporate political line without totally severing its connections with powerful financial interests.

The Republican Party needed, however, a solid electoral base if it was to colonize power effectively. It was around this time that Republicans sought an alliance with the Christian right. The latter had not been politically active in the past, but the foundation of Jerry Falwell's 'moral majority' as a political movement in 1978 changed all of that. The Republican Party now had its Christian base. It also appealed to the cultural nationalism of the white working classes and their besieged sense of moral righteousness (besieged because this class lived under conditions of chronic economic insecurity and felt excluded from many of the benefits that were being distributed through affirmative action and other state programmes). This political base could be mobilized through the positives of religion and cultural nationalism and negatively through coded, if not blatant, racism, homophobia, and anti-feminism. The problem was not capitalism and the neoliberalization of culture, but the 'liberals' who had used excessive state power to provide for special groups (blacks, women, environmentalists, etc.). A well-funded movement of neoconservative intellectuals (gathered around Irving Kristol and Norman Podhoretz and the journal *Commentary*), espousing morality and traditional values, gave credence to these theses. Supporting the neoliberal turn economically but not culturally, they excoriated the interventionist excesses of a so-called 'liberal elite'—thus greatly muddying what the term 'liberal' might mean. The effect was to divert attention from capitalism and corporate power as in any way having anything to do with either the economic or the cultural problems that unbridled commercialism and individualism were creating.

From then on the unholy alliance between big business and conservative Christians backed by the neoconservatives steadily consolidated, eventually eradicating all liberal elements (significant and influential in the 1960s) from the Republican Party, particularly after 1990, and turning it into the relatively homogeneous right-wing electoral force of present times.[18] Not for the first, nor, it is to be feared, for the last time in history has a social group been persuaded to vote against its material, economic, and class interests for cultural, nationalist, and religious reasons. In some cases, however, it is probably more appropriate to replace the word 'persuaded' with 'elected', since there is abundant evidence that the evangelical Christians (no more than 20 per cent of the population) who make up the core of the 'moral majority' eagerly embraced the alliance with big business and the Republican Party as a means to further promote their evangelical and moral agenda. This was certainly the case with the shadowy and secretive organization of

Christian conservatives that constituted the Council for National Policy, founded in 1981, 'to strategize how to turn the country to the right'.[19]

The Democratic Party, on the other hand, was fundamentally riven by the need to placate, if not succour, corporate and financial interests while at the same time making some gestures towards improving the material conditions of life for its popular base. During the Clinton presidency it ended up choosing the former over the latter and therefore fell directly into the neoliberal fold of policy prescription and implementation (as, for example, in the reform of welfare).[20] But, as in the case of Felix Rohatyn, it is doubtful if this was Clinton's agenda from the very beginning. Faced with the need to overcome a huge deficit and spark economic growth, his only feasible economic path was deficit reduction to achieve low interest rates. That meant either substantially higher taxation (which amounted to electoral suicide) or cutbacks in the budget. Going for the latter meant, as Yergin and Stanislaw put it, 'betraying their traditional constituencies in order to pamper the rich' or, as Joseph Stiglitz, once chair of Clinton's Council of Economic Advisors, later confessed, 'we did manage to tighten the belts of the poor as we loosened those on the rich'.[21] Social policy was in effect put in the care of the Wall Street bondholders (much as had happened in New York City earlier), with predictable consequences.

The political structure that emerged was quite simple. The Republican Party could mobilize massive financial resources and mobilize its popular base to vote against its material interests on cultural/religious grounds while the Democratic Party could not afford to attend to the material needs (for example for a national health-care system) of its traditional popular base for fear of offending capitalist class interests. Given the asymmetry, the political hegemony of the Republican Party became more sure.

Reagan's election in 1980 was only the first step in the long process of consolidating the political shift necessary to support Volcker's turn to monetarism and the prioritization of the fight against inflation. Reagan's policies, Edsall noted at the time, centred on 'an across the board drive to reduce the scope and

51

content of federal regulation of industry, the environment, the workplace, health care, and the relationship between buyer and seller'. Budget cuts and deregulation and 'the appointment of anti-regulatory, industry-oriented agency personnel' to key positions were the main means.[22]

The National Labour Relations Board, established to regulate capital–labour relations in the workplace in the 1930s, was converted by Reagan's appointments into a vehicle for attacking and regulating the rights of labour at the very moment when business was being deregulated.[23] It took less than six months in 1983 to reverse nearly 40 per cent of the decisions made during the 1970s that had been, in the view of business, too favourable to labour. Reagan construed all regulation (except of labour) as bad. The Office of Management and Budget was mandated to do thorough cost-benefit analyses of all regulatory proposals (past and present). If it could not be shown that the benefits of regulation clearly exceeded the costs then the regulations should be scrapped. To top it all, elaborate revisions of the tax code—mainly concerning depreciation on investments—allowed many corporations to get away without paying any taxes at all, while the reduction of the top tax rate for individuals from 78 to 28 per cent obviously reflected the intent to restore class power (see Figure 1.7). Worst of all, public assets were freely passed over into the private domain. Many of the key breakthroughs in pharmaceutical research, for example, had been funded by the National Institute of Health in collaboration with the drug companies. But in 1978 the companies were allowed to take all the benefits of patent rights without returning anything to the state, assuring the industry of high and highly subsidized profits ever after.[24]

But all of this required that labour and labour organization be brought to heel to conform to the new social order. If New York pioneered this by disciplining powerful municipal unions in 1975–7, Reagan followed at the national level by bringing down the air traffic controllers in 1981 and making it clear to the trade unions that they were unwelcome as participants in the inner councils of government. The uneasy social compact that had ruled between corporate and union power during the 1960s was over. With unemployment surging to 10 per cent in the mid-1980s, the moment was propitious to attack all forms of organized labour and to cut back on its privileges as well as its power. Transfer of industrial activity from the unionized north-east and midwest to the non-unionized and 'right-to-work' states of the south, if not beyond to Mexico and South-East Asia, became standard practice (subsidized by favourable taxation for new investment and aided by the shift in emphasis from production to finance as the centrepiece of capitalist class power). Deindustrialization of formerly unionized core industrial regions (the so-called 'rust belt') disempowered labour. Corporations could threaten plant closures, and risk—and usually win—strikes when necessary (for example in the coal industry).

But here too it was not merely the use of the big stick that mattered, for there were a number of carrots that could be offered to labourers as individuals to break with collective action. The unions' rigid rules and bureaucratic structures made them vulnerable to attack. The lack of flexibility was often as much a disadvantage for individual labourers as it was for capital. The virtuous claims for flexible specialization in labour processes and for flexitime arrangements could become part of the neoliberal rhetoric that could be persuasive to individual labourers, particularly those who had been excluded from the monopoly benefits that strong unionization sometimes conferred. Greater freedom and liberty of action in the labour market could be touted as a virtue for capital and labour alike, and here, too, it was not hard to integrate neoliberal values into the 'common sense' of much of the workforce. How this active potentiality was converted into a highly exploitative system of flexible accumulation (all the benefits accruing from increasing flexibility in labour allocations in both space and time go to capital) is key to explaining why real wages, except for a brief period during the 1990s, stagnated or fell (see Figure 1.6) and benefits diminished. Neoliberal theory conveniently holds that unemployment is always voluntary. Labour, the argument goes, has a 'reserve price' below which it prefers not to work. Unemployment arises because the reserve price of labour is too high. Since that reserve price is partly set by welfare payments (and stories of 'welfare queens' driving Cadillacs abounded) then it stands to reason that the neoliberal reform carried out by Clinton of 'welfare as we know it' must be a crucial step towards the reduction of unemployment.

All of this demanded some rationale, and to this end the war of ideas did play an important role. The economic ideas marshalled in support of the neoliberal turn amounted, Blyth suggests, to a complex fusion of monetarism (Friedman), rational expectations (Robert Lucas), public choice (James Buchanan, and Gordon Tullock), and the less respectable but by no means uninfluential 'supply-side' ideas of Arthur Laffer, who went so far as to suggest that the incentive effects of tax cuts would so increase economic activity as to automatically increase tax revenues (Reagan was enamoured of this idea). The more acceptable commonality to these arguments was that government intervention was the problem rather than the solution, and that 'a stable monetary policy, plus radical tax cuts in the top brackets, would produce a healthier economy' by getting the incentives for entrepreneurial activity aligned correctly.[25] The business press, with the *Wall Street Journal* very much in the lead, took up these ideas, becoming an open advocate for neoliberalization as the necessary solution to all economic ills. Popular currency was given to these ideas by prolific writers such as George Gilder (supported by think-tank funds), and the business schools that arose in prestigious universities such as Stanford and Harvard, generously funded by corporations and foundations, became centres of neoliberal orthodoxy from the very moment they opened. Charting the spread of ideas is always difficult, but by 1990 or so most economics departments in the major research universities as well as the business schools were dominated by neoliberal modes of thought. The importance of this should not be underestimated. The US research universities were and are training grounds for many foreigners who take what they learn back to their countries of origin—the key figures in Chile's and Mexico's adaptation to neoliberalism were US-trained economists for example—as well as into international institutions such as the IMF, the World Bank, and the UN.

The conclusion is, I think, clear. 'During the 1970s, the political wing of the nation's corporate sector', writes Edsall, 'staged one of the most remarkable campaigns in the pursuit of power in recent history.' By the early 1980s it 'had gained a level of influence and leverage approaching that of the boom days of the 1920s'.[26] And by the year 2000 it had used that leverage to restore its share of the national wealth and income to levels also not seen since the 1920s.

The construction of consent in Britain occurred in a very different way.[27] What happened in Kansas was quite different from what happened in Yorkshire. The cultural and political traditions were very different. In Britain, there is no Christian right to speak of to be mobilized into a moral majority. Corporate power there was little inclined to support overt political activism (its contributions to political parties were minimal), preferring instead to exercise influence through the networks of class and privilege that had long connected government, academia, the judiciary, and the permanent Civil Service (which at that time still maintained its tradition of independence) with the leaders of industry and finance. The political situation was also radically different, given that the Labour Party had largely been constructed as an instrument of working-class power, beholden to strong and sometimes quite militant trade unions. Britain had consequently developed a far more elaborate and all-encompassing welfare state structure than would have ever been dreamed of in the US. The commanding heights of the economy (coal, steel, automobiles) were nationalized, and a large proportion of the housing stock was in the public sector. And the Labour Party had, ever since the 1930s, built significant redoubts of power in the arena of municipal governance, with Herbert Morrison's London County Council being in the vanguard from the 1930s onwards. Social solidarities constructed through the union movement and municipal governance were strongly in evidence. Even when the Conservative Party took power for prolonged periods after the Second World War it largely refrained from any attempt at dismantling the welfare state it had inherited.

The Labour government of the 1960s had refused to send troops to Vietnam, thus saving the country from direct domestic traumas over participation in an unpopular war. After the Second World War, Britain had (albeit reluctantly and in some instances not without violent struggle and considerable prodding from the US) agreed to decolonization, and after the abortive Suez venture of 1956 gradually (and again often reluctantly) shed much of the mantle of direct imperial power. The withdrawal of its forces east of Suez in the 1960s was an important signifier of this process. Thereafter, Britain largely participated as a junior partner within NATO under the military shield of US power. But Britain did continue to project a neocolonial presence throughout much of what had been its empire, and in so doing frequently tangled with other great powers (as, for example, in the bloody Nigerian civil war when Biafra attempted to secede). The issue of Britain's relations with and responsibilities towards its ex-colonies was often fraught, both at home and abroad. Neocolonial structures of commercial exploitation were often deepened rather than eradicated. But migratory currents from the ex-colonies towards Britain were beginning to bring the consequences of empire back home in new ways.

The most important residual of Britain's imperial presence was the continuing role of the City of London as a centre of international finance. During the 1960s this became increasingly important as the UK moved to protect and enhance the position of the City with respect to the rising powers of globally oriented finance capital. This created a series of important contradictions. The protection of finance capital (through interest rate manipulations) more often than not conflicted with the needs of domestic manufacturing capital (hence provoking a structural division within the capitalist class) and sometimes inhibited the expansion of the domestic market (by restricting credit). The commitment to a strong pound undermined the export position of UK industry and helped create balance of payments crises in the 1970s. Contradictions arose between the embedded liberalism constructed within and the free market liberalism of London-based finance capital operating on the world stage. The City of London, the financial centre, had long favoured monetarist rather than Keynesian policies, and therefore formed a bastion of resistance to embedded liberalism.

The welfare state constructed in Britain after the Second World War was never to everyone's liking. Strong currents of criticism circulated through the media (with the highly respected *Financial Times* in the lead), which were increasingly subservient to financial interests. Individualism, freedom, and liberty were depicted as opposed to the stifling bureaucratic ineptitude of the state apparatus and oppressive trade union power. Such criticisms become widespread in Britain during the 1960s and became even more emphatic during the bleak years of economic stagnation during the 1970s. People then feared that Britain was becoming 'a corporatist state, ground down to a gray mediocrity'.[28] The undercurrent of thought represented by Hayek constituted a viable opposition and had its advocates in the universities and even more importantly dominated the work of the Institute of Economic Affairs (founded in 1955), where Keith Joseph, later to be a key adviser to Margaret Thatcher, rose to public prominence in the 1970s. The foundation of the Centre for Policy Studies (1974) and the Adam Smith Institute (1976), and the increasing commitment of the press to neoliberalization during the 1970s, significantly affected the climate of public opinion. The earlier rise of a significant youth movement (given to political satire) and the arrival of a freewheeling pop culture in the 'swinging London' of the 1960s both mocked and challenged the traditional structure of networked class relations. Individualism and freedom of expression became an issue and a left-leaning student movement, influenced in many ways by the complexities of coming to terms with Britain's entrenched class system as well as with its colonial heritage, became an active element within British politics, much as it did elsewhere in the movement of '68. Its disrespectful attitude towards class privileges (whether of aristocrats, politicians, or union bureaucrats) was to ground the later radicalism of the postmodern turn. Scepticism about politics was to prepare the way for suspicion of all metanarratives.

While there were many elements out of which consent for a neoliberal turn could be constructed, the Thatcher phenomenon would surely not have arisen, let alone succeeded, if it had not been for the serious crisis of capital accumulation during the 1970s. Stagflation was hurting everyone. In 1975 inflation surged to 26 per cent and unemployment topped one million (see Figure 1.1). The nationalized industries were draining resources from the Treasury. This set up a confrontation between the state and the unions. In 1972, and then again in 1974, the British miners (a nationalized industry) went on strike for the first time since 1926.

The miners had always been in the forefront of British labour struggles. Their wages were not keeping pace with accelerating inflation, and the public sympathized. The Conservative government, in the midst of power blackouts, declared a state of emergency, mandated a three-day working week, and sought public backing against the miners. In 1974 it called an election seeking public support for its stand. It lost, and the Labour government that returned to power settled the strike on terms favourable to the miners.

The victory was, however, pyrrhic. The Labour government could not afford the terms of the settlement and its fiscal difficulties mounted. A balance of payments crisis paralleled huge budget deficits. Turning for credits to the IMF in 1975–6, it faced the choice of either submitting to IMF-mandated budgetary restraint and austerity or declaring bankruptcy and sacrificing the integrity of sterling, thus mortally wounding financial interests in the City of London. It chose the former path, and draconian budgetary cutbacks in welfare state expenditures were implemented.[29] The Labour government went against the material interests of its traditional supporters. But it still had no solution to the crises of accumulation and stagflation. It sought, unsuccessfully, to mask the difficulties by appealing to corporatist ideals, in which everyone was supposed to sacrifice something for the benefit of the polity. Its supporters were in open revolt, and public sector workers initiated a series of crippling strikes in the 'winter of discontent' of 1978. 'Hospital workers went out, and medical care had to be severely rationed. Striking gravediggers refused to bury the dead. The truck drivers were on strike too. Only shop stewards had the right to let trucks bearing "essential supplies" cross picket lines. British Rail put out a terse notice "There are no trains today" . . . striking unions seemed about to bring the whole nation to a halt.'[30] The mainstream press was in full cry against greedy and disruptive unions, and public support fell away. The Labour government fell, and in the election that followed Margaret Thatcher won a significant majority with a clear mandate from her middle-class supporters to tame public sector trade union power.

The commonality between the US and the UK cases most obviously lies in the fields of labour relations and the fight against

58

inflation. With respect to the latter, Thatcher made monetarism and strict budgetary control the order of the day. High interest rates meant high unemployment (averaging more than 10 per cent in 1979–84, and the Trades Union Congress lost 17 per cent of its membership in five years). The bargaining power of labour was weakened. Alan Budd, an economic adviser to Thatcher, later suggested that 'the 1980s policies of attacking inflation by squeezing the economy and public spending were a cover to bash the workers'. Britain created what Marx called 'an industrial reserve army', he went on to observe, the effect of which was to undermine the power of labour and permit capitalists to make easy profits thereafter. And in an action that paralleled Reagan's provocation of PATCO in 1981, Thatcher provoked a miners' strike in 1984 by announcing a wave of redundancies and pit closures (imported coal was cheaper). The strike lasted for almost a year, and, in spite of a great deal of public sympathy and support, the miners lost. The back of a core element of the British labour movement had been broken.[31] Thatcher further reduced union power by opening up the UK to foreign competition and foreign investment. Foreign competition demolished much of traditional British industry in the 1980s—the steel industry (Sheffield) and shipbuilding (Glasgow) more or less totally disappeared within a few years, and with them a good deal of trade union power. Thatcher effectively destroyed the indigenous nationalized UK automobile industry, with its strong unions and militant labour traditions, instead offering the UK as an offshore platform for Japanese automobile companies seeking access to Europe.[32] These built on greenfield sites and recruited non-union workers who would submit to Japanese-style labour relations. The overall effect was to transform the UK into a country of relatively low wages and a largely compliant labour force (relative to the rest of Europe) within ten years. By the time Thatcher left office, strike activity had fallen to one-tenth of its former levels. She had eradicated inflation, curbed union power, tamed the labour force, and built middle-class consent for her policies in the process.

But Thatcher had to fight the battle on other fronts. A noble rearguard action against neoliberal policies was mounted in many a municipality—Sheffield, the Greater London Council (which

Thatcher had to abolish in order to achieve her broader goals in the 1980s), and Liverpool (where half the local councillors had to be gaoled) formed active centres of resistance in which the ideals of a new municipal socialism (incorporating many of the new social movements in the London case) were both pursued and acted upon until they were finally crushed in the mid-1980s.[33] She began by savagely cutting back central government funding to the municipalities, but several of them responded simply by raising property taxes, forcing her to legislate against their right to do so. Denigrating the progressive labour councils as 'loony lefties' (a phrase the Conservative-dominated press picked up with relish), she then sought to impose neoliberal principles through a reform of municipal finance. She proposed a 'poll tax'—a regressive head tax rather than a property tax—which would rein in municipal expenditures by making every resident pay. This provoked a huge political fight that played a role in Thatcher's political demise.

Thatcher also set out to privatize all those sectors of the economy that were in public ownership. The sales would boost the public treasury and rid the government of burdensome future obligations towards losing enterprises. These state-run enterprises had to be adequately prepared for privatization, and this meant paring down their debt and improving their efficiency and cost structures, often through shedding labour. Their valuation was also structured to offer considerable incentives to private capital—a process that was likened by opponents to 'giving away the family silver'. In several cases subsidies were hidden in the mode of valuation—water companies, railways, and even state-run enterprises in the automobile and steel industries held high-value land in prime locations that was excluded from the valuation of the enterprise as an ongoing concern. Privatization and speculative gains on the property released went hand in hand. But the aim here was also to change the political culture by extending the field of personal and corporate responsibility and encouraging greater efficiency, individual/corporate initiative, and innovation. British Aerospace, British Telecom, British Airways, steel, electricity and gas, oil, coal, water, bus services, railways, and a host of smaller state enterprises were sold off in a massive wave of privatizations. Britain pioneered the way in showing how to do this in a reasonably orderly and, for capital, profitable way. Thatcher was convinced that once these changes had been made they would become irreversible: hence the haste. The legitimacy of this whole movement was successfully underpinned, however, by the extensive selling off of public housing to tenants. This vastly increased the number of homeowners within a decade. It satisfied traditional ideals of individual property ownership as a working-class dream and introduced a new, and often speculative, dynamism into the housing market that was much appreciated by the middle classes, who saw their asset values rise—at least until the property crash of the early 1990s.

Dismantling the welfare state was, however, quite another thing. Taking on areas such as education, health care, social services, the universities, the state bureaucracy, and the judiciary proved difficult. Here she had to do battle with the entrenched and sometimes traditional upper-middle-class attitudes of her core supporters. Thatcher desperately sought to extend the ideal of personal responsibility (for example through the privatization of health care) across the board and cut back on state obligations. She failed to make rapid headway. There were, in the view of the British public, limits to the neoliberalization of everything. Not until 2003, for example, did a Labour government, against widespread opposition, succeed in introducing a fee-paying structure into British higher education. In all these areas it proved difficult to forge an alliance of consent for radical change. On this her Cabinet (and her supporters) were notoriously divided (between 'wets' and 'drys') and it took several years of bruising confrontations within her own party and in the media to win modest neoliberal reforms. The best she could do was to try to force a culture of entrepreneurialism and impose strict rules of surveillance, financial accountability, and productivity on to institutions, such as universities, that were ill suited to them.

Thatcher forged consent through the cultivation of a middle class that relished the joys of home ownership, private property, individualism, and the liberation of entrepreneurial opportunities. With working-class solidarities waning under pressure and job structures radically changing through deindustrialization, middle-class values spread more widely to encompass many of those who had once had a firm working-class identity. The opening of Britain to freer trade allowed a consumer culture to flourish, and the proliferation of financial institutions brought more and more of a debt culture into the centre of a formerly staid British life. Neoliberalism entailed the transformation of the older British class structure, at both ends of the spectrum. Moreover, by keeping the City of London as a central player in global finance it increasingly turned the heartland of Britain's economy, London and the south-east, into a dynamic centre of ever-increasing wealth and power. Class power had not so much been restored to any traditional sector but rather had gathered expansively around one of the key global centres of financial operations. Recruits from Oxbridge flooded into London as bond and currency traders, rapidly amassing wealth and power and turning London into one of the most expensive cities in the world.

While the Thatcher revolution was prepared by the organization of consent within the traditional middle classes who bore her to three electoral victories, the whole programme, particularly in her first administration, was far more ideologically driven (thanks largely to Keith Joseph) by neoliberal theory than was ever the case in the US. While from a solid middle-class background herself, she plainly relished the traditionally close contacts between the prime minister's office and the 'captains' of industry and finance. She frequently turned to them for advice and in some instances clearly delivered them favours by undervaluing state assets set for privatization. The project to restore class power—as opposed to dismantling working-class power—probably played a more subconscious role in her political evolution.

The success of Reagan and Thatcher can be measured in various ways.[34] But I think it most useful to stress the way in which they took what had hitherto been minority political, ideological, and intellectual positions and made them mainstream. The alliance of forces they helped consolidate and the majorities they led became a legacy that a subsequent generation of political leaders found hard to dislodge. Perhaps the greatest testimony to their success lies in the fact that both Clinton and Blair found themselves in a situation where their room for manoeuvre was so limited that they could not help but sustain the process of restoration of class power even against their own better instincts. And once neo-liberalism became that deeply entrenched in the English-speaking world it was hard to gainsay its considerable relevance to how capitalism in general was working internationally. This is not to say, as we shall see, that neoliberalism was merely imposed elsewhere by Anglo-American influence and power. For as these two case studies amply demonstrate, the internal circumstances and subsequent nature of the neoliberal turn were quite different in Britain and the US, and by extension we should expect that internal forces as well as external influences and impositions have played a distinctive role elsewhere.

Reagan and Thatcher seized on the clues they had (from Chile and New York City) and placed themselves at the head of a class movement that was determined to restore its power. Their genius was to create a legacy and a tradition that tangled subsequent politicians in a web of constraints from which they could not easily escape. Those who followed, like Clinton and Blair, could do little more than continue the good work of neoliberalization, whether they liked it or not.

3

The Neoliberal State

The role of the state in neoliberal theory is reasonably easy to define. The practice of neoliberalization has, however, evolved in such a way as to depart significantly from the template that theory provides. The somewhat chaotic evolution and uneven geographical development of state institutions, powers, and functions over the last thirty years suggests, furthermore, that the neoliberal state may be an unstable and contradictory political form.

The Neoliberal State in Theory

According to theory, the neoliberal state should favour strong individual private property rights, the rule of law, and the institutions of freely functioning markets and free trade.[1] These are the institutional arrangements considered essential to guarantee individual freedoms. The legal framework is that of freely negotiated contractual obligations between juridical individuals in the marketplace. The sanctity of contracts and the individual right to freedom of action, expression, and choice must be protected. The state must therefore use its monopoly of the means of violence to preserve these freedoms at all costs. By extension, the freedom of businesses and corporations (legally regarded as individuals) to operate within this institutional framework of free markets and free trade is regarded as a fundamental good. Private enterprise and entrepreneurial initiative are seen as the keys to innovation and wealth creation. Intellectual property rights are protected (for example through patents) so as to encourage technological changes. Continuous increases in productivity should then deliver higher living standards to everyone. Under the assumption that 'a rising tide lifts all boats', or of 'trickle down', neoliberal theory holds that the elimination of poverty (both domestically and worldwide) can best be secured through free markets and free trade.

Neoliberals are particularly assiduous in seeking the privatization of assets. The absence of clear private property rights—as in many developing countries—is seen as one of the greatest of all institutional barriers to economic development and the improvement of human welfare. Enclosure and the assignment of private property rights is considered the best way to protect against the so-called 'tragedy of the commons' (the tendency for individuals to irresponsibly super-exploit common property resources such as land and water). Sectors formerly run or regulated by the state must be turned over to the private sphere and be deregulated (freed from any state interference). Competition—between individuals, between firms, between territorial entities (cities, regions, nations, regional groupings)—is held to be a primary virtue. The ground-rules for market competition must be properly observed, of course. In situations where such rules are not clearly laid out or where property rights are hard to define, the state must use its power to impose or invent market systems (such as trading in pollution rights). Privatization and deregulation combined with competition, it is claimed, eliminate bureaucratic red tape, increase efficiency and productivity, improve quality, and reduce costs, both directly to the consumer through cheaper commodities and services and indirectly through reduction of the tax burden. The neoliberal state should persistently seek out internal reorganizations and new institutional arrangements that improve its competitive position as an entity vis-à-vis other states in the global market.

While personal and individual freedom in the marketplace is guaranteed, each individual is held responsible and accountable for his or her own actions and well-being. This principle extends into the realms of welfare, education, health care, and even pensions (social security has been privatized in Chile and Slovakia, and proposals exist to do the same in the US). Individual success or failure are interpreted in terms of entrepreneurial virtues or personal failings (such as not investing significantly enough in one's own human capital through education) rather than being attributed to any systemic property (such as the class exclusions usually attributed to capitalism).

The free mobility of capital between sectors, regions, and countries is regarded as crucial. All barriers to that free movement (such as tariffs, punitive taxation arrangements, planning and environmental controls, or other locational impediments) have to be removed, except in those areas crucial to 'the national interest', however that is defined. State sovereignty over commodity and capital movements is willingly surrendered to the global market. International competition is seen as healthy since it improves efficiency and productivity, lowers prices, and thereby controls inflationary tendencies. States should therefore collectively seek and negotiate the reduction of barriers to movement of capital across borders and the opening of markets (for both commodities and capital) to global exchange. Whether or not this applies to labour as a commodity is, however, controversial. To the degree that all states must collaborate to reduce barriers to exchange, so co-ordinating structures such as the group of advanced capitalist nations (the US, Britain, France, Germany, Italy, Canada, and Japan) known as the G7 (now the G8 with the addition of Russia) must arise. International agreements between states guaranteeing the rule of law and freedoms of trade, such as those now incorporated in the World Trade Organization agreements, are critical to the advancement of the neoliberal project on the global stage.

Neoliberal theorists are, however, profoundly suspicious of democracy. Governance by majority rule is seen as a potential threat to individual rights and constitutional liberties. Democracy is viewed as a luxury, only possible under conditions of relative affluence coupled with a strong middle-class presence to guarantee political stability. Neoliberals therefore tend to favour governance by experts and elites. A strong preference exists for government by executive order and by judicial decision rather than democratic and parliamentary decision-making. Neoliberals prefer to insulate key institutions, such as the central bank, from democratic pressures. Given that neoliberal theory centres on the rule of law and a strict interpretation of constitutionality, it follows that conflict and opposition must be mediated through the courts. Solutions and remedies to any problems have to be sought by individuals through the legal system.

Tensions and Contradictions

There are some shadowy areas as well as points of conflict within the general theory of the neoliberal state. First, there is the problem of how to interpret monopoly power. Competition often results in monopoly or oligopoly, as stronger firms drive out weaker. Most neoliberal theorists consider this unproblematic (it should, they say, maximize efficiency) provided there are no substantial barriers to the entry of competitors (a condition often hard to realize and which the state may therefore have to nurture). The case of so-called 'natural monopolies' is more difficult. It makes no sense to have multiple competing electrical power grids, gas pipelines, water and sewage systems, or rail links between Washington and Boston. State regulation of provision, access, and pricing seems unavoidable in such domains. While partial deregulation may be possible (permitting competing producers to feed electricity into the same grid or run trains on the same tracks, for example) the possibilities for profiteering and abuse, as the California power crisis of 2002 abundantly showed, or for deadly muddle and confusion, as the British rail situation has proven, are very real.

The second major arena of controversy concerns market failure. This arises when individuals and firms avoid paying the full costs attributable to them by shedding their liabilities outside the market (the liabilities are, in technical parlance, 'externalized'). The classic case is that of pollution, where individuals and firms avoid costs by dumping noxious wastes free of charge in the environment. Productive ecosystems may be degraded or destroyed as a result. Exposure to dangerous substances or physical dangers in the workplace may affect human health and even deplete the pool of healthy labourers in the workforce. While neoliberals admit the problem and some concede the case for limited state intervention, others argue for inaction because the cure will almost certainly be worse than the disease. Most would agree, however, that if there are to be interventions these should work through market mechanisms (via tax impositions or incentives, trading rights of pollutants, and the like). Competitive failures are approached in a similar fashion. Rising transaction costs can be incurred as contractual and subcontractual relations proliferate. The vast apparatus of currency speculation, to take just one example, appears more and more costly at the same time as it becomes more and more fundamental to capturing speculative profits. Other problems arise when, say, all competing hospitals in a region buy the same sophisticated equipment that remains underutilized, thus driving up aggregate costs. The case here for cost containment through state planning, regulation, and forced co-ordination is strong, but again neoliberals are deeply suspicious of such interventions.

All agents acting in the market are generally presumed to have access to the same information. There are presumed to be no asymmetries of power or of information that interfere with the capacity of individuals to make rational economic decisions in their own interests. This condition is rarely, if ever, approximated in practice, and there are significant consequences.[2] Better informed and more powerful players have an advantage that can all too easily be parlayed into procuring even better information and greater relative power. The establishment of intellectual property rights (patents), furthermore, encourages 'rent seeking'. Those who hold the patent rights use their monopoly power to set monopoly prices and to prevent technology transfers except at a very high cost. Asymmetric power relations tend, therefore, to increase rather than diminish over time unless the state steps in to counteract them. The neoliberal presumption of perfect information and a level playing field for competition appears as either innocently utopian or a deliberate obfuscation of processes that will lead to the concentration of wealth and, therefore, the restoration of class power.

The neoliberal theory of technological change relies upon the coercive powers of competition to drive the search for new products, new production methods, and new organizational forms. This drive becomes so deeply embedded in entrepreneurial common sense, however, that it becomes a fetish belief: that there is a technological fix for each and every problem. To the degree that this takes hold not only within corporations but also within the state apparatus (in the military in particular), it produces powerful independent trends of technological change that can become destabilizing, if not counterproductive. Technological developments can run amok as sectors dedicated solely to technological innovation create new products and new ways of doing things that as yet have no market (new pharmaceutical products are produced, for which new illnesses are then invented). Talented interlopers can, furthermore, mobilize technological innovations to undermine dominant social relations and institutions; they can, through their activities, even reshape common sense to their own pecuniary advantage. There is an inner connection, therefore, between technological dynamism, instability, dissolution of social solidarities, environmental degradation, deindustrialization, rapid shifts in time–space relations, speculative bubbles, and the general tendency towards crisis formation within capitalism.[3]

There are, finally, some fundamental political problems within neoliberalism that need to be addressed. A contradiction arises between a seductive but alienating possessive individualism on the one hand and the desire for a meaningful collective life on the other. While individuals are supposedly free to choose, they are not supposed to choose to construct strong collective institutions (such as trade unions) as opposed to weak voluntary associations (like charitable organizations). They most certainly should not choose to associate to create political parties with the aim of forcing the state to intervene in or eliminate the market. To guard against their greatest fears—fascism, communism, socialism, authoritarian populism, and even majority rule—the neoliberals have to put strong limits on democratic governance, relying instead upon undemocratic and unaccountable institutions (such as the Federal Reserve or the IMF) to make key decisions. This creates the paradox of intense state interventions and government by elites and 'experts' in a world where the state is supposed not to be interventionist. One is reminded of Francis Bacon's utopian tale *New Atlantis* (first published in 1626) where a Council of Wise Elders mandates all key decisions. Faced with social movements that seek collective interventions, therefore, the neoliberal state is itself forced to intervene, sometimes repressively, thus denying the very freedoms it is supposed to uphold. In this situation, however, it can marshal one secret weapon: international competition and globalization can be used to discipline movements opposed to the neoliberal agenda within individual states. If that fails, then the state must resort to persuasion, propaganda or, when necessary, raw force and police power to suppress opposition to neoliberalism. This was precisely Polanyi's fear: that the liberal (and by extension the neoliberal) utopian project could only ultimately be sustained by resort to authoritarianism. The freedom of the masses would be restricted in favour of the freedoms of the few.

The Neoliberal State in Practice

The general character of the state in the era of neoliberalization is hard to describe for two particular reasons. First, systematic divergences from the template of neoliberal theory quickly become apparent, not all of which can be attributed to the internal contradictions already outlined. Secondly, the evolutionary dynamic of neoliberalization has been such as to force adaptations that have varied greatly from place to place as well as over time. Any attempt to extract some composite picture of a typical neoliberal state from this unstable and volatile historical geography would seem to be a fool's errand. Nevertheless, I think it useful to sketch in some general threads of argument that keep the concept of a distinctively neoliberal state in play.

There are two arenas in particular where the drive to restore class power twists and in some respects even reverses neoliberal theory in its practice. The first of these arises out of the need to create a 'good business or investment climate' for capitalistic endeavours. While there are some conditions, such as political stability or full respect for the law and even-handedness in its application, that might plausibly be considered 'class neutral', there are others that are manifestly biased. The biases arise in particular out of the treatment of labour and the environment as mere commodities. In the event of a conflict, the typical neoliberal state will tend to side with a good business climate as opposed to either the collective rights (and quality of life) of labour or the capacity of the environment to regenerate itself. The second arena of bias arises because, in the event of a conflict, neoliberal states typically favour the integrity of the financial system and the solvency of financial institutions over the well-being of the population or environmental quality.

These systematic biases are not always easy to discern within the welter of divergent and often wildly disparate state practices. Pragmatic and opportunistic considerations play an important part. President Bush advocates free markets and free trade but imposed steel tariffs in order to bolster his electoral chances (successfully, it turned out) in Ohio. Quotas are arbitrarily placed on foreign imports to assuage domestic discontents. Europeans protect agriculture while insisting upon free trade in everything else for social, political, and even aesthetic reasons. Special interventions of the state favour particular business interests (for example armaments deals), and credits are arbitrarily extended from one state to another in order to gain political access and influence in geopolitically sensitive regions (such as the Middle East). For all these sorts of reasons it would be surprising indeed to find even the most fundamentalist of neoliberal states cleaving to neoliberal orthodoxy all of the time.

In other instances we may reasonably attribute divergences between theory and practice to frictional problems of transition reflecting the different state forms that existed prior to the neoliberal turn. The conditions that prevailed in central and eastern Europe after the collapse of communism were very special, for example. The speed with which privatization occurred under the 'shock therapy' that was visited upon those countries in the 1990s created enormous stresses that reverberate to this day. Social democratic states (such as those in Scandinavia or Britain in the immediate post-war period) had long taken key sectors of the economy such as health care, education, and even housing out of the market on the grounds that access to basic human needs should not be mediated through market forces and access limited by ability to pay. While Margaret Thatcher managed to change all that, the Swedes resisted far longer even in the face of strong attempts by capitalist class interests to take the neoliberal road. Developmental states (such as Singapore and several other Asian countries), for quite different reasons, rely on the public sector and state planning in tight association with domestic and corporate (often foreign and multinational) capital to promote capital accumulation and economic growth.[4] Developmental states typically pay considerable attention to social as well as physical infrastructures. This means far more egalitarian policies with respect to, for example, access to educational opportunities and health care. State investment in education is viewed, for example, as a crucial prerequisite to gaining competitive advantage in world trade. Developmental states become consistent with neoliberalization to the degree that they facilitate competition between firms, corporations, and territorial entities and accept the rules of free trade and rely on open export markets. But they are actively interventionist in creating the infrastructures for a good business climate. Neoliberalization therefore opens up possibilities for developmental states to enhance their position in international competition by developing new structures of state intervention (such as support for research and development). But, by the same token, neoliberalization creates conditions for class formation, and as that class power strengthens so the tendency arises (for example in contemporary Korea) for that class to seek to liberate itself from reliance upon state power and to reorient state power along neoliberal lines.

As new institutional arrangements come to define the rules of world trade—for example, the opening of capital markets is now a condition of membership of the IMF and the WTO—developmental states find themselves increasingly drawn into the neoliberal fold. One of the main effects of the Asian crisis of 1997–8, for example, was to bring developmental states more in line with standard neoliberal practices. And as we saw in the British case, it is hard to maintain a neoliberal posture externally (for example to facilitate the operations of finance capital) without accepting a modicum of neoliberalization on the inside (South Korea has struggled with exactly this sort of stress in recent times). But developmental states are by no means convinced that the neoliberal path is the right one, particularly since those states (like Taiwan and China) that had not freed up their capital markets suffered far less in the financial crisis of 1997–8 than those that had.[5]

Contemporary practices with respect to finance capital and financial institutions are perhaps the most difficult of all to reconcile with neoliberal orthodoxy. Neoliberal states typically facilitate the diffusion of influence of financial institutions through deregulation, but then they also all too often guarantee the integrity and solvency of financial institutions at no matter what cost. This commitment in part derives (legitimately in some versions of neoliberal theory) from reliance upon monetarism as the basis of state policy—the integrity and soundness of money is a central pinion of that policy. But this paradoxically means that the neoliberal state cannot tolerate any massive financial defaults even when it is the financial institutions that have made the bad decisions. The state has to step in and replace 'bad' money with its own supposedly 'good' money—which explains the pressure on central bankers to maintain confidence in the soundness of state money. State power has often been used to bail out companies or avert financial failures, such as the US savings and loans crisis of 1987–8, which cost US taxpayers an estimated $150 billion, or the collapse of the hedge fund Long Term Capital Management in 1997–8, which cost $3.5 billion.

Internationally, the core neoliberal states gave the IMF and the World Bank full authority in 1982 to negotiate debt relief, which meant in effect to protect the world's main financial institutions from the threat of default. The IMF in effect covers, to the best of its ability, exposures to risk and uncertainty in international financial markets. This practice is hard to justify according to neoliberal theory, since investors should in principle be responsible for their own mistakes. More fundamentalist-minded neoliberals therefore believe that the IMF should be abolished. This option was seriously considered during the early years of the Reagan administration, and Congressional Republicans raised it again in 1998. James Baker, Reagan's Secretary of the Treasury, breathed new life into the institution when he found himself faced with the potential bankruptcy of Mexico and serious losses for the main New York City investment banks that held Mexican debt in 1982. He used the IMF to impose structural adjustment on Mexico and protect the New York bankers from default. This practice of prioritizing the needs of the banks and financial institutions while diminishing the standard of living of the debtor country had already been pioneered during the New York City debt crisis. In the international context this meant extracting surpluses from impoverished Third World populations in order to pay off the international bankers. 'What a peculiar world', Stiglitz quizzically remarks, 'in which the poor countries are in effect subsidizing the richest.' Even Chile—the exemplar of 'pure' neoliberal practices after 1975—got hit in this way in 1982–3, with the result that gross domestic product fell by nearly 14 per cent and unemployment shot up to 20 per cent in one year. The inference that 'pure' neoliberalization does not work failed to be registered theoretically, although the pragmatic adaptations that followed in Chile (as well as in Britain after 1983) opened up a field of compromises that widened the gap even further between theory and practice.[6]

The extraction of tribute via financial mechanisms is an old imperial practice. It has proven very helpful to the restoration of class power, particularly in the world's main financial centres, and it does not always need a structural adjustment crisis to work. When entrepreneurs in developing countries borrow money from abroad, for example, the requirement that their own state should have sufficient foreign exchange reserves to cover their borrowings translates into the state having to invest in, say, US Treasury bonds. The difference between the interest rate on the money borrowed (for example 12 per cent) and the money deposited as collateral in US Treasuries in Washington (for example 4 per cent) yields a strong net financial flow to the imperial centre at the expense of the developing country.

This tendency on the part of the core states like the US to protect financial interests and to stand by as they suck in surpluses from elsewhere both promotes and reflects the consolidation of upper-class power within those states around processes of financialization. But the habit of intervening in the marketplace and bailing out financial institutions when they get into trouble cannot be reconciled with neoliberal theory. Reckless investments should be punished by losses to the lender, but the state makes lenders largely immune to losses. Borrowers have to pay up instead, no matter what the social cost. Neoliberal theory should warn 'Lender, beware', but the practice is 'Borrower, beware'.

There are limits to the capacity to squeeze out surpluses from developing countries' economies. Strapped by austerity measures that lock them into chronic economic stagnation, the prospect of their repaying debts has frequently receded into some distant future. Under these conditions, some measured losses may appear an attractive option. This happened under the Brady Plan of 1989.[7] Financial institutions agreed to write down 35 per cent of their outstanding debt as a loss in exchange for discounted bonds (backed by the IMF and the US Treasury), guaranteeing repayment of the rest (in other words creditors were guaranteed repayment of debts at the rate of 65 cents on the dollar). By 1994 some eighteen countries (including Mexico, Brazil, Argentina, Venezuela, and Uruguay) had agreed to deals that forgave them some $60 billion in debt. The hope, of course, was that this debt relief would spark an economic recovery that would permit the rest of the debt to be paid off in a timely way. The trouble was that the IMF also saw to it that all the countries that took advantage of this modicum of debt forgiveness (which many regarded as minimal in relation to what the banks could afford) were also required to swallow the poison pill of neoliberal institutional reforms. The peso crisis in Mexico in 1995, the Brazilian crisis of 1998, and the total collapse of the Argentine economy in 2001 were predictable results.

This brings us, finally, to the problematic issue of the neoliberal state's approach to labour markets. Internally, the neoliberal state is necessarily hostile to all forms of social solidarity that put restraints on capital accumulation. Independent trade unions or other social movements (such as the municipal socialism of the Greater London Council type), which acquired considerable power under embedded liberalism, have therefore to be disciplined, if not destroyed, and this in the name of the supposedly sacrosanct individual liberty of the isolated labourer. 'Flexibility' becomes the watchword with respect to labour markets. It is hard to argue that increased flexibility is all bad, particularly in the face of highly restrictive and sclerotic union practices. There are, therefore, reformists of a left persuasion who argue strongly for 'flexible specialization' as a way forward.[8] While some individual labourers may undoubtedly benefit from this, the asymmetries of information and of power that arise, coupled with the lack of easy and free mobility of labour (particularly across state borders), put labour at a disadvantage. Flexible specialization can be seized on by capital as a handy way to procure more flexible means of accumulation. The two terms—flexible specialization and flexible accumulation—have quite different connotations.[9] The general outcome is lower wages, increasing job insecurity, and in many instances loss of benefits and of job protections. Such trends are readily discernible in all states that have taken the neoliberal road. Given the violent assault on all forms of labour organization and labour rights and heavy reliance upon massive but largely disorganized labour reserves in countries such as China, Indonesia, India, Mexico, and Bangladesh, it would seem that labour control and maintenance of a high rate of labour exploitation have been central to neoliberalization all along. The restoration or formation of class power occurs, as always, at the expense of labour.

It is precisely in such a context of diminished personal resources derived from the job market that the neoliberal determination to transfer all responsibility for well-being back to the individual has doubly deleterious effects. As the state withdraws from welfare provision and diminishes its role in arenas such as health care, public education, and social services, which were once so fundamental to embedded liberalism, it leaves larger and larger segments of the population exposed to impoverishment.[10] The social safety net is reduced to a bare minimum in favour of a system that emphasizes personal responsibility. Personal failure is generally attributed to personal failings, and the victim is all too often blamed.

Behind these major shifts in social policy lie important structural changes in the nature of governance. Given the neoliberal suspicion of democracy, a way has to be found to integrate state decision-making into the dynamics of capital accumulation and the networks of class power that are in the process of restoration, or, as in China and Russia, in formation. Neoliberalization has entailed, for example, increasing reliance on public–private partnerships (this was one of the strong ideas pushed by Margaret Thatcher as she set up 'quasi-governmental institutions' such as urban development corporations to pursue economic development). Businesses and corporations not only collaborate intimately with state actors but even acquire a strong role in writing legislation, determining public policies, and setting regulatory frameworks (which are mainly advantageous to themselves). Patterns of negotiation arise that incorporate business and sometimes professional interests into governance through close and sometimes secretive consultation. The most blatant example of this was the persistent refusal of Vice-President Cheney to release the names of the consultative group that formulated the Bush administration's energy policy document of 2002; it almost certainly included Kenneth Lay, the head of Enron—a company accused of profiteering by deliberately fostering an energy crisis in California and which then collapsed in the midst of a huge accounting scandal. The shift from government (state power on its own) to governance (a broader configuration of state and key elements in civil society) has therefore been marked under neoliberalism.[11] In this respect the practices of the neoliberal and developmental state broadly converge.

The state typically produces legislation and regulatory frameworks that advantage corporations, and in some instances specific interests such as energy, pharmaceuticals, agribusiness, etc. In many of the instances of public–private partnerships, particularly at the municipal level, the state assumes much of the risk while the private sector takes most of the profits. If necessary, furthermore, the neoliberal state will resort to coercive legislation and policing tactics (anti-picketing rules, for example) to disperse or repress collective forms of opposition to corporate power. Forms of surveillance and policing multiply: in the US, incarceration became a key state strategy to deal with problems arising among discarded workers and marginalized populations. The coercive arm of the state is augmented to protect corporate interests and, if necessary, to repress dissent. None of this seems consistent with neoliberal theory. The neoliberal fear that special-interest groups would pervert and subvert the state is nowhere better realized than in Washington, where armies of corporate lobbyists (many of whom have taken advantage of the 'revolving door' between state employment and far more lucrative employment by the corporations) effectively dictate legislation to match their special interests. While some states continue to respect the traditional independence of the Civil Service, this condition has everywhere been under threat in the course of neoliberalization. The boundary between the state and corporate power has become more and more porous. What remains of representative democracy is overwhelmed, if not totally though legally corrupted by money power.

Since access to the judiciary is nominally egalitarian but in practice extremely expensive (be it an individual suing over negligent practices or a country suing the US for violation of WTO rules—a procedure that can cost up to a million dollars, a sum equivalent to the annual budget of some small, impoverished countries), the outcomes are often strongly biased towards those with money power. Class bias in decision-making within the judiciary is, in any case, pervasive if not assured.[12] It should not be surprising that the primary collective means of action under neoliberalism are then defined and articulated through non-elected (and in many instances elite-led) advocacy groups for various kinds of rights. In some instances, such as consumer protections, civil rights, or the rights of handicapped persons, substantive gains have been achieved by such means. Non-governmental and grassroots organizations (NGOs and GROs) have also grown and proliferated remarkably under neoliberalism, giving rise to the belief that opposition mobilized outside the state apparatus and within some separate entity called 'civil society' is the powerhouse of oppositional politics and social transformation.[13] The period in which the neoliberal state has become hegemonic has also been the period in which the concept of civil society—often cast as an entity in opposition to state power—has become central to the formulation of oppositional politics. The Gramscian idea of the state as a unity of political and civil society gives way to the idea of civil society as a centre of opposition, if not an alternative, to the state.

From this account we can clearly see that neoliberalism does not make the state or particular institutions of the state (such as the courts and police functions) irrelevant, as some commentators on both the right and the left have argued.[14] There has, however, been a radical reconfiguration of state institutions and practices (particularly with respect to the balance between coercion and consent, between the powers of capital and of popular movements, and between executive and judicial power, on the one hand, and powers of representative democracy on the other).

But all is not well with the neoliberal state, and it is for this reason that it appears to be either a transitional or an unstable political form. At the heart of the problem lies a burgeoning disparity between the declared public aims of neoliberalism—the well-being of all—and its actual consequences—the restoration of class power. But beyond this there lies a whole series of more specific contradictions that need to be highlighted.

1. On the one hand the neoliberal state is expected to take a back seat and simply set the stage for market functions, but on the other it is supposed to be activist in creating a good business climate and to behave as a competitive entity in global politics. In its latter role it has to work as a collective corporation, and this poses the problem of how to ensure citizen loyalty. Nationalism is an obvious answer, but this is profoundly antagonistic to the neoliberal agenda. This was Margaret Thatcher's dilemma, for it was only through playing the nationalism card in the Falklands/Malvinas war and, even more significantly, in the campaign against economic integration with Europe, that she could win re-election and promote further neoliberal reforms internally. Again and again, be it within the European Union, in Mercosur (where Brazilian and Argentine nationalisms inhibit integration), in NAFTA, or in ASEAN, the nationalism required for the state to function effectively as a corporate and competitive entity in the world market gets in the way of market freedoms more generally.

2. Authoritarianism in market enforcement sits uneasily with ideals of individual freedoms. The more neoliberalism veers towards the former, the harder it becomes to maintain its legitimacy with respect to the latter and the more it has to reveal its anti-democratic colours. This contradiction is paralleled by a growing lack of symmetry in the power relation between corporations and individuals such as you and me. If 'corporate power steals your personal freedom' then the promise of neoliberalism comes to nothing.[15] This applies to individuals in the workplace as well as in the living space. It is one thing to maintain, for example, that my health-care status is my personal choice and responsibility, but quite another when the only way I can satisfy my needs in the market is through paying exorbitant

premiums to inefficient, gargantuan, highly bureaucratized but also highly profitable insurance companies. When these companies even have the power to define new categories of illness to match new drugs coming on the market then something is clearly wrong.[16] Under such circumstances, maintaining legitimacy and consent, as we saw in Chapter 2, becomes an even more difficult balancing act that can easily topple over when things start to go wrong.

3. While it may be crucial to preserve the integrity of the financial system, the irresponsible and self-aggrandizing individualism of operators within it produces speculative volatility, financial scandals, and chronic instability. The Wall Street and accounting scandals of recent years have undermined confidence and posed regulatory authorities with serious problems of how and when to intervene, internationally as well as nationally. International free trade requires some global rules of the game, and that calls forth the need for some kind of global governance (for example by the WTO). Deregulation of the financial system facilitates behaviours that call for re-regulation if crisis is to be avoided.[17]

4. While the virtues of competition are placed up front, the reality is the increasing consolidation of oligopolistic, monopoly, and transnational power within a few centralized multinational corporations: the world of soft-drinks competition is reduced to Coca Cola versus Pepsi, the energy industry is reduced to five huge transnational corporations, and a few media magnates control most of the flow of news, much of which then becomes pure propaganda.

5. At the popular level, the drive towards market freedoms and the commodification of everything can all too easily run amok and produce social incoherence. The destruction of forms of social solidarity and even, as Thatcher suggested, of the very idea of society itself, leaves a gaping hole in the social order. It then becomes peculiarly difficult to combat anomie and control the resultant anti-social behaviours such as criminality, pornography, or the virtual enslavement of others. The reduction of 'freedom' to 'freedom of enterprise' unleashes all those 'negative freedoms' that Polanyi saw as inextricably tied in with the

positive freedoms. The inevitable response is to reconstruct social solidarities, albeit along different lines—hence the revival of interest in religion and morality, in new forms of association-ism (around questions of rights and citizenship, for example) and even the revival of older political forms (fascism, national-ism, localism, and the like). Neoliberalism in its pure form has always threatened to conjure up its own nemesis in varieties of authoritarian populism and nationalism. As Schwab and Smadja, organizers of the once purely celebratory neoliberal annual jamboree at Davos, warned as early as 1996:

Economic globalization has entered a new phase. A mounting backlash against its effects, especially in the industrial democracies, is threaten-ing a disruptive impact on economic activity and social stability in many countries. The mood in these democracies is one of helplessness and anxiety, which helps explain the rise of a new brand of populist politicians. This can easily turn into revolt.[18]

The Neoconservative Answer

If the neoliberal state is inherently unstable, then what might replace it? In the US there are signs of a distinctively neoconserva-tive answer to this question. Reflecting on the recent history of China, Wang also suggests that, theoretically,

such discursive narratives as 'neo-Authoritarianism', 'neoconservatism', 'classical liberalism', market extremism, national modernization . . . all had close relationships of one sort or another with the constitution of neoliberalism. The successive displacement of these terms for one another (or even the contradictions among them) demonstrate the shifts in the structure of power in both contemporary China and the con-temporary world at large.[19]

Whether or not this portends a more general reconfiguration of governance structures worldwide remains to be seen. It is, how-ever, interesting to note how neoliberalization in authoritarian states such as China and Singapore seems to be converging with the increasing authoritarianism evident in neoliberal states such as the US and Britain. Consider, then, how the neoconservative answer to the inherent instability of the neoliberal state has evolved in the US.

Like the neoliberals that preceded them, the 'neocons' had long been nurturing their particular views on the social order, in universities (Leo Strauss at the University of Chicago being particularly influential) and well-funded think-tanks, and through influential publications (such as *Commentary*).[20] US neoconservatives favour corporate power, private enterprise, and the restoration of class power. Neoconservatism is therefore entirely consistent with the neoliberal agenda of elite governance, mistrust of democracy, and the maintenance of market freedoms. But it veers away from the principles of pure neoliberalism and has reshaped neoliberal practices in two fundamental respects: first, in its concern for order as an answer to the chaos of individual interests, and second, in its concern for an overweening morality as the necessary social glue to keep the body politic secure in the face of external and internal dangers.

In its concern for order, neoconservatism appears as a mere stripping away of the veil of authoritarianism in which neoliberalism sought to envelop itself. But it also proposes distinctive answers to one of the central contradictions of neoliberalism. If 'there is no such thing as society but only individuals' as Thatcher initially put it, then the chaos of individual interests can easily end up prevailing over order. The anarchy of the market, of competition, and of unbridled individualism (individual hopes, desires, anxieties, and fears; choices of lifestyle and of sexual habits and orientation; modes of self-expression and behaviours towards others) generates a situation that becomes increasingly ungovernable. It may even lead to a breakdown of all bonds of solidarity and a condition verging on social anarchy and nihilism.

In the face of this, some degree of coercion appears necessary to restore order. The neoconservatives therefore emphasize militarization as an antidote to the chaos of individual interests. For this reason, they are far more likely to highlight threats, real or imagined, both at home and abroad, to the integrity and stability of the nation. In the US this entails triggering what Hofstadter refers to as 'the paranoid style of American politics' in which the nation is depicted as besieged and threatened by enemies from within and without.[21] This style of politics has had a long history in the US. Neoconservatism is not new, and since the Second World War it has found a particular home in a powerful military-industrial complex that has a vested interest in permanent militarization. But the end of the Cold War posed the question of where the threat to US security was coming from. Radical Islam and China emerged as the top two candidates externally, and dissident internal movements (the Branch Dravidians incinerated at Waco, militia movements that gave succour to the Oklahoma bombing, the riots that followed the beating of Rodney King in Los Angeles, and finally the disorders that broke out in Seattle in 1999) had to be targeted internally by stronger surveillance and policing. The very real emergence of the threat from radical Islam during the 1990s that culminated in the events of 9/11 finally came to the fore as the central focus for the declaration of a permanent 'war on terror' that demanded militarization both at home and abroad to guarantee the security of the nation. While, plainly, some sort of police/military response to the threat revealed by the two attacks on the World Trade Center in New York was called for, the arrival in power of neoconservatives guaranteed an overarching, and in the judgement of many an overreaching, response in the turn to extensive militarization at home and abroad.[22]

Neoconservatism has long hovered in the wings as a movement against the moral permissiveness that individualism typically promotes. It therefore seeks to restore a sense of moral purpose, some higher-order values that will form the stable centre of the body politic. This possibility is in a way presaged within the framework of neoliberal theories which, 'by questioning the very political foundation of interventionist models of economic management . . . have brought issues of morality, justice and power—although in their own peculiar ways—back into economics'.[23] What the neoconservatives do is to change the 'peculiar ways' in which such questions enter into debate. Their aim is to counteract the dissolving effect of the chaos of individual interests that neoliberalism typically produces. They in no way depart from the neoliberal agenda of a construction or restoration of a dominant class power. But they seek legitimacy for that power, as well as social control through construction of a climate of consent around a coherent set

83

of moral values. This immediately poses the question of which moral values should prevail. It would, for example, be entirely feasible to appeal to the liberal system of human rights since, after all, the aim of human rights activism, as Mary Kaldor argues, 'is not merely intervention to protect human rights but the creation of a moral community'.[24] In the US, doctrines of 'exceptionalism' and the long history of civil rights activism have certainly generated moral movements around issues such as civil rights, global hunger, and philanthropic engagement, as well as missionary zeal.

But the moral values that have now become central to the neoconservatives can best be understood as products of the particular coalition that was built in the 1970s, between elite class and business interests intent on restoring their class power, on the one hand, and an electoral base among the 'moral majority' of the disaffected white working class on the other. The moral values centred on cultural nationalism, moral righteousness, Christianity (of a certain evangelical sort), family values, and right-to-life issues, and on antagonism to the new social movements such as feminism, gay rights, affirmative action, and environmentalism. While this alliance was mainly tactical under Reagan, the domestic disorder of the Clinton years forced the moral values argument to the top of the agenda in the Republicanism of Bush the younger. It now forms the core of the moral agenda of the neoconservative movement.[25]

But it would be wrong to see this neoconservative turn as exceptional or peculiar to the US, even though there are special elements at work there that may not be present elsewhere. Within the US this assertion of moral values relies heavily on appeals to ideals of nation, religion, history, cultural tradition, and the like, and these ideals are by no means confined to the US. This brings one of the more troubling aspects of neoliberalization more sharply back into focus: the curious relationship between state and nation. In principle, neoliberal theory does not look with favour on the *nation* even as it supports the idea of a strong state. The umbilical cord that tied together state and nation under embedded liberalism had to be cut if neoliberalism was to flourish. This was particularly true for states, such as Mexico and France, that took a corporatist form. The Partido Revolucionario Institucional in

The Neoliberal State

Mexico had long ruled on the theme of unity of state and nation, but that increasingly fell apart, even turning much of the nation against the state, as a result of neoliberal reforms during the 1990s. Nationalism has, of course, been a long-standing feature of the global economy and it would have been strange indeed if had sunk without trace as a result of neoliberal reforms; in fact it has revived to some degree in opposition to what neoliberalization has been about. The rise of right-wing fascist parties expressive of strong anti-immigrant sentiments in Europe is a case in point. Even more distressing was the ethnic nationalism that arose in the wake of Indonesia's economic collapse, which resulted in a brutal assault upon the Chinese minority.

But, as we have seen, the neoliberal state needs nationalism of a certain sort to survive. Forced to operate as a competitive agent in the world market and seeking to establish the best possible business climate, it mobilizes nationalism in its effort to succeed. Competition produces ephemeral winners and losers in the global struggle for position, and this in itself can be a source of national pride or of national soul-searching. Nationalism around sports competitions between nations is a sign of this. In China, the appeal to nationalist sentiment in the struggle to procure the state's position (if not hegemony) in the global economy is overt (as is the intensity of its training programme for athletes for the Beijing Olympics). Nationalist sentiment is equally rife in South Korea and Japan, and in both instances this can be seen as an antidote to the dissolution of former bonds of social solidarity under the impact of neoliberalism. Strong currents of cultural nationalism are stirring within the old nation-states (such as France) that now constitute the European Union. Religion and cultural nationalism provided the moral heft behind the Hindu Nationalist Party's success in enhancing neoliberal practices in India in recent times. The invocation of moral values in the Iranian revolution and the subsequent turn to authoritarianism has not led to total abandonment of market-based practices there, even though the revolution was aimed at the decadence of unbridled market individualism. A similar impulse lies behind the long-standing sense of moral superiority that pervades countries such as Singapore and Japan in relationship to what they see as the 'decadent' individualism and the shapeless multiculturalism of the US. The case of Singapore is particularly instructive. It has combined neoliberalism in the marketplace with draconian coercive and authoritarian state power, while invoking moral solidarities based on the nationalist ideals of a beleaguered island state (after its ejection from the Malaysian federation), Confucian values, and, most recently, a distinctive form of the cosmopolitan ethic suited to its current position in the world of international trade.[26] The British case is particularly interesting. Margaret Thatcher, through the Falklands/Malvinas war and in her antagonistic posture towards Europe, invoked nationalist sentiment in support of her neoliberal project, though it was the idea of England and St George, rather than the United Kingdom, that animated her vision—which turned Scotland and Wales hostile.

Clearly, while there are dangers in the neoliberal dalliance with nationalism of a certain sort, the fierce neoconservative embrace of a national moral purpose is far more threatening. The picture of many states, each prepared to resort to draconian coercive practices while each espousing its own distinctive and supposedly superior moral values, competing on the world stage is not reassuring. What seems like an answer to the contradictions of neoliberalism can all too easily turn into a problem. The spread of neoconservative, if not outright authoritarian, power (of the sort Vladimir Putin exercises in Russia and the Communist Party exercises in China), albeit grounded very differently in different social formations, highlights the dangers of descent into competing and perhaps even warring nationalisms. If there is an inevitability at work, then it arises more out of the neoconservative turn than out of eternal truths attaching to supposed national differences. To avoid catastrophic outcomes therefore requires rejection of the neoconservative solution to the contradictions of neoliberalism. This presumes, however, that there is some alternative: and that question will be addressed later.

4

Uneven Geographical Developments

The Moving Map of Neoliberalization

A moving map of the progress of neoliberalization on the world stage since 1970 would be hard to construct. To begin with, most states that have taken the neoliberal turn have done so only partially—the introduction of greater flexibility into labour markets here, a deregulation of financial operations and embrace of monetarism there, a move towards privatization of state-owned sectors somewhere else. Wholesale changes in the wake of crises (such as the collapse of the Soviet Union) can be followed by slow reversals as the unpalatable aspects of neoliberalism become more evident. And in the struggle to restore or establish a distinctive upper-class power all manner of twists and turns occur as political powers change hands and as the instruments of influence are weakened here or strengthened there. Any moving map would therefore feature turbulent currents of uneven geographical development that need to be tracked in order to understand how local transformations relate to broader trends.[1]

Competition between territories (states, regions, or cities) as to who had the best model for economic development or the best business climate was relatively insignificant in the 1950s and 1960s. Competition of this sort heightened in the more fluid and open systems of trading relations established after 1970. The general progress of neoliberalization has therefore been increasingly impelled *through* mechanisms of uneven geographical developments. Successful states or regions put pressure on everyone else to follow their lead. Leapfrogging innovations put this or that state (Japan, Germany, Taiwan, the US, or China), region (Silicon Valley, Bavaria, Third Italy, Bangalore, the Pearl River delta, or

Botswana), or even city (Boston, San Francisco, Shanghai, or Munich) in the vanguard of capital accumulation. But the competitive advantages all too often prove ephemeral, introducing an extraordinary volatility into global capitalism. Yet it is also true that powerful impulses of neoliberalization have emanated, and even been orchestrated, from a few major epicentres.

Clearly, the UK and the US led the way. But in neither country was the turn unproblematic. While Thatcher could successfully privatize social housing and the public utilities, core public services such as the national health-care system and public education remained largely immune. In the US, the 'Keynesian compromise' of the 1960s had never got close to the achievements of social democratic states in Europe. The opposition to Reagan was therefore less combative. Reagan was, in any case, heavily preoccupied with the Cold War. He launched a deficit-funded arms race ('military Keynesianism') of specific benefit to his electoral majority in the US south and west. While this certainly did not accord with neoliberal theory, the rising Federal deficits did provide a convenient excuse to gut social programmes (a neoliberal objective).

In spite of all the rhetoric about curing sick economies, neither Britain nor the US achieved high levels of economic performance in the 1980s, suggesting that neoliberalism was not the answer to the capitalists' prayers. To be sure, inflation was brought down and interest rates fell, but this was all purchased at the expense of high rates of unemployment (averaging 7.5 per cent in the US during the Reagan years and more than 10 per cent in Thatcher's Britain). Cutbacks in state welfare and infrastructural expenditures diminished the quality of life for many. The overall result was an awkward mix of low growth and increasing income inequality. And in Latin America, where the first wave of forced neoliberalization struck in the early 1980s, the result was for the most part a whole 'lost decade' of economic stagnation and political turmoil.

The 1980s in fact belonged to Japan, the East Asian 'tiger' economies, and West Germany as competitive powerhouses of the global economy. Their success in the absence of any wholesale neoliberal reforms makes it difficult to argue that neoliberalization progressed on the world stage as a proven palliative of economic stagnation. To be sure, the central banks in these countries generally followed a monetarist line (the West German Bundesbank was particularly assiduous in combating inflation). And gradual reductions in trade barriers created competitive pressures that resulted in a subtle process of what might be called 'creeping neoliberalization' even in countries generally resistant to it. The Maastricht agreement of 1991, for example, which set a broadly neoliberal framework for the internal organization of the European Union, would not have been possible had there not been pressure from those states, such as Britain, that had committed themselves to neoliberal reforms. But in West Germany the trade unions remained strong, social protections were kept in place, and wage levels continued to be relatively high. This stimulated the technological innovation that kept West Germany well ahead of the field in international competition in the 1980s (though it also produced technologically induced unemployment). Export-led growth powered the country forward as a global leader. In Japan, independent unions were weak or non-existent and rates of labour exploitation were high, but state investment in technological change and the tight relationship between corporations and banks (an arrangement that also proved felicitous in West Germany) generated an astonishing export-led growth performance in the 1980s, very much at the expense of the UK and the US. Such growth as there was in the 1980s did not depend, therefore, on neoliberalization except in the shallow sense that greater openness in global trade and markets provided the context in which the export-led success stories of Japan, West Germany, and the Asian 'tigers' could more easily unfold in the midst of intensifying international competition. By the end of the 1980s those countries that had taken the stronger neoliberal path still seemed to be in economic difficulty. It was hard not to conclude that the West German and Asian 'regimes' of accumulation were deserving of emulation. Many European states therefore resisted neoliberal reforms and embraced the West German model. In Asia, the Japanese model was broadly emulated first by the 'Gang of Four' (South Korea, Taiwan, Hong Kong, and Singapore) and then by Thailand, Malaysia, Indonesia, and the Philippines.

The West German and the Japanese models did not, however, facilitate the restoration of class power. The increases in social inequality to be found in the UK and particularly in the US during the 1980s were held in check. While rates of growth were low in the US and the UK, the standard of living of labour was declining significantly and the upper classes were beginning to do well. The rates of remuneration of US CEOs, for example, were becoming the envy of Europeans in comparable positions. In Britain, a new wave of entrepreneurial financiers began to consolidate large fortunes. If the project was to restore class power to the top elites, then neoliberalism was clearly the answer. Whether or not a country could be pushed towards neoliberalization then depended upon the balance of class forces (powerful union organization in West Germany and Sweden held neoliberalization in check) as well as upon the degree of dependency of the capitalist class on the state (very strong in Taiwan and South Korea).

The means whereby class power could be transformed and restored were gradually but unevenly put into place during the 1980s and consolidated in the 1990s. Four components were critical in this. First, the turn to more open financialization that began in the 1970s accelerated during the 1990s. Foreign direct investment and portfolio investment rose rapidly throughout the capitalist world. But it was spread unevenly (Figure 4.1), often depending on how good the business climate was here as opposed to there. Financial markets experienced a powerful wave of innovation and deregulation internationally. Not only did they become far more important instruments of co-ordination, but they also provided the means to procure and concentrate wealth. They became the privileged means for the restoration of class power. The close tie between corporations and the banks that had served the West Germans and the Japanese so well during the 1980s was undermined and replaced by an increasing connectivity between corporations and financial markets (the stock exchanges). Here Britain and the US had the advantage. In the 1990s, the Japanese economy went into a tailspin (led by a collapse in speculative land and property markets), and the banking sector was found to be in a parlous state. The hasty reunification of Germany created stresses, and the technological advantage that the Germans had earlier commanded dissipated, making it necessary to challenge more deeply its social democratic tradition in order to survive.

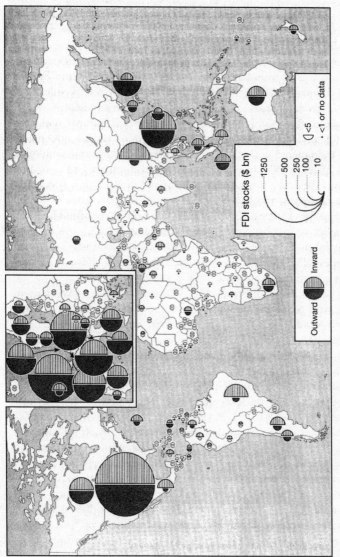

Figure 4.1 Global pattern of foreign direct investments, 2000
Source: Dicken, *Global Shift*.

Uneven Geographical Developments

Secondly, there was the increasing geographical mobility of capital. This was in part facilitated by the mundane but critical fact of rapidly diminishing transport and communications costs. The gradual reduction in artificial barriers to movement of capital and of commodities, such as tariffs, exchange controls, or, even more simply, waiting times at borders (the abolition of which in Europe had dramatic effects) also played an important role. While there was considerable unevenness (Japan's markets remained highly protected, for example), the general thrust was towards standardization of trade arrangements through international agreements that culminated in the World Trade Organization agreements that took effect in 1995 (more than a hundred countries had signed on within the year). This greater openness to capital flow (primarily US, European, and Japanese) put pressures on all states to look to the quality of their business climate as a crucial condition for their competitive success. Since degree of neoliberalization was increasingly taken by the IMF and the World Bank as a measure of a good business climate, the pressure on all states to adopt neoliberal reforms ratcheted upwards.[2]

Thirdly, the Wall Street–IMF–Treasury complex that came to dominate economic policy in the Clinton years was able to persuade, cajole, and (thanks to structural adjustment programmes administered by the IMF) coerce many developing countries to take the neoliberal road.[3] The US also used the carrot of preferential access to its huge consumer market to persuade many countries to reform their economies along neoliberal lines (in some instances through bilateral trade agreements). These policies helped produce a boom in the US in the 1990s. The US, riding a wave of technological innovation that underpinned the rise of a so-called 'new economy', looked as if it had the answer and that its policies were worthy of emulation, even though the relatively full employment achieved was at low rates of pay under conditions of diminishing social protections (the number of people without health insurance grew). Flexibility in labour markets and reductions in welfare provision (Clinton's draconian overhaul of 'the welfare system as we know it') began to pay off for the US and put competitive pressures on the more rigid labour markets that prevailed in most of Europe (with the exception of Britain) and Japan. The

92

real secret of US success, however, was that it was now able to pump high rates of return into the country from its financial and corporate operations (both direct and portfolio investments) in the rest of the world. It was this flow of tribute from the rest of the world that founded much of the affluence achieved in the US in the 1990s (Figures 1.8 and 1.9).[4]

Lastly, the global diffusion of the new monetarist and neoliberal economic orthodoxy exerted an ever more powerful ideological influence. As early as 1982, Keynesian economics had been purged from the corridors of the IMF and the World Bank. By the end of the decade most economics departments in the US research universities—and these helped train most of the world's economists—had fallen into line by broadly cleaving to the neoliberal agenda that emphasized the control of inflation and sound public finance (rather than full employment and social protections) as primary goals of economic policy.

All of these strands came together in the so-called 'Washington Consensus' of the mid-1990s.[5] The US and UK models of neoliberalism were there defined as the answer to global problems. Considerable pressure was put even on Japan and Europe (to say nothing of the rest of the world) to take the neoliberal road. It was, therefore, Clinton and then Blair who, from the centre-left, did the most to consolidate the role of neoliberalism both at home and internationally. The formation of the World Trade Organization was the high point of this institutional thrust (though the creation of NAFTA and the earlier signing of the Maastricht accords in Europe were also significant regional institutional adjustments). Programmatically, the WTO set neoliberal standards and rules for interaction in the global economy. Its primary objective, however, was to open up as much of the world as possible to unhindered capital flow (though always with the caveat clause of the protection of key 'national interests'), for this was the foundation of the capacity of the US financial power as well as that of Europe and Japan, to exact tribute from the rest of the world.

None of this is particularly consistent with neoliberal theory except for the emphasis on budgetary restraints and the continued fight against what by the 1990s was an almost non-existent inflation. Of course, there were always considerations of national security which would inevitably upset any attempt to apply neoliberal theory in pure terms. While the fall of the Berlin Wall and the end of the Cold War generated a seismic geopolitical shift in imperial rivalries, they did not end the sometimes deadly dance of geopolitical jockeying for power and influence between major powers on the world stage, particularly in those regions, such as the Middle East, that controlled key resources, or in regions of marked social and political instability (such as the Balkans). It did, however, lessen the US commitment to support Japan and the East Asian economies as bastions in the frontline of the Cold War. The supportive economic role that the US had played in South Korea and Taiwan before 1989 was not available to Indonesia and Thailand in the 1990s. But even within the neoliberal frame there were many elements, such as the activities of the IMF or of the G7, which functioned less as neoliberal institutions than as centres of raw power mobilized by particular powers or collections of powers seeking particular advantage. The theoretical neoliberal critique of the IMF never went away. The preparedness to intervene in currency markets by agreements such as the Plaza Accord of 1985, which artificially lowered the dollar against the Japanese yen, followed shortly thereafter by the Reverse Plaza Accord, which sought to rescue Japan from its depressed state in the 1990s, were instances of orchestrated interventions attempting to stabilize global financial markets.[6]

Financial crises were both endemic and contagious. The debt crisis of the 1980s was not limited to Mexico but had global manifestations (see Figure 4.2).[7] And in the 1990s there were two sets of interrelated financial crises that yielded a negative trace of uneven neoliberalization. The 'tequila crisis' that hit Mexico in 1995, for example, spread almost immediately, with devastating effects on Brazil and Argentina. But its reverberations were also felt to some degree in Chile, the Philippines, Thailand, and Poland. Why, exactly, this particular pattern of contagion occurred is hard to explain because speculative movements and expectations in financial markets do not necessarily rely on hard facts. But unregulated financialization plainly posed a serious danger of contagious crises. The 'herd mentality' of the financiers (no one wants to be the last one holding on to a currency before devaluation) could produce

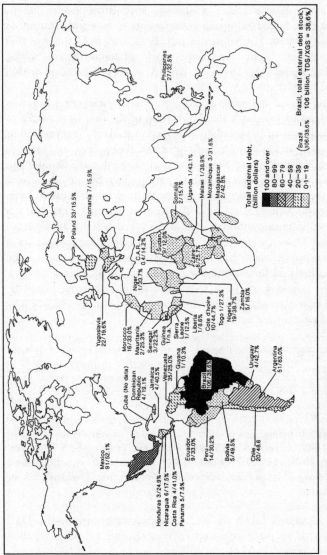

Figure 4.2 The international debt crisis of 1982–1985
Source: Corbridge, *Debt and Development.*

self-fulfilling expectations. These could have aggressive as well as defensive manifestations. Currency speculators made billions when they forced European governments to loosen the European Exchange Rate Mechanism in July 1993, and, in October of that year, George Soros alone made nearly $1 billion in two weeks, betting against the ability of Britain to keep the pound within ERM limits.

The second and much broader wave of financial crises began in Thailand in 1997 with the devaluation of the *baht* in the wake of the collapse of a speculative property market. The crisis first spread to Indonesia, Malaysia, and the Philippines, and then to Hong Kong, Taiwan, Singapore, and South Korea. Estonia and Russia were then hit hard, and shortly afterwards Brazil fell apart, with serious and long-lasting consequences for Argentina. Even Australia, New Zealand, and Turkey were affected. Only the US seemed immune, although even there a hedge fund, Long Term Capital Management (with two Nobel prizewinning economists as key advisers), which had bet the wrong way on Italian currency movements, had to be bailed out to the tune of $3.5 billion.

The whole 'East Asian regime' of accumulation facilitated by 'developmental states' was being put to the test in 1997–8. The social effects were devastating:

As the crisis progressed, unemployment soared, GDP plummeted, banks closed. The unemployment rate was up fourfold in Korea, threefold in Thailand, tenfold in Indonesia. In Indonesia, almost 15 per cent of males working in 1997 had lost their jobs by August 1998, and the economic devastation was even worse in the urban areas of the main island, Java. In South Korea, urban poverty almost tripled, with almost a quarter of the population falling into poverty; in Indonesia, poverty doubled ... In 1998, GDP in Indonesia fell by 13.1 per cent, in Korea by 6.7 per cent, and in Thailand by 10.8 per cent. Three years after the crisis, Indonesia's GDP was still 7.5 per cent below that before the crisis, Thailand's 2.3 per cent lower.[8]

As Indonesia's GDP fell and unemployment surged, the IMF stepped in to mandate austerity by abolishing subsidies on food and kerosene. The riots and violence that followed 'tore the coun-try's social fabric' apart. The capitalist classes, mainly ethnic

Chinese, were widely blamed for the debacle. While the wealthiest Chinese business elite decamped to Singapore, a wave of revenge killings and attacks on property engulfed the rest of the Chinese minority, as ethnonationalism reared its ugly head in search of a scapegoat for the social collapse.[9]

The standard IMF/US Treasury explanation for the crisis was too much state intervention and corrupt relationships between state and business ('crony capitalism'). Further neoliberalization was the answer. The Treasury and the IMF acted accordingly, with disastrous consequences. The alternative view of the crisis was that impetuous financial deregulation and the failure to construct adequate regulatory controls over unruly and speculative portfolio investments lay at the heart of the problem. The evidence for this latter view is substantial: those countries that had not liberated their capital markets—Singapore, Taiwan, and China—were far less affected than those countries, such as Thailand, Indonesia, Malaysia, and the Philippines, that had. Furthermore, the one country that ignored the IMF and imposed capital controls—Malaysia—recovered faster.[10] After South Korea likewise rejected IMF advice on industrial and financial restructuring it also staged a faster recovery. Why the IMF and the US Treasury continues to insist on neoliberalization is an apparent mystery. The victims increasingly propose a conspiratorial answer:

The IMF first told countries in Asia to open up their markets to hot short-term capital. The countries did it and money flooded in, but just as suddenly flowed out. The IMF then said interest rates should be raised and there should be fiscal contraction, and a deep recession was induced. Asset prices plummeted, the IMF urged affected countries to sell their assets even at bargain basement prices . . . The sales were handled by the same financial institutions that had pulled out their capital, precipitating the crisis. These banks then got large commissions from their work selling the troubled companies or splitting them up, just as they had got large commissions when they had originally guided the money into the countries in the first place.[11]

Behind this conspiratorial view lies the shadowy and largely unexamined role of the New York-based hedge funds. If Soros and other speculators could make billions at the expense of European

97

governments by betting against their ability to stay within the guidelines of the ERM, then why could not the hedge funds, armed with trillions of dollars of leveraged funds from the banks, engineer an attack upon not only East and South-East Asian governments but some of the most successful corporations in global capitalism, simply by denying them liquidity at a point of minor difficulty? The resulting flow of tribute to Wall Street was immense, boosting stock prices at a time when internal savings rates in the US were plunging. And after bankruptcy had been declared throughout much of the region, a wave of foreign direct investment could flood back in to buy up perfectly viable companies, or (as in the case of Daewoo) bits of companies, for a song. Stiglitz rejects the conspiratorial view and proposes a 'simpler' explanation: the IMF was simply 'reflecting the interests and ideology of the Western financial community'.[12] But he ignores the role of the hedge funds, and it never occurs to him that the increasing social inequality that he so frequently bemoans as a side-product of neoliberalization might have been its *raison d'être* all along.

Dispatches from the Frontlines

Mexico

The Partido Revolucionario Institucional (PRI) was the sole governing party in Mexico from 1929 until Vicente Fox's election in 2000. The party created a corporatist state that proved adept at organizing, co-opting, buying off, and if necessary suppressing oppositional movements among the workers, peasants, and middle classes that had formed the basis of the revolution. The PRI pursued a state-led modernization and economic development model mainly focused on import substitution and a vigorous export trade with the US. A significant monopoly state sector emerged in transport, energy, and public utilities, as well as in some basic industries (such as steel). Controlled entry of foreign capital under the maquila programme, which allowed mainly US capital to produce in Mexico's border zone, using cheap labour unhindered by any tariffs or restrictions on commodity movements, had begun in 1965. In spite of relatively strong economic development in the

1950s and 1960s, the benefits of growth had not spread very far. Mexico was not a good example of embedded liberalism, but episodic pay-offs to restive groups (peasants, workers, middle classes) did redistribute incomes to some degree. The violent suppression of the student movement protesting social inequalities in 1968 left a bitter legacy that threatened the PRI's legitimacy. But the balance of class forces began to shift in the 1970s. Business interests strengthened their independent position and deepened their links to foreign capital.

The global crisis of the 1970s hit Mexico badly. The PRI's response was to extend the public sector by taking over failing private enterprises, maintaining them as sources of employment to stave off the threat of working-class unrest. The number of state enterprises more than doubled between 1970 and 1980, as did the number of their employees. But these enterprises were losing money and the state had to borrow to fund them. The New York investment banks, awash with petrodollars to invest, obliged. Mexico's oil discoveries made lending to it an attractive bet. The foreign debt rose from \$6.8 billion in 1972 to \$58 billion by 1982.[13]

Then came Volcker's high interest rate policy, the recession in the US that diminished demand for Mexican products, and the slump in oil prices. Mexican state revenues fell and the cost of servicing the debt soared. Mexico declared bankruptcy in August 1982. The massive capital flight already under way in anticipation of a devaluation of the peso accelerated, and President Portillo nationalized the banks as an emergency measure.[14] The business elite and the bankers disapproved. De la Madrid, who assumed the presidency just a few months later, had to make a political choice. He sided with business. One could say this was inevitable, but the political power of the PRI did not necessarily make it so. De la Madrid was reform-minded, less embedded in the traditional politics of the PRI, and had close relations with capitalist class and foreign interests. The new combination of the IMF, the World Bank, and the US Treasury pulled together by James Baker to bail Mexico out of its difficulties put additional pressure on him. They not only insisted on budgetary austerity; they insisted, for the first time, on broad neoliberal reforms, such as privatization, reorganization of the financial system in ways more consistent with foreign interests, the opening of internal markets to foreign capital, lowering tariff barriers, and the construction of more flexible labour markets. In 1984 the World Bank, for the first time in its history, granted a loan to a country in return for structural neoliberal reforms. De la Madrid then opened Mexico to the global economy by joining GATT and implementing an austerity programme. The effects were wrenching:

From 1983 to 1988 Mexico's per capita income fell at a rate of 5 per cent per year; the value of workers' real wages fell between 40 per cent and 50 per cent; inflation, which had oscillated between 3 and 4 per cent per year in the 1960s, had gone up to the mid teens after 1976, and surpassed 100 per cent in several of those years . . . At the same time, due to government fiscal problems and the re-orientation of the country's governing economic model, state expenditure on public goods declined. Food subsidies were restricted to the poorest segments of the population, and the quality of public education and health care stagnated or declined.[15]

In Mexico City in 1985 this meant that resources were 'so scarce that expenditures on critical urban services in the capital plummeted 12 per cent on transport, 25 per cent on potable water, 18 per cent on health services, 26 per cent on trash collection'.[16] The crime wave that followed turned Mexico City from one of the more tranquil into one of the most dangerous of all Latin American cities within a decade. This was a rerun, though in many respects more devastating, of what had happened to New York City ten years before. Much later, in a symbolic event, Mexico City awarded a multi-million-dollar contract to Giuliani's consultancy organization to teach them how to deal with crime.

De la Madrid saw that one way out of the debt dilemma was to sell off public enterprises and use the proceeds to pay down the debt. But the initial steps towards privatization were both tentative and relatively minor. Privatization entailed the wholesale restructuring of labour contracts and this provoked conflict. Fierce labour struggles broke out in the late 1980s only to be put down ruthlessly by the government. The attack on organized labour intensified under the Salinas presidency that took over in 1988. Several labour leaders were gaoled for corruption, and new and more compliant leaders were installed in key labour organizations under the PRI's control. Troops were called out more than once to break strikes, and the independent power of organized labour, such as it was, was diminished at every turn. Salinas accelerated and formalized the process of privatization. He was US-trained and looked to US-trained economists for advice.[17] His economic development programme was couched in language close to neoliberal orthodoxy.

Opening Mexico up further to foreign direct investment and competition became one of the key elements in Salinas's reform programme. The maquila programme expanded rapidly along the northern border to become fundamental to Mexico's industrial and employment structure (Figure 4.3). He began and successfully completed the negotiations with the US that produced NAFTA. Privatization proceeded apace. Employment in the state sector was cut in half between 1988 and 1994. By 2000 the number of state-owned firms had been reduced to barely 200 compared to the 1,100 that had existed in 1982.[18] The terms of privatization were increasingly set to encourage foreign ownership. The banks that had been so hastily nationalized in 1982 were re-privatized in 1990. To conform with NAFTA, Salinas also had to open up the peasant sector and agriculture to foreign competition. He had, therefore, to attack the powers of the peasantry that had long formed one of the key pillars of the PRI's support. The 1917 Constitution from the Mexican Revolution protected the legal rights of indigenous peoples and enshrined those rights in the *ejido* system that allowed land to be collectively held and used. In 1991 the Salinas government passed a reform law that both permitted and encouraged privatization of the *ejido* lands, opening them up to foreign ownership. Since the *ejido* provided the basis of collective security among indigenous groups, the government was, in effect, divesting itself of its responsibilities to maintain that security. The subsequent lowering of import barriers delivered yet another blow, as cheap imports from the efficient but also highly subsidized agribusinesses in the United States drove down the price of corn and other products to the point where only the most efficient and affluent Mexican farmers could compete. Close to starvation, many peasants were forced off the land, only to augment the pool of unemployed in already overcrowded cities, where the so-called

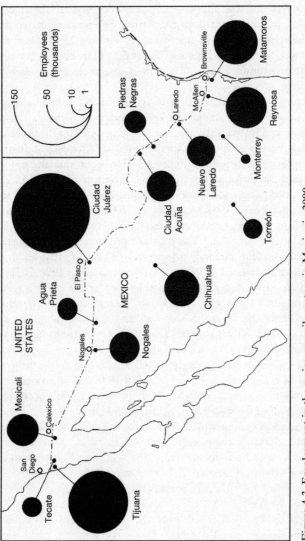

Figure 4.3 Employment in the major maquila sectors in Mexico in 2000
Source: Dicken, *Global Shift.*

informal economy (for example street vendors) grew by leaps and bounds. Resistance to the *ejido* reform was, however, widespread, and several peasant groups supported the Zapatista rebellion that broke out in Chiapas in 1994.[19]

Having signed on to what became known as the Brady Plan for partial debt forgiveness in 1989, Mexico had to swallow, mainly voluntarily as it turned out, the IMF's poison pill of deeper neo-liberalization. The result was the 'tequila crisis' of 1995, sparked, as had happened in 1982, by the US Federal Reserve raising inter-est rates. This put speculative pressure on the peso, which was devalued. The trouble was that Mexico had earlier taken to issuing dollar-denominated debt (called *tesobonos*) to encourage foreign investment, and after the devaluation could not mobilize enough dollars to pay them off. The US Congress refused to help, but Clinton exercised executive powers to put together a $47.5 billion rescue package. He feared a loss of jobs in those US industries exporting to Mexico, the prospect of increasing illegal immigra-tion, and, above all, the loss of legitimacy for neoliberalization and the NAFTA agreements. As a convenient side-effect of the devaluation, US capital could then rush in and buy up all manner of assets at fire-sale prices. While only one of the Mexican banks privatized in 1990 was foreign-owned, by 2000 twenty-four out of thirty were in foreign hands. The exaction of tribute from Mexico by foreign capitalist class interests then became unstoppable. But foreign competition also began to be a problem. Mexico lost a significant number of maquila jobs after 2000 as China became a much cheaper and therefore preferred location for many foreign firms looking to employ low-wage labour.[20]

The effects of all this, particularly the privatizations, on concentrations of wealth within Mexico were marked:

In 1994, Forbes magazine's list of the richest people in the world revealed that Mexico's economic restructuring had produced twenty-four billion-aires. Of these, at least seventeen participated in the privatization programme, buying banks, steel mills, sugar refineries, hotels and restaurants, chemical plants, and a telecommunications firm as well as concessions to operate firms within newly privatized sectors of the economy, such as ports, private toll highways, and cellular and long distance telephony.[21]

Carlos Slim, Mexico's richest man, was twenty-fourth on the Forbes list, and he controlled four of Mexico's twenty-five largest firms. His entrepreneurial interests spread beyond Mexico's borders and he became a major player in telecommunications throughout all of Latin America, as well as in the US. His strategy for cellphone service became renowned: capture and monopolize the high-density and affluent markets and leave the low-density and poorer markets without service. By 2005 Mexico ranked ninth in the world (ahead of Saudi Arabia) for its number of billionaires. It is a moot point whether we call this the *restoration* or the *creation de novo* of class power. Plainly, the attack on labour, on the peasantry, and on the standard of living of the population had worked in Mexico. Their lot became markedly worse as wealth accumulated both within Mexico and beyond in the hands of a small group of magnates backed by their financial and legal apparatuses of power.

The Argentinian Collapse

Argentina emerged from its period of military dictatorship heavily indebted and rigidly locked into a corporatist, authoritarian, and quite corrupt system of governance. Democratization proved difficult, but in 1992 Carlos Menem came to power. Though a Peronist, Menem set about liberalizing the economy, partly to curry favour with the US but also to re-establish Argentina's credentials in the international community in the wake of the revelations of the 'dirty war' that sullied its reputation. Menem opened the country to foreign trade and capital flows, introduced greater flexibility into labour markets, privatized state-owned companies and social security, and pegged the peso to the dollar in order to bring inflation under control and provide security for foreign investors. Unemployment rose, putting a downward pressure on wages, while the elite used privatization to amass new fortunes. Money flooded into the country and it boomed from 1992 until the 'tequila crisis' spilled over from Mexico:

Within weeks, the Argentine banking system lost 18 per cent of its deposits. The economy that had grown at an average annual rate of 8 per cent from the second half of 1990 to the second half of 1994 fell into a steep recession. Gross domestic product contracted by 7.6 per cent from the last quarter of 1994 to the first quarter of 1996 . . . the government's interest burden increased by more than 50 per cent from 1994 to 1996. There was a massive capital outflow and shrinkage of foreign exchange reserves.[22]

Unemployment soared to 18 per cent. While the peso was clearly overvalued, devaluation (in contrast to the situation in Mexico) was precluded by insistence upon maintaining the security of the dollar peg. A brief recovery based on foreign capital inflows followed, until the effects of the Asian economic crisis of 1997–8 spread first to Russia and then to neighbouring Brazil. With that and high interest rates pushing the domestic budget into deficit, an unbearable pressure was put upon the Argentine peso. Foreign and domestic capital began to decamp in anticipation of devaluation. Argentina's debt more than doubled between 1995 and September 2001, while foreign exchange reserves were fast disappearing. The interest payment due on the debt soared to $9.5 billion by 2000. The IMF, which had backed the dollar peg and which was firmly set against devaluation for fear of inflationary consequences (as it had been in Russia and Brazil with, in Stiglitz's judgement, disastrous consequences in both cases), bailed Argentina out with a $6 billion loan (the second largest in IMF history).

But even this could not stanch the outflow. In 2001 the Argentine banking system lost more than 17 per cent of its deposits ($14.5 billion). Perhaps as much as $2 billion was lost on 30 November alone. The IMF refused an emergency loan on the grounds that Argentina had not cured its budgetary imbalance. Argentina defaulted on its debt. The government restricted bank withdrawals on 1 December to $250 per week and regulated all foreign account transactions over $1,000. The riots that ensued left twenty-seven people dead, and President de la Rua resigned, along with Domingo Carvallo, the architect of his economic policy. By 6 January 2002, the new president, Duhalde, had abandoned the dollar peg and devalued the peso. But he also decided to freeze all savings accounts above $3,000 and eventually to treat the dollar deposits as if they were pesos, thus reducing savings to about one-third of their former value. $16 billion in purchasing power had been transferred from savers to the banks and through them to a political–economic elite. The consequences in terms of social unrest were dramatic and far-reaching. Unemployment soared and incomes fell. Idle factories were occupied by militant workers and set to work, neighbourhood solidarity committees were set up to seek better collective means of survival and the *piqueteros* (street pickets) blocked transportation networks and mobilized around key political demands.[23]

In the face of popular opinion, which held the banks, foreign investors, and the IMF in total contempt, Kirchner, the newly elected populist president who succeeded Duhalde, could only snub the IMF, default on $88 billion in debts, and initially offer to pay off outraged creditors at the rate of 25 cents on the dollar.[24] Interestingly, Kirchner's economics team does not have a single US-trained economist in it. Locally trained, they take the 'heterodox' view that while the repayment of the external debt is important it should not entail a collapse of living standards in Argentina. With signs of recovery in 2004, particularly in the manufacturing sector helped by the devaluation, the big problem for Argentina is to face down fierce competition from Brazil and, in the near future, from China as the latter conforms to WTO rules and gains open access to Argentine markets.

This story of Argentina's rollercoaster experience with neoliberalization illustrates all too well how little neoliberal theory has to do with practice. As a member of the neoliberal Ludwig von Mises Institute has pointed out, the 'confiscatory deflation' that occurred in Argentina was quite properly interpreted by its Argentine victims as 'bank robbery by the political elites'.[25] Or, as Veltmeyer and Petras prefer to characterize it, the whole episode reeks of 'a new imperialism: pillage of the economy, growth of vast inequalities, economic stagnation followed by profound and enduring depression and massive impoverishment of the population as a consequence of the greatest concentration of wealth in Argentine history'.[26]

South Korea

South Korea emerged from the war of 1950–3 a devastated country in a parlous economic and geopolitical position. Its economic turn-around is usually dated from the military coup of 1961 which brought General Park Chung Hee to power. Per capita income was less than $100 in 1960 but now stands at more than $12,000. This astonishing economic performance is often cited as the perfect example of what any developmental state might do. South Korea had, however, two initial geopolitical advantages. Since the country was at the frontline of the Cold War the US was prepared to support it militarily and economically, particularly in the early years. But, less obviously, the ex-colonial relationship with Japan conferred benefits that varied from familiarity with Japanese economic and military organizational strategies (Park was trained in the Japanese Military Academy) to active Japanese assistance in penetrating foreign markets.

Korea was still basically an agrarian country in 1960. Under Park's dictatorial rule, the state set out to industrialize. The capitalist class was weak but by no means insignificant. After arresting the main business leaders for corruption, Park came to an accommodation with them. He reformed the state bureaucracy, set up an economic planning ministry (following the successful Japanese model), and nationalized the banks to gain control over credit allocation. He then relied on the entrepreneurial vigour and investment strategies of a nascent group of industrial capitalists who were invited to enrich themselves in the process.[27] During the early 1960s industrialists became export-oriented because Japan increasingly used them as an offshore platform to re-export its own partially manufactured goods to the US market. Joint ventures with the Japanese flourished. Koreans used them to gain technology and experience of foreign markets. The Korean state supported this export-led strategy by mobilizing internal savings, rewarding successful businesses, and encouraging their merger into *chaebols* (large integrated firms such as Hyundai, Daewoo, and Samsung) through easy access to credit, tax advantages, procurement of inputs, control over the labour force, and support in gaining access to foreign (particularly US) markets. With support from a heavy-industry development strategy (focusing on steel, shipbuilding, petrochemicals, electronics, automobiles, and machinery) several *chaebols* switched focus and became global players in these industries from the mid-1970s on. They also became the locus of power of an ever more wealthy domestic capitalist class. As their size and resources grew (by the mid-1980s three *chaebols* accounted for one-third of the national product) the relationship between *chaebol* and state changed. By the mid-1980s, they 'wielded enough power and influence to launch a successful campaign for the steady dismantling of the state's impressive regulatory apparatus'. No longer dependent on the state given their well-established position in international trade and independent access to credit, the capitalist class came to favour its own version of neoliberalization.[28]

This version rested on protecting its privileges while shedding regulatory controls. The banks were in effect privatized. The close and often corrupt nexus of power that bound the leadership of the *chaebols* and the state so closely together proved very hard to break, and the Korean banks lent as much on the basis of political favours as they did for sound investment reasons. Korean businesses also needed liberalization of trade relations and of capital flows (something that was also forced from outside through the Uruguay Round in 1986) so that they could invest surplus capital freely abroad (Figure 4.4). Korean capital explored offshore production using cheaper and more compliant labour forces. So began the export of degrading labour practices through Korean-owned subcontracting networks that reached into Latin America and South Africa as well as across much of East and South-East Asia. After the revaluation of the yen in 1995, Japan shifted to offshore production in lower-cost locations in Thailand, Indonesia, and Malaysia. This, together with China's entry into the world market, intensified intra-regional competition. While the Chinese initially challenged South Korea (and other countries in the region) in low-value-added sectors of production (such as textiles) it quickly moved up the value-added chain. The South Korean response was to offshore a lot of production into China through direct investment, which may have been good for Korean corporations but was not good for employment at home.

After a boom in exports in the late 1980s, Korean industry succumbed to the competition, experiencing a loss of export markets and a collapse of profitability after 1990. The *chaebols* resorted to borrowing, increasingly from foreign banks. Korean businesses acquired a very high debt-to-equity ratio and therefore became

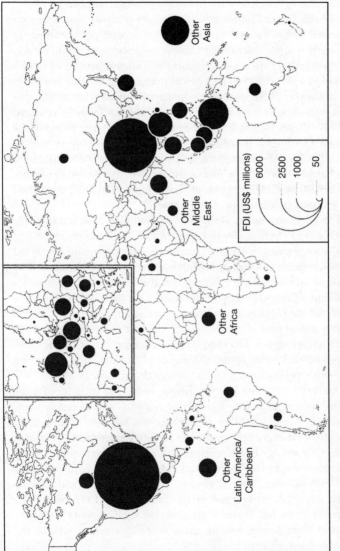

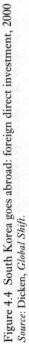

Figure 4.4 South Korea goes abroad: foreign direct investment, 2000
Source: Dicken, *Global Shift.*

vulnerable to any rapid rise in interest rates.[29] Internally, South Korea also had to deal with the rising power of organized labour. Massive industrialization entailed equally massive proletarianization and urbanization, which favoured labour organization. In the early years, independent union organizations were fiercely repressed. But Park's assassination (by his own director of intelligence) in 1979, followed by a brutal massacre of civilian protesters in Kwangju in 1980, sparked a popular movement of students, citizens, and workers for democratization. This was formally achieved in 1987. Wages then rose as unions consolidated their power in the face of continuing governmental repression. Employers wanted more flexible labour markets, but successive governments found this hard to deliver. The formation and legalization of the democratic Korean Confederation of Trade Unions in 1995 confirmed the growing power of organized labour.[30]

The declining ability of the state to discipline capital during the 1990s was exacerbated by the crisis of 1997–8. Foreign capital had long campaigned for easier access to a traditionally protected domestic market as well as for further financial liberalization. The evolving architecture of international trade and finance ensured a modicum of success on that front during the early 1990s. Clinton's price for supporting Korea's incorporation into the OECD had been a strong dose of financial liberalization. The outbreak of the crisis was preceded, however, by labour unrest targeting the *chaebols* (then seeking to lay off thousands of workers) and protesting repressive government policies towards the unions. In March 1997 the government passed a new labour code that introduced a far higher level of flexibility into labour relations and so tacitly sanctioned the lay-offs.[31] Many of the *chaebols*, however, were heavily indebted to increasingly suspicious foreign lenders and to national banks that already had a preponderance of non-performing loans. The government had such a weak foreign reserve position that it could do nothing. Several *chaebols*, such as Hansin and Hambo Steel, declared bankruptcy in the first half of 1997 before the currency crisis hit. When it erupted, the foreign banks withdrew support from Korea, forcing many more *chaebols*, as well as the country itself, close to bankruptcy.[32]

The US saw no reason to offer financial support (the Cold War was over) and instead followed the dictates of Wall Street, which had long pushed for financial liberalization for its own specific reasons of profitability. Stiglitz recognized that US national interests were being sacrificed for narrow Wall Street financial gains.[33] When the Asian crisis broke, South Korea was encouraged by the IMF to raise interest rates to defend its currency and in so doing plunged its own economy even deeper into recession. This forced many companies with a high debt-to-equity ratio into bankruptcy. High unemployment, falling wage rates, and even more *chaebol* bankruptcies (Daewoo went under, and Hyundai came very close) immediately followed. The government appealed to the IMF and the US. In exchange for a $55 billion bail-out it agreed to open up financial services to foreign ownership and to let foreign firms operate freely. These bail-out terms were not convincing, and ten days later, in the face of imminent default, another agreement had to be struck in which the lending banks rescheduled Korean debt (a 'bail-in') in return for a privileged lock on future income (shades of the New York City solution). As a result 'Koreans suffered through massive bankruptcies of big and small firms, and a recession that contracted national income by seven per cent, bringing down wages for the average worker by ten per cent and sending the jobless rate to nearly nine per cent'.[34] From this two lessons can be drawn. First, 'Koreans learned in the hardest possible way that at the moment of their financial ruination, the United States had chosen to further its parochial self-interest'; secondly, the US now defined that self-interest entirely in terms of Wall Street and finance capital.[35] The Wall Street–Treasury–IMF alliance had, in effect, done to South Korea what the investment bankers had done in the mid-1970s to New York City. The subsequent revival of the Korean economy (in part based on ignoring IMF advice on restructuring as well as on a much less militant labour situation) has first and foremost augmented the flow of tribute into the coffers of Wall Street and thereby augmented concentrated elite class power in the US. The power of the *chaebols* has been either shattered or reconstituted as foreign capital moved in on a wave of mergers and acquisitions engineered by what became impolitely known as 'vulture capital' from abroad. The internal class structure is in flux as South Korean capital transforms relations to both the state and the global market. But behind this the data show that income inequality and impoverishment surged during and after the crisis. The increasing casualization and 'flexibilization' of the labour force (particularly deleterious for women), backed by yet another round of state repression of labour and community movements, signals a renewed class offensive against the least well off that can only presage the usual consequences for the accumulation of class power both within and without the country.

Sweden

Probably nowhere in the Western world was the power of capital more democratically threatened in the 1970s than in Sweden. Ruled by the Social Democrats since the 1930s, Sweden's balance of class forces had been stabilized around a strong centralized trade union structure that bargained collectively with the Swedish capitalist class directly over wage rates, benefits, conditions of contract, and the like. Politically, the Swedish welfare state had been organized around the ideals of a redistributive socialism with progressive taxation and a reduction of income inequality and poverty achieved in part through the provision of elaborate welfare services. The capitalist class, though small, was extremely powerful. Unlike many other social democratic and dirigiste states, Sweden had refrained from nationalizing any of the commanding heights of the economy (with the exception of transportation and public utilities). While there were many small businesses, a few families owned a disproportionate share of the means of production.

As in almost all advanced capitalist societies, labour unrest burgeoned in the late 1960s, sparking a wave of regulatory reform that curbed the power of capital and extended the power of labour even into the workplace. The proposal that most threatened the capitalist class was the Rehn–Meidner plan. A 20 per cent tax on corporate profits would flow into wage earner funds controlled by the unions to be reinvested in the corporations. The effect would be to steadily reduce the significance of private ownership and to build towards collective ownership managed by the representatives of the workers. This amounted to 'a frontal assault on the sanctity of private ownership'. However generous the terms of the buy-out may have been, the capitalist class was threatened with gradual annihilation as a distinctive class. And it responded accordingly.[36]

From the mid-1970s onwards, the Swedish Employers' Federation (doubtless emulating its counterpart in the US) increased its membership, mobilized a massive war-chest, and launched a propaganda campaign against excessive regulation and for the increasing liberalization of the economy, the reduction of the tax burden, and the rolling back of excessive welfare state commitments which, in its view, caused economic stagnation. But when a centre-right Conservative Party came to power in 1976, replacing the Social Democrats for the first time since the 1930s, it failed to act on the employers' proposals. The labour unions were too strong and the public was not persuaded. When it became clear that direct confrontation with the labour unions through lock-outs and non-collaboration in wage negotiations did not work either, the employers moved more towards undermining rather than confronting the institutional arrangements of the corporatist state. In 1983 they refused to participate in central bargaining. Thenceforth, wage and benefits negotiations would have to proceed on a company-by-company basis. They managed to persuade one union to go along with this, and so seriously damaged the collective power of labour.

But most efficacious of all was the propaganda campaign waged by the employers. They used their control over the Nobel Prize in Economics to consolidate neoliberalism within Swedish economic thinking. Long-standing complaints on the part of intellectuals and professionals regarding the oppressive universalisms and high taxation policies of the Swedish state were assiduously cultivated through a rising tide of rhetoric lauding individual liberties and freedoms. These debates reverberated throughout the media and gained increasing currency in the popular imagination. Above all, the employers' think-tank—the Center for Business and Policy Studies (SNS)—funded serious research on economic structures and prospects (like the NBER in the US) that again and again proved 'scientifically' to policy elites and to the public that the welfare state was the fundamental cause of economic stagnation.[37]

The real shift towards neoliberalism came with the election of a Conservative government in 1991. But the way had already been partially prepared by the Social Democrats, who were increasingly pressed to find ways out of the economic stagnation. Their partial implementation of some parts of the neoliberal agenda suggested acceptance of the persuasive analyses of the SNS. It was the left rather than the right that now lacked ideas. The unions were persuaded to exercise wage restraint in order to raise profits and encourage investment. Deregulation of banking (which led to a classic speculative bubble in credit allocation and the housing market) and tax cuts for the wealthiest (again supposedly to encourage investment) had already occurred in the late 1980s. The central bank (always Conservative) finally switched its mission to fighting inflation rather than maintaining full employment. The collapse of the speculative bubble in asset prices that followed upon the oil price rise of 1991 led to capital flight and internal bankruptcies that cost the Swedish government dear. The blame for the crash was instinctively placed upon the inefficiencies of the welfare state and the Conservative government that came to power listened sympathetically to the Swedish Chamber of Commerce's plan for the complete privatization of the welfare state.

Blyth considers that the proposed remedies were wholly inappropriate to the circumstances. The problem, he argues, was 'cognitive locking'—the inability to think of any other policy solution than that prescribed by neoliberal orthodoxy. 'It was this homogeneity of personnel and ideas, coupled with the politicization of business, that thrust these new ideas onto the agenda and ultimately led to the transformation of Swedish liberalism.' The practical result was a serious depression that diminished output and doubled unemployment rates in two years. With the government losing public confidence, another way had to be found to sustain the neoliberal reforms. The answer was to join the European Union, a move that is 'perhaps best understood as an attempt by business and the Conservatives to let the economic ideas and institutions of the EU achieve by international convergence what they had failed to do through domestic reform'. Joining the EU in 1993–4 deprived the state of many of the tools it had previously maintained to fight unemployment and advance the social wage.[38] The result was that even when the Social Democrats returned to power in 1994, the neoliberal programme of 'deficit reduction, inflation control and balanced budgets rather than full employment and an equitable distribution of income became cornerstones of macroeconomic policy'.[39] Privatization of pensions and of welfare provision was accepted as inevitable. Blyth interprets this as a case of 'path dependency'—a certain logic of decision-making powered by hegemonic ideas carries all before it. Embedded liberalism was eroded, but by no means fully dismantled. The public still remained broadly attached to its welfare structures. Inequality certainly increased, but by no means to the levels seen in the US or the UK. Poverty levels remained low and levels of social provision remained high. Sweden is an example of what might be called 'circumscribed neoliberalization', and its generally superior social condition reflects that fact.

Forces and Fluxes

The evidence assembled here suggests that uneven development was as much an outcome of diversification, innovation, and competition (sometimes of the monopolistic sort) between national, regional, and in some instances even metropolitan models of governance as it was an imposition by some hegemonic outside power, such as the US. A more fine-grained analysis suggests a wide range of factors that affected the degree of neoliberalization in particular instances. Most conventional analyses of the forces at work concentrate on some combination of the power of neoliberal ideas (held to be particularly strong in the cases of Britain and Chile), the need to respond to financial crises of various sorts (as in Mexico and South Korea) and a more pragmatic approach to reform of the state apparatus (as in France and China) to improve competitive position in the global market. While these have all been elements of some significance, the lack of any examination of the class forces that might be at work is quite startling. The possibility, for example, that the ruling ideas might be those of some ruling class is not even considered, even though there is overwhelming evidence for massive interventions on the part of business elites and financial interests in the production of ideas and ideologies: through investment in think-tanks, in the training of technocrats, and in the command of the media. The possibility that financial crises might be caused by capital strikes, capital flight, or financial speculation, or that financial crises are deliberately engineered to facilitate accumulation by dispossession, is ruled out as far too conspiratorial even in the face of innumerable suspicious signs of co-ordinated speculative attacks on this or that currency. We need, it seems, a somewhat broader frame for interpreting the complicated and geographically uneven paths of neoliberalization.

Some attention must be paid to contextual conditions and institutional arrangements, since these vary greatly from Singapore to Mexico, Mozambique, Sweden, and Britain, and the ease of conversion to neoliberalism has varied as a consequence. The South African case is particularly troubling. Emerging in the midst of all of the hopes generated out of the collapse of apartheid and desperate to reintegrate into the global economy, it was partly persuaded and partly coerced by the IMF and the World Bank to embrace the neoliberal line, with the predictable result that economic apartheid now broadly confirms the racial apartheid that preceded it.[40] The changing internal balance of class forces within a particular state over time has also been a crucial determinant. To the degree that organized labour has managed to maintain or acquire (in the case of South Korea) a powerful presence, neoliberalization has faced strong and in some instances insurmountable barriers. Weakening (as in Britain and the US), bypassing (as in Sweden), or violently destroying (as in Chile) the powers of organized labour is a necessary precondition for neoliberalization. By the same token, neoliberalization has frequently depended upon the increasing power, autonomy, and cohesion of businesses and corporations and their capacity as a class to put pressure on state power (as in the US and Sweden). This capacity is most easily exercised directly via financial institutions, market behaviours, capital strikes, or capital flight, and indirectly through influencing elections, lobbying, bribery and corruption or, even more subtly, through commanding the power of economic ideas. The degree to which neoliberalism has become integral to common-sense understandings among the populace at large has varied greatly depending on the strength of belief in the power of social solidarities and the importance of traditions of collective social responsibility and provision. Cultural and political traditions that underpin popular common sense have therefore had their role to play in differentiating the degree of political acceptance of ideals of individual liberty and free market determinations as opposed to other forms of sociality.

But perhaps the most interesting aspect of neoliberalization arises out of the complex interplay of internal dynamics and external forces. While in certain instances the latter may reasonably be construed as dominant, in most cases the relationships are far more intricate. In Chile, after all, it was the upper classes that sought US help in mounting the coup, and it was they who accepted neoliberal restructuring as the path forward, albeit on the basis of advice from US-trained technocrats. And in Sweden it was the employers who sought European integration as the means to lock in a neoliberal domestic agenda that was in difficulty. Even the most draconian of IMF restructuring programmes is unlikely to go forward without a modicum of internal support from someone. It sometimes seems as if the IMF merely takes the responsibility for doing what some internal class forces want to do anyway. And there are enough successful cases of rejections of IMF advice to suggest that the US Treasury–Wall Street–IMF complex is not as all-powerful as is sometimes claimed. It is only when the internal power structure has been reduced to a hollow shell and when internal institutional arrangements are in total chaos, either because of collapse (as in the ex-Soviet Union and central Europe), or because of civil wars (as in Mozambique, Senegal, or Nicaragua), or because of degenerative weakness (as in the Philippines), that we see external powers freely orchestrating neoliberal restructurings. And in these instances the success rate tends to be poor precisely because neoliberalism cannot function without a strong state and strong market and legal institutions.

It has undoubtedly also been the case that the burden on all states to create 'a good business climate' to attract and retain geographically mobile capital has played its part, particularly in the advanced capitalist countries (such as France). But what is odd here is the way in which neoliberalization and a good business climate are so often held as equivalent, as in the 2004 World Bank *Development Report*.[41] If neoliberalization produces social unrest and political instability of the order of that in Indonesia or

Argentina in recent years, or if it results in depression and restrictions on the growth of internal markets, then it could just as easily be said that neoliberalization repels rather than encourages investment.[42] Even when some aspect of neoliberal policy with respect to, say, flexible labour markets or financial liberalization has been solidly implanted it is not clear that this is in itself sufficient to lure mobile capital. And beyond this there is the even more serious problem of what kind of capital is being attracted. Portfolio capital is just as easily attracted by a speculative boom as it is by solid institutional and infrastructural arrangements that might attract high-value-added industries. Attracting 'vulture capital' hardly seems a worthwhile venture, but this in effect is what neo-liberalization has all too frequently accomplished (as critics like Stiglitz freely acknowledge).

Contingent geopolitical considerations have also played their part. South Korea's position as a frontline state in the Cold War initially gave it US protection for its developmentalism. Mozambique's position as a frontline state led to a civil war fomented by South Africa to undermine Frelimo's attempt to construct socialism. Heavily indebted as a result of the war, Mozambique fell an easy prey to the IMF's penchant for neoliberal restructuring.[43] US-backed counter-revolutionary governments in Central America, Chile, and elsewhere have frequently produced similar outcomes. Even a particular geographical position, such as Mexico's proximity to the US and its peculiar vulnerability to US pressures, has played its part. And the fact that the US no longer needs to defend against the threat of communism means that it no longer has to worry unduly if neoliberal restructurings spark massive unemployment and social unrest in this place or that. It failed, much to the chagrin of loyal Thais who had supported the US throughout the Vietnam War, to bail out Thailand in its distress. Indeed, US as well as other financial institutions acted the part of vulture capital with considerable relish.

But one persistent fact within this complex history of uneven neoliberalization has been the universal tendency to increase social inequality and to expose the least fortunate elements in any society—be it in Indonesia, Mexico, or Britain—to the chill winds of austerity and the dull fate of increasing marginalization. While such a trend has been ameliorated here and there by social policies, the effects at the other end of the social spectrum have been quite spectacular. The incredible concentrations of wealth and power that now exist in the upper echelons of capitalism have not been seen since the 1920s. The flows of tribute into the world's major financial centres have been astonishing. What, however, is even more astonishing is the habit of treating all of this as a mere and in some instances even unfortunate byproduct of neoliberalization. The very idea that this might be—just might be—the fundamental core of what neoliberalization has been about all along appears unthinkable. It has been part of the genius of neoliberal theory to provide a benevolent mask full of wonderful-sounding words like freedom, liberty, choice, and rights, to hide the grim realities of the restoration or reconstitution of naked class power, locally as well as transnationally, but most particularly in the main financial centres of global capitalism.

5

Neoliberalism 'with Chinese Characteristics'

In December 1978, faced with the dual difficulties of political uncertainty in the wake of Mao's death in 1976 and several years of economic stagnation, the Chinese leadership under Deng Xiaoping announced a programme of economic reform. We may never know for sure whether Deng was all along a secret 'capitalist roader' (as Mao had claimed during the Cultural Revolution) or whether the reforms were simply a desperate move to ensure China's economic security and bolster its prestige in the face of the rising tide of capitalist development in the rest of East and South-East Asia. The reforms just happened to coincide—and it is very hard to consider this as anything other than a conjunctural accident of world-historical significance—with the turn to neoliberal solutions in Britain and the United States. The outcome in China has been the construction of a particular kind of market economy that increasingly incorporates neoliberal elements interdigitated with authoritarian centralized control. Elsewhere, as in Chile, South Korea, Taiwan, and Singapore, the compatability between authoritarianism and the capitalist market had already been clearly established.

While egalitarianism as a long-term goal for China was not abandoned, Deng argued that individual and local initiative had to be unleashed in order to increase productivity and spark economic growth. The corollary, that certain levels of inequality would inevitably arise, was well understood as something that would need to be tolerated. Under the slogan of *xiaokang*—the concept of an ideal society that provides well for all its citizens—Deng focused on 'four modernizations': in agriculture, industry, education, and science and defence. The reforms strove to bring market forces to bear internally within the Chinese economy. The idea was to

120

stimulate competition between state-owned firms and thereby spark, it was hoped, innovation and growth. Market pricing was introduced, but this was probably far less significant than the rapid devolution of political-economic power to the regions and to the localities. This last move proved particularly astute. Confrontation with traditional power centres in Beijing was avoided and local initiatives could pioneer the way to a new social order. Innovations that failed could simply be ignored. To supplement this effort, China was also opened up, albeit under strict state supervision, to foreign trade and foreign investment, thus ending China's isolation from the world market. Experimentation was initially limited, mainly to Guangdong province close to Hong Kong, conveniently remote from Beijing. One aim of this opening to the outside was to procure technology transfers (hence the emphasis on joint ventures between foreign capital and Chinese partners). The other was to gain enough foreign reserves to buy in the necessary means to support a stronger internal dynamic of economic growth.[1]

These reforms would not have assumed the significance we now accord to them, nor would China's extraordinary subsequent economic evolution have taken the path and registered the achievements it did, had there not been significant and seemingly unrelated parallel shifts in the advanced capitalist world with respect to how the world market worked. The gathering strength of neoliberal policies on international trade during the 1980s opened up the whole world to transformative market and financial forces. In so doing it opened up a space for China's tumultuous entry and incorporation into the world market in ways that would not have been possible under the Bretton Woods system. The spectacular emergence of China as a global economic power after 1980 was in part an unintended consequence of the neoliberal turn in the advanced capitalist world.

Internal Transformations

To put it this way in no way diminishes the significance of the tortuous path of the internal reform movement within China itself. For what the Chinese had to learn (and to some degree are still learning), among many other things, was that the market can do

121

little to transform an economy without a parallel shift in class relations, private property, and all the other institutional arrangements that typically ground a thriving capitalist economy. The evolution along this path was both fitful and frequently marked by tensions and crises, in which impulses and even threats from outside certainly played their part. Whether it was all a matter of conscious though adaptive planning ('groping the stones while crossing the river' as Deng called it) or the working out, behind the backs of the party politicians, of an inexorable logic deriving from the initial premises of Deng's market reforms, will doubtless long be debated.[2]

What can be said with precision, is that China, by not taking the 'shock therapy' path of instant privatization later foisted on Russia and central Europe by the IMF, the World Bank, and the 'Washington Consensus' in the 1990s, managed to avert the economic disasters that beset those countries. By taking its own peculiar path towards 'socialism with Chinese characteristics' or, as some now prefer to call it, 'privatization with Chinese characteristics', it managed to construct a form of state-manipulated market economy that delivered spectacular economic growth (averaging close to 10 per cent a year) and rising standards of living for a significant proportion of the population for more than twenty years.[3] But the reforms also led to environmental degradation, social inequality, and eventually something that looks uncomfortably like the reconstitution of capitalist class power.

It is hard to make sense of the details of this transformation without a rough map of its general path. The politics are difficult to fathom, masked as they are by the mysteries of power struggles within a Communist Party determined to maintain its singular and unique hold on power. Key decisions ratified at party congresses set the stage for each step on the reform trail. It is unlikely, however, that the party would have easily countenanced the active reconstitution of capitalist class power in its midst. It almost certainly embraced economic reforms in order to amass wealth and upgrade its technological capacities so as to be better able to manage internal dissent, to better defend itself against external aggression, and to project its power outwards onto its immediate geopolitical sphere of interest in a rapidly developing East and

South-East Asia. Economic development was seen as a means to these ends rather than as an end in itself. Furthermore, the actual developmental path taken seems to fit with the aim of preventing the formation of any coherent capitalist class power bloc within China itself. Heavy reliance upon foreign direct investment (a completely different economic development strategy to that taken by Japan and South Korea) has kept the power of capitalist class ownership offshore (Table 5.1), making it somewhat easier, at least in the Chinese case, for the state to control.[4] The barriers erected to foreign portfolio investment effectively limit the powers of international finance capital over the Chinese state. The reluctance to permit forms of financial intermediation other than the state-owned banks—such as stock markets and capital markets—deprives capital of one of its key weapons vis-à-vis state power. The long-standing attempt to keep structures of state ownership intact while liberating managerial autonomy likewise smacks of an attempt to inhibit capitalist class formation.

But the party also had to face a number of awkward dilemmas. The Chinese business diaspora provided key external links and Hong Kong, reabsorbed into the Chinese polity in 1997, was already structured along capitalistic lines. China had to compromise with both, as well as with the neoliberal rules of international trade set up through the WTO, which China joined in 2001. Political demands for liberalization also began to emerge. Worker protests surfaced in 1986. A student movement, sympathetic to the workers but also expressive of its own demands for greater freedoms, climaxed in 1989. The tremendous tension in the political realm that paralleled economic neoliberalization culminated in the massacre of students in Tiananmen Square. Deng's violent crackdown, carried out against the wishes of party reformers, clearly indicated that neoliberalization in the economy was not to be accompanied by any progress in the fields of human, civil, or democratic rights. While Deng's faction repressed the political it had to initiate yet another wave of neoliberal reforms to survive. Wang summarizes these as follows:

monetary policy became a prime means of control; there was a significant readjustment in the foreign currency exchange rate, moving towards a

Table 5.1. Measures of capital inflows: foreign loans, foreign direct investments, and contractual alliances, 1979–2002

	Amount (US$100 million)				Percentage shares of total capital inflows		
	Total	Foreign loans	Actual FDI inflows	Con-tractual alliances	Foreign loans	Actual FDI inflows	Con-tractual alliances
1979–1982	124.57	106.90	11.66	6.01	85.82	9.36	4.82
1983	19.81	10.65	6.36	2.80	53.76	32.10	14.13
1984	27.05	12.86	12.58	1.61	47.54	46.51	5.95
1985	46.45	26.88	16.61	2.96	57.87	35.76	6.37
1986	72.57	50.14	18.74	3.69	69.09	25.82	5.08
1987	84.52	58.05	23.14	3.33	68.68	27.38	3.94
1988	102.27	64.87	31.94	5.46	63.43	31.23	5.34
1989	100.59	62.86	33.92	3.81	62.49	33.72	3.79
1990	102.89	65.34	34.87	2.68	63.50	33.89	2.60
1991	115.55	68.88	43.66	3.01	59.61	37.78	2.60
1992	192.03	79.11	110.07	2.85	41.20	57.32	1.48
1993	389.60	111.89	275.15	2.56	28.72	70.62	0.66
1994	432.13	92.67	337.67	1.79	21.44	78.14	0.41
1995	481.33	103.27	375.21	2.85	21.46	77.95	0.59
1996	548.04	126.69	417.26	4.09	23.12	76.14	0.75
1997	587.51	120.21	452.57	14.73	20.46	77.03	2.51
1998	579.36	110.00	454.63	14.72	18.99	78.47	2.54
1999	526.6	102.12	403.19	15.18	19.4	76.6	2.88
2000	594.5	100	407.1	17.71	16.8	68.5	2.98
2001	496.8	—	468.8	18.4	—	94.4	3.7
2002	550.1	—	527.4	21.3	—	95.9	3.87

Source: Huang, 'Is China Playing by the Rules?'.

unified rate; exports and foreign trade came to be managed by mechanisms of competition and assumption of responsibility for profits or losses; the 'dual track' pricing system was reduced in scope; the Shanghai Pudong development zone was fully opened and the various regional development zones were all put on track.[5]

After an ageing Deng toured the southern region in 1992 to see for himself what effect the opening to the outside was having on economic development, he pronounced himself fully satisfied. 'To get rich is glorious' he said, adding: 'What does it matter if it is a ginger cat or a black cat as long as it catches mice?' The whole of China was opened up, though still under the watchful eye of the party, to market forces and foreign capital. A democracy of consumption was encouraged in urban areas to forestall social unrest. Market-based economic growth then accelerated in ways that sometimes seemed to be beyond party control.

When Deng initiated the reform process in 1978, almost everything of significance in China lay within the state sector. State-owned enterprises (SOEs) dominated the leading sectors of the economy. By most accounts these were reasonably profitable. They offered not only security of employment to their workers but a wide range of welfare and pension benefits (known as 'the iron rice bowl' or the state's guarantee of a livelihood). There were in addition a variety of local state enterprises under provincial, city, or local government control. The agrarian sector was organized according to a commune system, and most accounts agree it was lagging in productivity and badly in need of reform. Welfare arrangements and social provision were internalized within each of these sectors, though unevenly. Rural dwellers were the least privileged and were kept separate from urban populations by way of a residency permit system which conferred many welfare benefits and rights on the latter while denying them to the former. This system also helped hold back any mass rural migration to the cities. Each sector was integrated into a regionally organized state planning system in which output targets were assigned and inputs allocated according to plan. State-owned banks largely existed as a depository for savings and provided investment moneys outside of the state budget.

The SOEs were long maintained as the stable centrepieces of state control of the economy. The security and benefits they conferred on their workers, though whittled away over time, kept a social safety net under a significant sector of the population for many years. A more open market economy was created around them by dissolving the agricultural communes in favour of an individualized 'personal responsibility system'. Township and village enterprises (TVEs) were created out of the assets held by the communes, and these became centres of entrepreneurialism, flexible labour practices, and open market competition. A wholly private sector was permitted at first only in small-scale production, trade, and service activities, with limits (gradually relaxed over time) on the employment of wage labour. Finally, foreign capital flowed in, gathering momentum during the 1990s. Initially limited to joint ventures and certain regions, it ultimately bore down everywhere, though unevenly. The state-owned banking system expanded during the 1980s and gradually substituted for the central state in providing lines of credit to the SOEs, the TVEs, and the private sector. These different sectors did not evolve independently of each other. The TVEs drew their initial finance from the agrarian sector and provided markets for outputs or furnished intermediate inputs to the SOEs. Foreign capital integrated into the TVEs and the SOEs as time went on, and the private sector became much more significant both directly (in the form of owners) and indirectly (in the form of stockholders). When the SOEs became less profitable they received cheap credit from the banks. As the market sector gained in strength and significance, so the whole economy moved towards a neoliberal structure.[6]

Consider, then, how each distinctive sector evolved over time. In agriculture, peasants were given the right to use communal lands under a 'personal responsibility' system in the early 1980s. Initially, they could sell surpluses (over and above the commune target) at free market rather than state-controlled prices. By the end of the 1980s the communes had been totally dissolved. Though the peasants could not formally own the land, they could lease it and rent it out, hire in labour, and sell their product at market prices (the dual price system effectively collapsed). As a result, rural incomes increased at the astonishing rate of 14 per cent annually and output similarly surged between 1978 and 1984. Thereafter, rural incomes stagnated and even fell in real terms (particularly after 1995) in all but a few select areas and lines of production. The disparity between rural and urban incomes increased markedly. Urban incomes that averaged just $80 a year in 1985 soared to over $1,000 in 2004, while rural incomes rose from around $50 to around $300 in the same period. Furthermore the loss of the collective social rights earlier established within the communes—weak though they may have been—meant the peasants had to face burdensome user charges for schools, medical care, and the like. This was not the case for most permanent urban residents, who were also favoured after 1995 when an urban real-estate law conferred real-estate ownership rights on urban residents, who could then speculate on property values. The urban/rural differential in real incomes is now, according to some estimates, greater than in any other country in the world.[7]

Forced to seek work elsewhere, rural migrants—many of them young women—have consequently flooded—illegally and without the rights of residency—into the cities to form an immense labour reserve (a 'floating' population of indeterminate legal status). China is now 'in the midst of the largest mass migration the world has ever seen' which 'already dwarfs the migrations that reshaped America and the modern Western world'. By official count, it has '114 million migrant workers who have left rural areas, temporarily or for good, to work in cities', and government experts 'predict the number will rise to 300 million by 2020, eventually to 500 million'. Shanghai alone 'has 3 million migrant workers; by comparison, the entire Irish migration to America from 1820 to 1930 is thought to have involved perhaps 4.5 million people'.[8] This labour force is vulnerable to super-exploitation and puts downward pressure on the wages of urban residents. But urbanization is hard to stop, and the rate of urbanization stands at something like 15 per cent per year. Given the lack of dynamism in the rural sector, it is now widely accepted that whatever problems there are will be solved in the cities or not at all. Remittances back to the rural regions are now a crucial element in the survival of rural populations. The dire condition of the rural sector and the instability it is generating is today one of the most serious problems facing the Chinese government.[9]

When the communes were dissolved their previous political and administrative powers were turned over to newly created township and village governments set up under the Constitution of December 1982. Later legislation allowed these governments to take possession of the communes' industrial assets and restructure them as TVEs. Liberated from central state control, local administrations typically took an entrepreneurial stance. The initial surge in rural incomes provided savings that could be ploughed back into the TVEs. Depending on location, joint ventures with foreign capital (particularly from Hong Kong or through the Chinese business diaspora) also flourished. TVEs were particularly active in rural peripheries of large cities, such as Shanghai and in the provincial zones, such as Guangdong, that had been liberated for foreign investment. The TVEs became an incredible source of dynamism in the economy during the first decade and a half of the reform period. By 1995 they were employing 128 million people (see Table 5.2). They centred grassroots experimentation, functioning as proving grounds for reforms.[10] Whatever worked with the TVEs could later become the basis of state policy. And what largely worked was a surge of development in light industry producing consumer goods for export, thus leading China down the export-led industrialization path. Only in 1987, however, did the state finally commit to the idea that development should be export-led.

Accounts as to what these TVEs were about vary greatly. Some

Table 5.2. Changing employment structure in China, 1980–2002 (millions)

	1980	1990	1995	2000	2002
Total	**423.6**	**647.5**	**680.7**	**720.9**	**737.4**
Urban	105.3	170.4	190.4	231.5	247.8
state	80.2	103.5	112.6	81.0	71.6
(SOEs)	67.0	73.0	76.4	43.9	35.3
collective	24.3	35.5	31.5	15.0	11.2
joint-owned	0	1.0	3.7	13.4	18.3
foreign	0	0.7	5.1	6.4	7.6
private	0.8	6.7	20.6	34	42.7
residual	0	23.1	16.9	81.6	96.4
Rural	318.4	477.1	490.3	489.3	489.6
TVEs	30.0	92.7	128.6	128.2	132.9
private		1.1	4.7	11.4	14.1
self-employed		14.9	30.5	29.3	24.7
farmers	288.4	368.4	326.4	320.4	317.9

Source: Prasad, *China's Growth and Integration into the World Economy*, table 8.1.

cite evidence that they were private operations 'in all but name', exploiting dirt-cheap rural or migrant labour—particularly young women—and operating outside of all forms of regulation. The TVEs often paid dismally low wages and offered no benefits and no legal protections. But some TVEs provided limited welfare and pension benefits as well as legal protections. In the chaos of transition, all manner of differences emerged, and these frequently had marked local and regional manifestations.[11]

During the 1980s it became clear that most of China's phenomenal growth rate was being powered from outside the SOE sector. In the revolutionary period the SOEs provided job security and social protections for their workforces. But in 1983 SOEs were allowed to hire 'contract workers' with no social protections and limited tenure.[12] They were also granted greater managerial autonomy from state ownership. Managers could retain a certain proportion of their profits and sell any surplus they produced over their targets at free market prices. The latter were much higher than the official prices, thus setting up an awkward and, it turned out, short-lived dual pricing system. In spite of these incentives, the SOEs did not flourish. Many of them fell into debt and had to be supported either by the central government or by the state-owned banks, which were encouraged to lend to them on favourable terms. This later posed serious problems for the banks as the volume of non-performing loans to the SOEs grew exponentially. Pressure for further reform of the SOE sector mounted. In 1993, therefore, the state decided 'to turn targeted large and medium state enterprises into limited liability or shareholding companies'. The former would have 'two to fifty shareholders' while the latter would have 'more than fifty shareholders and could offer public issues'. A year later a far more extensive programme of corporatization was announced: all but the most important of the SOEs were to be converted into 'share-based co-operatives' in which all employees had the nominal right to purchase shares. Further waves of privatization/conversion of the SOEs occurred in the late 1990s so that, by 2002, SOEs accounted for only 14 per cent of total manufacturing employment relative to the 40 per cent share they had held in 1990. The most recent step has been to open both the TVEs and the SOEs to full foreign ownership.[13]

Neoliberalism 'with Chinese Characteristics'

Foreign direct investment, for its part, met with very mixed results in the 1980s. It was initially channelled into four special economic zones in southern coastal regions. These zones 'had the initial objective of producing goods for export to earn foreign exchange. They also acted as social and economic laboratories where foreign technologies and managerial skills could be observed. They offered a range of inducements to foreign investors, including tax holidays, early remittances of profits and better infrastructure facilities.'[14] But initial attempts by foreign firms to colonize the internal China market in areas such as automobiles and manufactured goods did not do well. While Volkswagen and Ford (barely) survived, General Motors failed in the early 1990s. The only sectors where clear initial successes were recorded were in those sectors exporting goods with high labour content. More than two-thirds of the foreign direct investment that came in during the early 1990s (and an even great percentage of the business ventures that survived) was organized by the overseas Chinese (particularly operating out of Hong Kong but also from Taiwan). The weak legal protections for capitalist enterprises put a premium on informal local relations and trust networks that the overseas Chinese were in a privileged position to exploit.[15]

Subsequently the Chinese government designated several 'open coastal cities' as well as 'open economic regions' for foreign investment (Figure 5.1). After 1995 it virtually opened the whole country up to foreign direct investment of any type. The wave of bankruptcies that hit some of the TVEs in the manufacturing sector in 1997–8, spilling over into many of the SOEs in the main urban centres, proved a turning-point. Competitive pricing mechanisms then took over from the devolution of power from the central state to the localities as the core process impelling the restructuring of the economy. The effect was to severely damage, if not destroy, many of the SOEs and create a vast wave of unemployment. Reports of considerable labour unrest abounded (see below) and the Chinese government was faced with the problem of absorbing vast labour surpluses if it was to survive.[16] It could not solely rely on an ever-expanding inflow of foreign direct investment to solve the problem, important though this might be.

Since 1998, the Chinese have sought in part to confront this

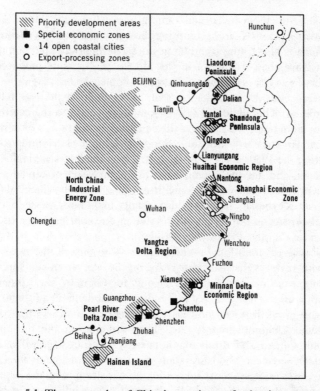

Figure 5.1 The geography of China's opening to foreign investment in the 1980s
Source: Dicken, *Global Shift*.

problem through debt-financed investments in huge mega-projects to transform physical infrastructures. They are proposing a far more ambitious project (costing at least $60 billion) than the already huge Three Gorges Dam to divert water from the Yangtze to the Yellow River. Astonishing rates of urbanization (no fewer than forty-two cities have expanded beyond the 1 million population mark since 1992) required huge investments of fixed capital. New subway systems and highways are being built in major cities, and 8,500 miles of new railroad are proposed to link the interior to the economically dynamic coastal zone, including a high-speed link between Shanghai and Beijing and a link into Tibet. The Olympic Games are prompting heavy investment in Beijing. 'China is also trying to build an interstate highway system more extensive than America's in just fifteen years, while practically every large city is building or has just completed a big new airport.' At last count, China had 'more than 15,000 highway projects in the works, which will add 162,000 kilometers of road to the country, enough to circle the planet at the equator four times'.[17] This effort is far larger *in toto* than that which the United States undertook during the 1950s and 1960s in constructing the interstate highway system, and has the potential to absorb surpluses of capital and labour for several years to come. It is, however, deficit-financed (in classic Keynesian style). It also entails high risks, since if the investments do not return their value in due course, then a fiscal crisis of the state will quickly ensue.

Rapid urbanization provides one way to absorb the massive labour reserves that have converged on the cities from rural areas. Dongguan, just north of Hong Kong, for example, has exploded from a mere town to a city of 7 million inhabitants in a little over twenty years. But 'city officials are not content with a 23 per cent annual economic growth rate. They are putting the finishing touches on a vast, entirely new annex city that they hope will draw 300,000 engineers and researchers, the vanguard of a new China'.[18] It is also the site of construction for what is slated to be the largest shopping mall in the world (built by a Chinese billionaire, it has seven zones modelled on Amsterdam, Paris, Rome, Venice, Egypt, the Caribbean, and California, each constructed with such close attention to detail as to be indistinguishable, we are told, from the real thing).

Such new tier cities are locked in ferocious inter-urban competition. In the Pearl River delta, for example, each city is now trying to capture as much business as possible 'by outbuilding its neighbors, often with duplicative results. Five international airports were built in the late 1990s in a 100–kilometer radius, and a similar boom is starting for ports and bridges'.[19] Provinces and cities resist Beijing's efforts to rein in their investments, in part because they have the power to fund their own projects by selling rights to develop real estate.

Neoliberalism 'with Chinese Characteristics'

Cities have also become venues for frenzied real-estate development and property speculation:

During the early to mid 1990s when a 'casino mentality' gripped the country, banks and other financial institutions imprudently funded massive property developments throughout China. First class office spaces, luxury villas, ostentatious town houses, and apartments sprang up overnight, not only in major cities like Beijing, Shanghai, Shenzhen, but also in many of the smaller provincial and coastal towns ... The so-called 'Shanghai bubble' transformed this once drab city into one of the world's most glamorous metropolises. By the end of 1995, Shanghai boasted over a thousand skyscrapers, some one hundred five-star hotels, about 13.5 million square feet of office space—five times the 2.7 million feet in 1994—and a 'hot' real estate market that was adding stock at a faster rate than new York City ... By late 1996 the bubble had burst, in large part because of inefficient allocation of resources and overcapacity.[20]

But the boom resumed even more vigorously in the late 1990s only to be followed by rumours of overbuilding in key urban markets in 2004.[21]

Behind much of this lay the financial role of China's largely state-owned banking system. This sector expanded rapidly after 1985. By 1993, for example, the number of branches of state banks had risen 'from 60,785 to 143,796 and the number of employees increased from 973,355 to 1,893,957. During the same period deposits increased from 427.3 billion yuan (US$51.6) to 2.3 trillion yuan while total loans increased from 590.5 billion yuan to 2.6 trillion yuan.'[22] By then the banks' disbursements exceeded government budget expenditures by a factor of five. A lot of money went to failing SOEs and the banks clearly 'played a leading role in creating "asset bubbles", especially in the volatile real estate and construction sectors'. Non-performing loans became a problem and in the end the central government had to spend 'almost as much to clean up bad loans' as the US did to rescue the savings and loan industry in 1987 (the cost of that bail-out was '$123.8 billion in public funds and $29.1 billion in supplemental deposit insurance premiums from financial institutions'). In 2003, for example, China announced a complex transfer of $45 billion from its foreign exchange reserves to two big government banks, and this was 'the third largest bailout in the banking system in less than six years'.[23] Although the non-performing loan portfolio accounts for perhaps 35 per cent of China's GDP, this pales in comparison with the overhang of US federal government and consumer debt that stands at more than 300 per cent of GDP.[24]

In one key respect China evidently learned from Japan. The modernization of education and science had to go hand in hand with a definitive strategy of research and development for both military and civilian purposes. Chinese investment in these fields has been significant. It now even offers its services as a commercial satellite provider (much to the irritation of the US). But from the late 1990s on, foreign corporations began to transfer a significant amount of their research and development activity into China. Microsoft, Oracle, Motorola, Siemens, IBM, and Intel have all set up research laboratories in China because of its 'growing importance and sophistication as a market for technology' and its 'large reservoir of skilled but inexpensive scientists, and its consumers, still relatively poor but growing richer and eager for new technology'.[25] More than 200 major foreign corporations, including such giants as BP and General Motors, have now placed a significant part of their research effort in China. These corporations often complain at what they consider the illegal pirating of their technologies and designs by indigenous Chinese companies. But they can do little about it given the reluctance of the Chinese government to intervene and the power of the Chinese state to make things difficult for them to operate in the world's largest market if they press too hard on such issues. And it is not only foreign companies that have been active. Both Japan and South Korea have invested in large-scale 'research cities' in China to position themselves to take advantage of highly skilled but low-cost labour. The overall effect is to make China a much more attractive location for high-tech sector activities.[26] Even Indian high-tech companies find it cheaper to offshore some of their activities to China. An indigenous high-tech sector has also taken off in a number of areas. In Shenzhen, for example, 'with dozens of sleek stone and glass buildings that would not look out of place in Silicon Valley, the expanding campus houses many of the 10,000 engineers working to establish Huawei as China's first international player in the communications equipment business'. Beginning in the late 1990s 'Huawei invested heavily in establishing sales networks in Asia, the Middle East and Russia; it now sells products in 40 countries, often at prices as much as a third lower than its rivals'.[27] And in personal computer marketing and production Chinese corporations now have a very active presence.

External Relations

Foreign trade accounted for only 7 per cent of China's GNP in 1978 but by the early 1990s it had soared to 40 per cent and it has stayed at that level ever since. China's share of world trade quadrupled during the same period. By 2002, over 40 per cent of China's GDP was accounted for by foreign direct investment (and manufacturing accounted for half). By then China had become the largest recipient of foreign direct investment in the developing world, and multinationals were exploiting the China market profitably. General Motors, which had lost on its failed venture in the early 1990s, re-entered the market at the end of the decade and by 2003 was reporting far higher profits on its Chinese venture than on its domestic US operations.[28]

It seemed as if an export-led development strategy had succeeded brilliantly. But none of this had been planned in 1978. Deng had signalled a departure from Mao's policies of internal self-reliance, but the first openings towards the outside were tentative and confined to special economic zones in Guangdong. It was not until 1987 that the party, noting the success of the Guangdong experiment, accepted that growth should be export-led. And it was only after Deng's 'southern tour' in 1992 that the full force of the central government was put behind the opening to foreign trade and foreign direct investment.[29] In 1994, for example, the dual currency exchange rate (official and market) was abolished by a 50 per cent devaluation of the official rate. While the devaluation sparked something of an internal inflationary crisis, it paved the way for massive growth in trade and of capital inflows that have now positioned China as the world's most dynamic and successful economy. What this betokens for the future of neoliberalization, given the latter's penchant for change through competitive uneven geographical developments, remains to be seen.

The initial success of Deng's strategy depended upon the Hong Kong connection. As one of the first of Asia's 'tiger' economies, Hong Kong was already a significant centre of capitalist dynamism. Unlike the other states in the region (Singapore, Taiwan, and South Korea), which resorted to high levels of state planning, Hong Kong had developed in a more chaotic entrepreneurial way without significant state guidance. It conveniently stood at the centre of a Chinese business diaspora that already had significant global connections. Hong Kong's manufacturing had developed along labour-intensive and low-value-added lines (textiles being in the lead). But by the late 1970s it was suffering from severe foreign competition and acute labour shortages. Guangdong, just across the border in China, had all the cheap labour in the world. Deng's opening therefore came as a godsend. Hong Kong capital seized the opportunity. It took advantage of its many hidden connections across the border into China, its function as an intermediary for whatever foreign trade China already had, and its marketing network into the global economy through which Chinese-made goods could easily flow.

As late as the mid-1990s, some two-thirds of foreign direct investment (FDI) in China came through Hong Kong. And although some of this was Hong Kong business expertise intermediating for more diverse sources of foreign capital, there is no question that the fortuitous fact of Hong Kong's proximity was critical to the developmental path that unfolded in China as a whole. The provincial government's economic development zone in urban Shenzhen, for example, was unsuccessful in the early 1980s. What attracted the Hong Kong capitalists were the newly created TVEs in rural areas. Hong Kong capital provided the machinery, the inputs, and the marketing while the TVEs did the work. Once established, this style of operation could be emulated by other foreign capitalists (particularly Taiwanese, mainly around Shanghai after it was opened up). The sources of FDI diversified greatly during the 1990s as Japanese and South Korean as well as US corporations began to use China as an offshore production centre in a big way.

Neoliberalism 'with Chinese Characteristics'

By the mid-1990s, it became clear that China's huge internal market was becoming more and more attractive to foreign capital. While only 10 per cent of the population may have possessed the purchasing power of a nascent and growing middle class, 10 per cent of more than a billion people constituted a huge internal market. The competitive race was on to provide them with automobiles, mobile phones, DVDs, televisions, and washing machines, as well as with shopping centres, highways, and 'luxury' homes. Monthly car production rose gradually from around 20,000 in 1993 to just over 50,000 in 2001, but thereafter leapt upwards to nearly 250,000 monthly by mid-2004. A flood of foreign investment—everything from Wal-Mart and McDonald's to computer chip production—poured into China in anticipation of rapid future internal market growth, in spite of institutional uncertainties, the uncertainties of state policy, and the evident dangers of overcapacity.[30]

The heavy reliance on FDI makes China a special case, very different from Japan or South Korea. Chinese capitalism is not well integrated as a result. Inter-regional trade is rather weakly developed, even though there have been massive investments in new means of communication. Provinces such as Guangdong trade far more with the outside world than they do with the rest of China. Capital does not flow easily from one part of China to another, in spite of a recent spate of merger activity and state-led efforts to create regional alliances among different provinces.[31] Reliance on FDI will therefore diminish only to the extent that resource allocation and capitalist interlinkages improve within China itself.[32]

China's external trading relations have mutated over time, but particularly over the last four years. While accession to the WTO in 2001 has had a lot to do with it, the sheer dynamism of Chinese economic growth and the shifting structures of international competition have made a major realignment of trading relations inevitable. In the 1980s China's position in global markets was mainly through low-value-added production, selling cheap textiles, toys, and plastics in international markets in large volume. Maoist policies had left China self-sufficient in energy and many raw materials (it is one of the largest cotton producers in the world). It merely needed to import the machinery and the technology and gain access to markets (with Hong Kong conveniently obliging). It could use its cheap labour to great competitive advantage. Hourly wages in textile production in China in the late 1990s stood at 30 cents compared to Mexico's and South Korea's $2.75, Hong Kong's and Taiwanese levels hovering around $5, and the US's cost of more than $10.[33] Chinese production was, however, largely subservient in the initial stages to the Taiwanese and Hong Kong merchants, who commanded the access to global markets, took the lion's share of the trading profits, and increasingly achieved backward integration into production by buying out or investing in the TVEs or SOEs. Production facilities employing as many as 40,000 workers are not uncommon in the Pearl River delta. Furthermore, low rates of pay make capital-saving innovations possible. Highly productive US plants use expensive automated systems, but 'Chinese factories reverse this process by taking capital out of the production process and reintroducing a greater role for labor'. The total capital required is typically reduced by one-third. 'The combination of lower wages and less capital typically raises the return on capital above the US factory levels.'[34]

Incredible wage labour advantages of this sort mean that China can compete against other low-cost locations such as Mexico, Indonesia, Vietnam, and Thailand in low-value-added production sectors (such as textiles). Mexico lost 200,000 jobs in just two years as China (in spite of NAFTA) overtook it as the major supplier of the US market in consumer goods. During the 1990s China began to move up the value-added ladder of production and to compete with South Korea, Japan, Taiwan, Malaysia, and Singapore in spheres such as electronics and machine tools. This occurred in part as corporations in those countries decided to move their production offshore to take advantage of the large pool of low-cost and highly skilled labourers being churned out by the Chinese university system. Initially, the biggest inflow came from Taiwan. As many as 1 million Taiwanese entrepreneurs and engineers are now thought to be living and working in China, taking a lot of production capacity with them. The inflow from South Korea has also been strong (see Figure 4.4). Korean electronics corporations now have substantial operations in China. In September 2003, for example, Samsung Electronics announced it was moving its entire PC-making business to China, having previously invested $2.5 billion there, 'creating 10 sales subsidiaries and 26 production companies, employing a total of 42,000 people'.[35] Japanese outsourcing of production to China contributed to the decline in Japanese manufacturing employment from 15.7 million in 1992 to 13.1 million in 2001. Japanese companies also began to withdraw from Malaysia, Thailand, and elsewhere in order to relocate in China. They are now so heavily invested in China that 'more than half of China–Japan trade is conducted among Japanese companies'.[36] As happened in the US, corporations can do very well while their home countries suffer. China has displaced more manufacturing jobs from Japan, South Korea, Mexico, and elsewhere than it has from the US. China's spectacular growth both internally as well as in its international trading position has corresponded with long-lasting recession in Japan, and lagging growth, stagnating exports, and periodic crises in the rest of East and South-East Asia. The negative competitive effects on many countries will likely deepen in time.[37]

China's dramatic growth has, on the other hand, made it more dependent upon foreign sources of raw materials and energy. In 2003 China took '30 per cent of the world's coal production, 36 per cent of the world's steel and 55 per cent of the world's cement'.[38] It went from relative self-sufficiency in 1990 to being the second largest importer of oil after the US in 2003. Its energy companies sought stakes in Caspian Basin oil and opened negotiations with Saudi Arabia to secure access to Middle Eastern oil supplies. Its energy interests in the Sudan as well as in Iran have created tension with the US in both arenas. It competed with Japan over access to Russian oil. Its imports from Australia quadrupled in the 1990s as it sought new sources of metals. In its desperate need for strategic metals such as copper, tin, iron ore, platinum, and aluminium it scurried to cut deals with Chile, Brazil, Indonesia, Malaysia, and many other countries. It sought agricultural and timber imports from everywhere (massive purchases of soy beans from Brazil and Argentina helped breathe new life into those economies), and Chinese demand for scrap metal became so enormous as to raise prices all over the globe. Even US manufacturing has benefited from the Chinese demand for earth-moving equipment (Caterpillar) and turbines (GE). Asian exports to China have also grown at startling rates. China is now the primary export destination for South Korea and rivals the US in Japan's export market. The rapidity of the reorientation of trade relations is best illustrated by the case of Taiwan. China overtook the US as the prime destination of Taiwanese exports (mainly of intermediate manufacturing goods) in 2001, but by the end of 2004 Taiwan was exporting twice as much to China as to the US.[39]

China effectively dominates the whole of East and South–East Asia as a regional hegemon with enormous global influence. It is not above reasserting its imperial traditions in the region and beyond. When confronted by Argentina's worries about cheap Chinese imports destroying the vestiges of its indigenous textile, shoe, and leather industries that began to revive in 2004, the Chinese advice was simply to let such industries die and concentrate on being a raw material and agricultural commodity producer for the booming China market. It was not lost on the Argentines that this was exactly how Britain had approached its Indian empire in the nineteenth century. Nevertheless, the massive infrastructural investments under way in China have entrained much of the global economy. Conversely, China's slower growth in 2004 has been

roiling commodity and financial markets everywhere. Nickel prices have plunged from 15-year highs, copper has tumbled from 8-year highs. The currencies of commodity-driven economies like Australia, Canada and New Zealand have also suffered. And markets in Asia's other export-driven economies have trembled amid concern that China might buy fewer semiconductors from Taiwan and fewer steel rods from South Korea as well as less Thai rubber, Vietnamese rice and Malaysian tin.[40]

As invariably happens with the dynamics of successful capital accumulation, there comes a point at which internally accumulated surpluses require external outlets. One path has been to fund the US debt and thereby keep the market for Chinese products buoyant while keeping the yuan conveniently pegged to the value of the dollar. But Chinese trading companies have long been active globally, and they expanded their scope and range markedly from the mid-1990s on. Chinese businesses also invest overseas to secure their position in foreign markets. Chinese television sets are now being assembled in Hungary to assure access to the European market and in North Carolina to assure access to the US. A Chinese auto company plans to assemble cars and eventually build a factory in Malaysia. Chinese companies are even investing in Pacific region tourism to meet their own surging demand.[41]

But in one respect the Chinese depart glaringly from the neoliberal template. China has massive labour surpluses, and if it is to achieve social and political stability it must either absorb or violently repress that surplus. It can do the former only by debt-financing infrastructural and fixed-capital formation projects on a massive scale (fixed-capital investment increased by 25 per cent in 2003). The danger lurks of a severe crisis of over-accumulation of fixed capital (particularly in the built environment). Abundant signs exist of excess production capacity (for example in automobile production and electronics) and a boom and bust cycle in urban investments has already occurred. But all of this requires that the Chinese state depart from neoliberal orthodoxy and act like a Keynesian state. This requires that it maintain capital and exchange rate controls. These are inconsistent with the global rules of the IMF, the WTO, and the US Treasury. While China is exempt from these rules as a transitional condition for WTO membership, it cannot remain so in perpetuity. The enforcement of capital flow controls is becoming increasingly difficult as Chinese yuan seep across a highly porous border via Hong Kong and Taiwan into the global economy. It is worthwhile recalling that one of the conditions that broke up the whole Keynesian post-war Bretton Woods system was the formation of a eurodollar market as US dollars escaped the discipline of its own monetary authorities.[42] The Chinese are already well on their way to replicating that problem, and their Keynesianism is correspondingly threatened.

The Chinese banking system, which is at the heart of the current deficit financing, cannot currently withstand integration into the global financial system because as much as half its loan portfolio is non-performing. Fortunately, the Chinese have a balance of payments surplus that can be applied, as we have already seen, to wiping the banks' slates clean. But it is at this point that the other shoe is liable to drop, because the only way the Chinese can afford this is by piling up balance of payments surpluses against the US. A peculiar symbiosis emerges, in which China, along with Japan, Taiwan, and other Asian central banks, fund the US debt so that the US can conveniently consume their surplus output. But this renders the US vulnerable to the whims of Asian central bankers. Conversely, Chinese economic dynamism is held hostage to US fiscal and monetary policy. The US is also currently behaving in a Keynesian fashion—running up enormous federal deficits and consumer debt while insisting that everyone else must obey neoliberal rules. This is not a sustainable position, and there are now many influential voices in the US suggesting that it is steering right into the hurricane of a major financial crisis.[43] For China, this would entail switching from a politics of labour absorption to a politics of overt repression. Whether or not such a tactic can succeed, as it did in Tiananmen Square in 1989, will depend crucially upon the balance of class forces and how the Communist Party positions itself in relation to those forces.[44]

Towards a Reconstitution of Class Power?

On 9 June 2004 a certain Mr Wang purchased a $900,000 Maybech ultra-luxury sedan from Daimler Chrysler in Beijing. The market in luxury cars of this sort is, apparently, quite brisk. The inference is that 'a few Chinese families have accumulated extraordinary wealth'.[45] Further down the car status-ranking, China is now the largest market in the world for Mercedes-Benz cars. Somebody, somewhere and somehow, is getting very rich.

Though China may have one of the world's fastest-growing economies it has also become one of its most unequal societies (Figure 5.2). The benefits of growth 'have been bestowed mainly on urban residents and government and party officials. In the past five years, the income divide between the urban rich and the rural poor has widened so sharply that some studies now compare China's social cleavage unfavourably with Africa's poorest nations.'[46] Social inequality was never eradicated in the revolutionary era. The differentiation between town and country was even written into law. But with reform, writes Wang, 'this structural

Neoliberalism 'with Chinese Characteristics'

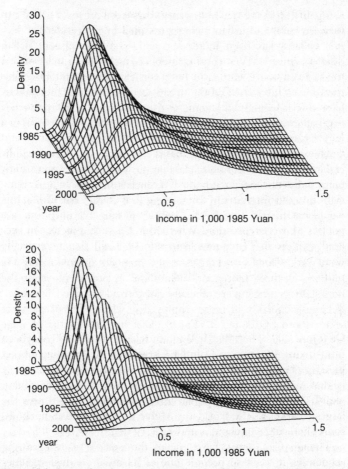

Figure 5.2 Increasing income inequality in China: rural (above) and urban (below), 1985–2000

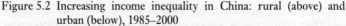

Source: Wu and Perloff, *China's Income Distribution Over Time*.

inequality quickly transformed itself into disparities in income among different classes, social strata, and regions, leading rapidly to social polarization'.[47] Formal measures of social inequality, such as the Gini coefficient, confirm that China has travelled the path from one of the poorest and most egalitarian societies to chronic inequality, all in the space of twenty years (see Figure 5.2). The gap between rural and urban incomes (ossified by the residential permit system) has been increasing rapidly. While affluent urban dwellers drive BMWs, rural farmers are lucky to eat meat once a week. Even more emphatic has been the increasing inequality *within* both the rural and the urban sectors. Regional inequalities have also deepened, with some of the southern coastal zone cities surging ahead while the interior and the 'rust belt' of the northern region have either failed to take off or floundered badly.[48]

Mere increases in social inequality constitute an uncertain indicator of the reconstitution of class power. The evidence on this last point is largely anecdotal and by no means secure. We can, however, proceed inferentially by looking first at the situation at the bottom of the social ladder. 'In 1978 there were 120 million workers in China. By 2000 there were 270 million. Adding the 70 million peasants that have moved to the cities and found long-term wage work, China's working class now numbers approximately 350 million.' Of these 'more than 100 million' are now employed in the non-state sectors and are officially categorized as wage labourers.[49] A large proportion of those employed in what is left of the state sector (both SOEs and TVEs) in effect have the status of wage labourers also. There has, therefore, been a wholesale process of proletarianization going on in China, marked by the stages of privatization and the steps taken to impose greater flexibility on the labour market (including the shedding of welfare and pension obligations on the part of public enterprises). The government has 'gutted' services as well. According to China Labor Watch, 'Rural governments get almost no support from wealthier areas. They tax local farmers and impose endless fees to finance schools, hospitals, road building, even the police.' Poverty is intensifying among those left behind even as growth roars ahead at 9 per cent. Between 1998 and 2002, 27 million workers were let go from SOEs as their numbers fell from 262,000 to 159,000. Even more surprising, the net loss of manufacturing jobs in China over the past decade or so has been around 15 million.[50] In so far as neoliberalism requires a large, easily exploited, and relatively powerless labour force, then China certainly qualifies as a neoliberal economy, albeit 'with Chinese characteristics'.

Neoliberalism 'with Chinese Characteristics'

The accumulation of wealth at the other end of the social scale is a more complicated story. It seems to have proceeded in part via a combination of corruption, hidden ruses, and overt appropriation of rights and assets that were once held in common. As local governments transferred shares of enterprises to management as part of their restructuring strategy, so many managers 'have overnight come to hold shares worth tens of millions of yuan through various means, forming a new group of tycoons'. When SOEs were restructured into joint stock corporations 'the managers were given significant portions of the shares' and sometimes received a yearly salary one hundred times that of their average worker.[51] The chief managers of the Tsingtao Brewery, which became a stock-holding company in 1993, not only came to own a large slice of the shares of a lucrative business (that is augmenting its national presence and oligopolistic power through takeovers of many local breweries) but also pay themselves handsomely as managers. The privileged relationships between party members, government officials, and private entrepreneurs and the banks have also played an important role. Managers of newly privatized businesses who have received a certain number of shares may borrow from banks (or from friends) to buy up the remaining shares from the workers (sometimes coercively, by threatening layoffs for example). Since a large number of bank loans are non-performing, the new owners either run the companies into the ground (asset-stripping for personal gain along the way) or find ways to renege on their debts without declaring bankruptcy (bankruptcy law is not well developed in China). When the state takes $45 billion of foreign exchange earned off the backs of highly exploited labour and bails out the banks to cover their non-earning loans then it may well be redistributing wealth from the lower to the upper classes rather than writing off bad investments. Unscrupulous managers can gain control over newly privatized corporations and their assets all too easily and use them for their own personal enrichment.

Indigenous capital is also playing an increasingly important role in wealth creation. Having benefited from more than twenty years of technology transfer through joint ventures, blessed with access to large pools of skilled labour and managerial skills and above all harnessing the 'animal spirits' of entrepreneurial ambition, many

Neoliberalism 'with Chinese Characteristics'

Chinese firms have now positioned themselves to compete with foreign rivals not only in the domestic market but also in the international arena. And this no longer occurs only in the low-value-added sectors. What is now the eighth-ranked computer maker in the world, for example, was set up in 1984 by a group of Chinese scientists backed by government funds. By the late 1990s it had transformed itself from a distributor to a maker and held the largest share of the Chinese market. Lenovo, as it is now called, is currently locked in fierce competition with major players, and has now taken over IBM's personal computer line to gain better access to the global market. The deal (which, incidentally, threatens Taiwan's position in the computer business) enables IBM to build a firmer bridge into the Chinese software market at the same time as it builds a huge Chinese-based company in the computer industry with a global reach.[52] While the state may hold shares in companies like Lenovo, their managerial autonomy guarantees an ownership and reward system that permits increasing concentrations of executive officer wealth on a par with that found elsewhere around the world.

Real-estate development, particularly in and around the large cities and in the export development zones, appears to be another privileged path towards amassing immense wealth in a few hands. Since peasant cultivators did not hold title to the land, they could easily be dispossessed and the land converted to lucrative urban uses, leaving the cultivators with no rural base for a livelihood and forcing them off the land and into the labour market. The compensation offered to the farmers is usually a small fraction of the value of the land then passed on to developers by government officials. As many as 70 million farmers may have lost their land in this way over the past decade. Commune leaders, for example, frequently asserted de facto property rights over communal land and assets in negotiations with foreign investors or developers. These rights were later confirmed as belonging to them as individuals, in effect enclosing the commons to the benefit of the few. In the confusion of transition, writes Wang, 'a significant amount of national property "legally" and illegally was transferred to the personal economic advantage of a small minority'.[53] Speculation in land and property markets, particularly in urban areas, became rife even in the absence of clear systems of property rights. So serious had the loss of arable land become that the central government had to put a moratorium on conversions in 1998 until more rational land-use planning could be implemented. But a lot of the damage had already been done. Valuable land had been assembled, and developers (utilizing privileged relationships with the banks) had gone to work, accumulating immense wealth in a few hands. Even on a small scale, much more money was to be made in real-estate ventures than in production.[54] The fact that the $900,000 car was purchased by someone who had made his money in real estate is significant.

Speculation in asset values, often using credit granted on favourable terms, has also played its part. This has been particularly marked in urban real estate in and around the large cities such as Beijing, Shanghai, Shenzhen, Dongguang, and the like. The gains, which have been huge for certain brief periods of boom, typically belong to the speculator, and the losses during the crashes are largely borne by the banks. In all of these arenas, including that hidden zone of corruption that is beyond measure, the appropriation of assets, often by key party leaders or government officials, has transformed them from agents of state power to independent and extremely wealthy businessmen well able to protect their new-found wealth, if necessary by spiriting it out of the country via Hong Kong.

A surging consumer culture has emerged in the main urban centres, to which the increasing inequalities add their particular features, such as gated and protected communities of high-income housing (with names like Beverly Hills) for the rich, and spectacular privileged consumption zones, restaurants and nightclubs, shopping malls, and theme parks in many cities. Postmodern culture has arrived in Shanghai, big time. All of the trappings of Westernization are there to be found, including transformations in social relations that have young women trading on their sexuality and good looks at every turn and cultural institutions (ranging from Miss World beauty pageants to blockbuster art exhibits) forming at an astonishing rate to create exaggerated versions, even to the point of parody, of New York, London, or Paris. What is now called 'the rice bowl of youth' takes over as everyone speculates on the desires of others in the Darwinian struggle for position. The gender consequences of this have been marked. 'In the coastal cities, women encounter the extremes of greater opportunities to earn unprecedented levels of income and professional employment, and, on the other hand, relatively low wages in manufacturing or low-status service sector jobs in restaurants, domestic service, and prostitution.'[55]

The other source for amassing wealth arises out of the super-exploitation of labour power, particularly of young women migrants from rural areas. Wage levels in China are extremely low, and conditions of labour are sufficiently unregulated, despotic, and exploitative to put to shame the descriptions that Marx assembled long ago in his devastating account of factory and domestic labour conditions in Britain in the early stages of the Industrial Revolution there. Even more invidious is the non-payment of wages and pension obligations. Lee reports that,

in the heart of the NE rustbelt, Shenyang, between 1996–2001, 23.1% of employed workers experienced wage arrears, 26.4% of retirees experienced pension arrears. Nationwide, the total number of workers who were owed unpaid wages increased from 2.6 million in 1993 to 14 million in 2000. The problem is not restricted to old and bankrupt industrial bases with retirees and laid off workers. Government surveys showed 72.5% of the country's nearly 100 million migrant workers were owed wages. The total amount of owed pay was estimated to be about $12 billion (or about 100 billion yuan). 70% of these are in the construction trade.[56]

Much of the capital accumulated by private and foreign firms comes from unpaid labour. The result has been the eruption of fierce labour protests in many areas. While Chinese workers seem prepared to accept the long hours, the appalling working conditions, and the low wages as part of the price of modernization and economic growth, the non-payment of wages and of pensions is something else. Petitions and complaints to the central government on this score have mounted in recent years, and the failure of the government to respond adequately has led to direct action.[57] In the north-eastern city of Liaoyang more than 30,000 workers from some twenty factories protested for several days in 2002 in what was the 'largest demonstration of its kind since the Tiananmen crackdown'. In Jiamasu, in northern China, where about 80 per cent of the town's population was unemployed and living on less than $20 week after a textile factory employing 14,000 suddenly closed, direct action erupted after months of unanswered petitions. 'On some days retirees blocked all traffic on the main highway into town, squatting in rows on the pavement. On other days, thousands of laid off textile workers sat on railway tracks, disrupting service. In late December, workers from an ailing pulp mill lay like frozen soldiers on Jiamasu's only runway, preventing planes from landing.'[58] Police data show that 'some three million took part in protests' in 2003. Until recently, conflicts of this sort have been successfully managed by keeping them isolated, fragmented, unorganized, and certainly under-reported. But recent accounts suggest that more widespread conflicts are erupting. In Anhui province, for example, 'about 10,000 textile workers and retirees recently protested decreases in pension payments, the lack of medical insurance and compensation for injuries'. In Dongguan, Stella International Ltd, a Taiwanese-owned shoe manufacturer employing 42,000 people 'faced strikes this spring that turned violent. At one point more than 500 rampaging workers sacked company facilities and severely injured a Stella executive, leading police to enter the factory and round up ringleaders.'[59]

All manner of protests, 'many of them violent, have broken out with increasing frequency across the country in recent months'. Riots and protests have also erupted all over China over the land seizures occurring in rural areas. Whether or not this will all give rise to a mass movement is hard to predict. But the party is clearly fearful of the potential breakdown in order and is mobilizing party and police powers to forestall the proliferation of any general social movement that may arise. Lee's conclusions as to the nature of political subjectivity are here of interest. Both state and migrant workers, she suggests, reject the term working class and refuse 'class as the discursive frame to constitute their collective experience'. Nor do they see themselves as 'the contractual, juridical, and abstract labour subject normally assumed in theories of capitalist modernity', bearing individual legal rights. They typically appeal instead to the traditional Maoist notion of the masses constituted

by 'workers, the peasantry, the intelligentsia and the national bourgeoisie whose interests were harmonious with each other and also
with the state'. In this way workers 'can make moral claims for
state protection, reinforcing the leadership and responsibility of
the state to those it rules'.[60] The aim of any mass movement,
therefore, would be to make the central state live up to its revolutionary mandate against foreign capitalists, private interests, and
local authorities.

Whether or not the Chinese state is currently able or willing to
live up to such moral claims and thereby retain its legitimacy is by
no means certain. In rising to the defence of a worker brought to
trial for leading a violent factory walk-out, a prominent lawyer
observed that before the revolution 'the Communist Party stood
alongside the workers in their fight against capitalist exploitation,
whereas today the Communist Party is fighting shoulder to shoulder with the cold-blooded capitalists in their struggle against the
workers'.[61] While there are several aspects of Communist Party
policy that were designed to frustrate capitalist class formation,
the party has also acceded to the massive proletarianization of
China's workforce, the breaking of the 'iron rice bowl', the evisceration of social protections, the imposition of user fees, the creation
of a flexible labour market regime, and the privatization of assets
formerly held in common. It has created a social system where
capitalist enterprises can both form and function freely. In so doing
it has achieved rapid growth and alleviated the poverty of many,
but it has also embraced great concentrations of wealth in the
upper echelons of society. Moreover, business membership within
the party has been growing (up from 13.1 per cent in 1993 to 19.8
per cent by 2000). It is, however, hard to tell whether this reflects
an influx of capitalist entrepreneurs or the fact that many party
members have used their privileges to become capitalists by dubious means. In any case what this signals is the growing integration
of party and business elites in ways that are all too common in the
US. The links between workers and the party organization have,
on the other hand, become strained.[62] Whether this internal transformation of party structure will consolidate the ascendance of the
same sort of technocratic elite that led the Mexican PRI towards
total neoliberalization remains to be seen. But it cannot be ruled

out either that 'the masses' will seek a restoration of their own unique form of class power. For the party is now lined up against them and is plainly prepared to use its monopoly of violence to quell dissent, throw peasants off the land, and suppress the rising demands not only for democratization but also for a modicum of distributive justice. China, we may conclude, has definitely moved towards neoliberalization and the reconstitution of class power, albeit 'with distinctly Chinese characteristics'. The authoritarianism, the appeal to nationalism, and the revival of certain strains of imperialism suggest, however, that China may be moving, though from a quite different direction, towards a confluence with the neoconservative tide now running strongly in the US. That does not bode well for the future.

6

Neoliberalism on Trial

The two economic engines that have powered the world through the global recession that set in after 2001 have been the United States and China. The irony is that both have been behaving like Keynesian states in a world supposedly governed by neoliberal rules. The US has resorted to massive deficit-financing of its militarism and its consumerism, while China has debt-financed with non-performing bank loans massive infrastructural and fixed-capital investments. True blue neoliberals will doubtless claim that the recession is a sign of insufficient or imperfect neoliberalization, and they could well point to the operations of the IMF and the army of well-paid lobbyists in Washington that regularly pervert the US budgetary process for their special-interest ends as evidence for their case. But their claims are impossible to verify, and, in making them, they merely follow in the footsteps of a long line of eminent economic theorists who argue that all would be well with the world if only everyone behaved according to the precepts of their textbooks.[1]

But there is a more sinister interpretation of this paradox. If we lay aside, as I believe we must, the claim that neoliberalization is merely an example of erroneous theory gone wild (*pace* the economist Stiglitz) or a case of senseless pursuit of a false utopia (*pace* the conservative political philosopher John Gray[2]), then we are left with a tension between sustaining capitalism, on the one hand, and the restoration/reconstitution of ruling class power on the other. If we are at a point of outright contradiction between these two objectives, then there can be no doubt as to which side the current Bush administration is leaning, given its avid pursuit of tax cuts for the corporations and the rich. Furthermore, a global financial crisis in part provoked by its own reckless economic policies would permit the US government to finally rid itself of any obligation whatsoever to provide for the welfare of its citizens except for the ratcheting up of that military and police power that might be needed to quell social unrest and compel global discipline. Saner voices within the capitalist class, having listened carefully to the warnings of the likes of Paul Volcker that there is a high probability of a serious financial crisis in the next five years, may prevail.[3] But this will mean rolling back some of the privileges and power that have over the last thirty years been accumulating in the upper echelons of the capitalist class. Previous phases of capitalist history—one thinks of 1873 or the 1920s—when a similarly stark choice arose, do not augur well. The upper classes, insisting on the sacrosanct nature of their property rights, preferred to crash the system rather than surrender any of their privileges and power. In so doing they were not oblivious of their own interest, for if they position themselves aright they can, like good bankruptcy lawyers, profit from a collapse while the rest of us are caught most horribly in the deluge. A few of them may get caught and end up jumping out of Wall Street windows, but that is not the norm. The only fear they have is of political movements that threaten them with expropriation or revolutionary violence. While they can hope that the sophisticated military apparatus they now possess (thanks to the military industrial complex) will protect their wealth and power, the failure of that apparatus to easily pacify Iraq on the ground should give them pause. But ruling classes rarely, if ever, voluntarily surrender any of their power and I see no reason to believe they will do so this time. Paradoxically, a strong and powerful social democratic and working-class movement is in a better position to redeem capitalism than is capitalist class power itself. While this may sound a counter-revolutionary conclusion to those on the far left, it is not without a strong element of self-interest either, because it is ordinary people who suffer, starve, and even die in the course of capitalist crises (examine Indonesia or Argentina) rather than the upper classes. If the preferred policy of ruling elites is *après moi le déluge*, then the deluge largely engulfs the powerless and the unsuspecting while elites have well-prepared arks in which they can, at least for a time, survive quite well.

153

Neoliberalism on Trial

Neoliberal Achievements

What I have written above is speculative. But we can usefully scrutinize the historical-geographical record of neoliberalization for evidence of its powers as a potential cure-all for the political-economic ills that currently threaten us. To what degree, then, has neoliberalization succeeded in stimulating capital accumulation? Its actual record turns out to be nothing short of dismal. Aggregate global growth rates stood at 3.5 per cent or so in the 1960s and even during the troubled 1970s fell only to 2.4 per cent. But the subsequent growth rates of 1.4 per cent and 1.1 per cent for the 1980s and 1990s (and a rate that barely touches 1 per cent since 2000) indicate that neoliberalization has broadly failed to stimulate worldwide growth (see Figure 6.1).[4] In some cases, such as the territories of the ex-Soviet Union and those countries in central Europe that submitted to neoliberal 'shock therapy', there have been catastrophic losses. During the 1990s, Russian per capita income declined at the rate of 3.5 per cent annually. A large proportion of the population fell into poverty, and male life expectancy declined by five years as a result. Ukraine's experience was similar. Only Poland, which flouted IMF advice, showed any marked improvement. In much of Latin America neoliberalization produced either stagnation (in the 'lost decade' of the 1980s) or spurts of growth followed by economic collapse (as in Argentina). And in Africa it has done nothing at all to generate positive changes. Only in East and South-East Asia, followed now to some extent by India, has neoliberalization been associated with any positive record of growth, and there the not very neoliberal developmental states played a very significant role. The contrast between China's growth (nearly 10 per cent annually) and Russian decline (−3.5 per cent annually) is stark. Informal employment has soared worldwide (estimates suggest it rose from 29 per cent of the economically active population in Latin America during the 1980s to 44 per cent during the 1990s) and almost all global indicators on health levels, life expectancy, infant mortality, and the like show losses rather than gains in well-being since the 1960s. The proportion of the world's population in poverty has, however, fallen but this is almost entirely due to improvements in India and China

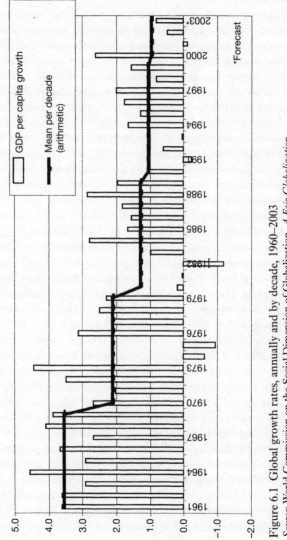

Figure 6.1 Global growth rates, annually and by decade, 1960–2003
Source: World Commission on the Social Dimension of Globalization, *A Fair Globalization*.

alone.[5] The reduction and control of inflation is the only systematic success neoliberalization can claim.

Comparisons are always odious, of course, but this is particularly so for neoliberalization. Circumscribed neoliberalization in Sweden, for example, has achieved far better results than sustained neoliberalization in the UK. Swedish per capita incomes are higher, inflation lower, the current account position with the rest of the world better, and all indices of competitive position and of business climate superior. Quality of life indices are higher. Sweden ranks third in the world in life expectancy compared to the UK's ranking of twenty-ninth. The poverty rate is 6.3 per cent in Sweden as opposed to 15.7 per cent in the UK, while the richest 10 per cent of the population in Sweden gain 6.2 times the incomes of the bottom 10 per cent, whereas in the UK the figure is 13.6. Illiteracy is lower in Sweden and social mobility greater.[6]

Were these sorts of facts widely known the praise for neoliberalization and its distinctive form of globalization would surely be much muted. Why, then, are so many persuaded that neoliberalization through globalization is the 'only alternative' and that it has been so successful? Two reasons stand out. First, the volatility of uneven geographical development has accelerated, permitting certain territories to advance spectacularly (at least for a time) at the expense of others. If, for example, the 1980s belonged largely to Japan, the Asian 'tigers', and West Germany, and if the 1990s belonged to the US and the UK, then the fact that 'success' was to be had somewhere obscured the fact that neoliberalization was generally failing to stimulate growth or improve well-being. Secondly, neoliberalization, the process rather than the theory, has been a huge success from the standpoint of the upper classes. It has either restored class power to ruling elites (as in the US and to some extent in Britain—see Figure 1.3) or created conditions for capitalist class formation (as in China, India, Russia, and elsewhere). With the media dominated by upper-class interests, the myth could be propagated that states failed economically because they were not competitive (thereby creating a demand for even more neoliberal reforms). Increased social inequality within a territory was construed as necessary to encourage the entrepreneurial risk and innovation that conferred competitive power and stimulated growth. If conditions among the lower classes deteriorated, this was because they failed, usually for personal and cultural reasons, to enhance their own human capital (through dedication to education, the acquisition of a Protestant work ethic, submission to work discipline and flexibility, and the like). Particular problems arose, in short, because of lack of competitive strength or because of personal, cultural, and political failings. In a Darwinian neoliberal world, the argument went, only the fittest should and do survive.

Of course there have been a number of spectacular shifts of emphasis under neoliberalization and these give it the appearance of incredible dynamism. The rise of finance and of financial services has been paralleled by a remarkable shift in the remuneration of financial corporations (see Figure 6.2) as well as a tendency for the larger corporations (such as General Motors) to fuse the two functions. Employment in these sectors has burgeoned remarkably. But there are serious questions as to how productive this has been. Much of the business of finance turns out to be about finance and nothing else. Speculative gains are perpetually being sought, and to the degree that they can be had all manner of shifts in power can be accomplished. So-called global cities of finance and command functions have become spectacular islands of wealth and privilege, with towering skyscrapers and millions upon millions of square feet of office space to house these operations. Within these towers, trading between floors creates a vast amount of fictitious wealth. Speculative urban property markets, furthermore, have become prime engines of capital accumulation. The rapidly evolving skylines of Manhattan, Tokyo, London, Paris, Frankfurt, Hong Kong, and now Shanghai are marvels to behold.

Along with this has gone an extraordinary burst in information technologies. In 1970 or so investment in that field was on a par with the 25 per cent going into production and to physical infrastructures respectively, but, by 2000, IT accounted for around 45 per cent of all investment, while the relative shares of investment in production and physical infrastructures declined. During the 1990s this was thought to betoken the rise of a new information economy.[7] It in fact represented an unfortunate bias in the path of technological change away from production and infrastructure formation into lines required by the market-driven financialization

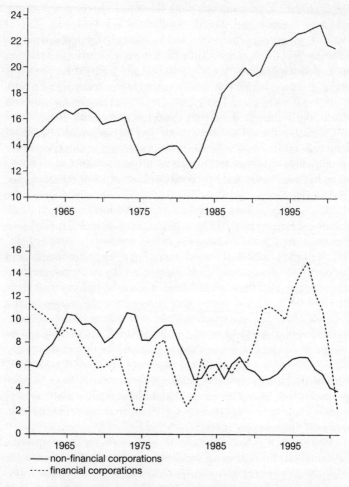

Figure 6.2 The hegemony of finance capital: net worth and rates of profit for financial and non-financial corporations in the US, 1960–2001

Source: Duménil and Lévy, *Capital Resurgent*, 111, 134. Reproduced courtesy Harvard University Press.

that was the hallmark of neoliberalization. Information technology is the privileged technology of neoliberalism. It is far more useful for speculative activity and for maximizing the number of short-term market contracts than for improving production. Interestingly, the main arenas of production that gained were the emergent cultural industries (films, videos, video games, music, advertising, art shows), which use IT as a basis for innovation and the marketing of new products. The hype around these new sectors diverted attention from the failure to invest in basic physical and social infrastructures. Along with all of this went the hype about 'globalization' and all that it supposedly stood for in terms of the construction of an entirely different and totally integrated global economy.[8]

The main substantive achievement of neoliberalization, however, has been to redistribute, rather than to generate, wealth and income. I have elsewhere provided an account of the main mechanisms whereby this was achieved under the rubric of 'accumulation by dispossession'.[9] By this I mean the continuation and proliferation of accumulation practices which Marx had treated of as 'primitive' or 'original' during the rise of capitalism. These include the commodification and privatization of land and the forceful expulsion of peasant populations (compare the cases, described above, of Mexico and of China, where 70 million peasants are thought to have been displaced in recent times); conversion of various forms of property rights (common, collective, state, etc.) into exclusive private property rights (most spectacularly represented by China); suppression of rights to the commons; commodification of labour power and the suppression of alternative (indigenous) forms of production and consumption; colonial, neocolonial, and imperial processes of appropriation of assets (including natural resources); monetization of exchange and taxation, particularly of land; the slave trade (which continues particularly in the sex industry); and usury, the national debt and, most devastating of all, the use of the credit system as a radical means of accumulation by dispossession. The state, with its monopoly of violence and definitions of legality, plays a crucial role in both backing and promoting these processes. To this list of mechanisms we may now add a raft of techniques such as the extraction of rents from patents and intellectual property rights and the diminution or erasure of various forms of common property rights (such as state pensions, paid vacations, and access to education and health care) won through a generation or more of class struggle. The proposal to privatize all state pension rights (pioneered in Chile under the dictatorship) is, for example, one of the cherished objectives of the Republicans in the US.

Accumulation by dispossession comprises four main features:

1. *Privatization and commodification.* The corporatization, commodification, and privatization of hitherto public assets has been a signal feature of the neoliberal project. Its primary aim has been to open up new fields for capital accumulation in domains hitherto regarded off-limits to the calculus of profitability. Public utilities of all kinds (water, telecommunications, transportation), social welfare provision (social housing, education, health care, pensions), public institutions (universities, research laboratories, prisons) and even warfare (as illustrated by the 'army' of private contractors operating alongside the armed forces in Iraq) have all been privatized to some degree throughout the capitalist world and beyond (for example in China). The intellectual property rights established through the so-called TRIPS agreement within the WTO defines genetic materials, seed plasmas, and all manner of other products as private property. Rents for use can then be extracted from populations whose practices had played a crucial role in the development of these genetic materials. Biopiracy is rampant and the pillaging of the world's stockpile of genetic resources is well under way to the benefit of a few large pharmaceutical companies. The escalating depletion of the global environmental commons (land, air, water) and proliferating habitat degradations that preclude anything but capital-intensive modes of agricultural production have likewise resulted from the wholesale commodification of nature in all its forms. The commodification (through tourism) of cultural forms, histories, and intellectual creativity entails wholesale dispossessions (the music industry is notorious for the appropriation and exploitation of grassroots culture and creativity). As in the past, the

160

power of the state is frequently used to force such processes even against popular will. The rolling back of regulatory frameworks designed to protect labour and the environment from degradation has entailed the loss of rights. The reversion of common property rights won through years of hard class struggle (the right to a state pension, to welfare, to national health care) into the private domain has been one of the most egregious of all policies of dispossession, often procured against the broad political will of the population. All of these processes amount to the transfer of assets from the public and popular realms to the private and class-privileged domains.[10]

2. *Financialization*. The strong wave of financialization that set in after 1980 has been marked by its speculative and predatory style. The total daily turnover of financial transactions in international markets, which stood at $2.3 billion in 1983, had risen to $130 billion by 2001. The $40 trillion annual turnover in 2001 compares to the estimated $800 billion that would be required to support international trade and productive investment flows.[11] Deregulation allowed the financial system to become one of the main centres of redistributive activity through speculation, predation, fraud, and thievery. Stock promotions, ponzi schemes, structured asset destruction through inflation, asset-stripping through mergers and acquisitions, the promotion of levels of debt incumbency that reduced whole populations, even in the advanced capitalist countries, to debt peonage, to say nothing of corporate fraud, dispossession of assets (the raiding of pension funds and their decimation by stock and corporate collapses) by credit and stock manipulations—all of these became central features of the capitalist financial system. Innumerable ways exist to skim off values from within the financial system. Since brokers get a commission for each transaction, they can maximize their incomes by frequent trading on their accounts (a practice known as 'churning') no matter whether the trades add value to the account or not. High turnover on the stock exchange may simply reflect churning rather than confidence in the market. The emphasis on stock values, which arose out of bringing together the interests of owners and managers of capital through the

remuneration of the latter in stock options, led, as we now know, to manipulations in the market that brought immense wealth to a few at the expense of the many. The spectacular collapse of Enron was emblematic of a general process that dispossessed many of their livelihoods and their pension rights. Beyond this, we also have to look at the speculative raiding carried out by hedge funds and other major institutions of finance capital, for these formed the real cutting edge of accumulation by dispossession on the global stage, even as they supposedly conferred the positive benefit of 'spreading risks'.[12]

3. *The management and manipulation of crises.* Beyond the speculative and often fraudulent froth that characterizes much of neoliberal financial manipulation, there lies a deeper process that entails the springing of 'the debt trap' as a primary means of accumulation by dispossession.[13] Crisis creation, management, and manipulation on the world stage has evolved into the fine art of deliberative redistribution of wealth from poor countries to the rich. I documented the impact of Volcker's interest rate increase on Mexico earlier. While proclaiming its role as a noble leader organizing 'bail-outs' to keep global capital accumulation on track, the US paved the way to pillage the Mexican economy. This was what the US Treasury–Wall Street–IMF complex became expert at doing everywhere. Greenspan at the Federal Reserve deployed the same Volcker tactic several times in the 1990s. Debt crises in individual countries, uncommon during the 1960s, became very frequent during the 1980s and 1990s. Hardly any developing country remained untouched, and in some cases, as in Latin America, such crises became endemic. These debt crises were orchestrated, managed, and controlled both to rationalize the system and to redistribute assets. Since 1980, it has been calculated, 'over fifty Marshall Plans (over $4.6 trillion) have been sent by the peoples at the Periphery to their creditors in the Center'. 'What a peculiar world', sighs Stiglitz, 'in which the poor countries are in effect subsidizing the richest.' What neoliberals call 'confiscatory deflation' is, furthermore, nothing other than accumulation by dispossession. Wade and Veneroso capture the essence of this when they write of the Asian crisis of 1997–8:

Neoliberalism on Trial

Financial crises have always caused transfers of ownership and power to those who keep their own assets intact and who are in a position to create credit, and the Asian crisis is no exception . . . there is no doubt that Western and Japanese corporations are the big winners . . . The combination of massive devaluations, IMF-pushed financial liberalization, and IMF-facilitated recovery may even precipitate the biggest peacetime transfer of assets from domestic to foreign owners in the past fifty years anywhere in the world, dwarfing the transfers from domestic to US owners in Latin America in the 1980s or in Mexico after 1994. One recalls the statement attributed to Andrew Mellon: 'In a depression assets return to their rightful owners.'[14]

The analogy with the deliberate creation of unemployment to produce a labour surplus convenient for further accumulation is exact. Valuable assets are thrown out of use and lose their value. They lie fallow until capitalists possessed of liquidity choose to breathe new life into them. The danger, however, is that crises might spin out of control and become generalized, or that revolts will arise against the system that creates them. One of the prime functions of state interventions and of international institutions is to control crises and devaluations in ways that permit accumulation by dispossession to occur without sparking a general collapse or popular revolt (as happened in both Indonesia and Argentina). The structural adjustment programme administered by the Wall Street–Treasury–IMF complex takes care of the first while it is the job of the comprador state apparatus (backed by military assistance from the imperial powers) in the country that has been raided to ensure that the second does not occur. But the signs of popular revolt are everywhere, as illustrated by the Zapatista uprising in Mexico, innumerable anti-IMF riots, and the so-called 'anti-globalization' movement that cut its teeth in the revolts at Seattle, Genoa, and elsewhere.

4. *State redistributions*. The state, once neoliberalized, becomes a prime agent of redistributive policies, reversing the flow from upper to lower classes that had occurred during the era of embedded liberalism. It does this in the first instance through pursuit of privatization schemes and cutbacks in those state expenditures that support the social wage. Even when privatization

appears to be beneficial to the lower classes, the long-term effects can be negative. At first blush, for example, Thatcher's programme for the privatization of social housing in Britain appeared as a gift to the lower classes, whose members could now convert from rental to ownership at a relatively low cost, gain control over a valuable asset, and augment their wealth. But once the transfer was accomplished housing speculation took over, particularly in prime central locations, eventually bribing or forcing low-income populations out to the periphery in cities like London and turning erstwhile working-class housing estates into centres of intense gentrification. The loss of affordable housing in central areas produced homelessness for some and long commutes for those with low-paying service jobs. The privatization of the *ejidos* in Mexico during the 1990s had analogous effects upon the prospects for the Mexican peasantry, forcing many rural dwellers off the land into the cities in search of employment. The Chinese state has sanctioned the transfer of assets to a small elite to the detriment of the mass of the population and provoking violently repressed protests. Reports now indicate that as many as 350,000 families (a million people) are being displaced to make way for the urban renewal of much of old Beijing, with the same outcome as that in Britain and Mexico outlined above. In the US, revenue-strapped municipalities are now regularly using the power of eminent domain to displace low- and even moderate-income property owners living in perfectly good housing stock in order to free land for upper-income and commercial developments that will enhance the tax base (in New York State there are more than sixty current cases of this).[15]

The neoliberal state also redistributes wealth and income through revisions in the tax code to benefit returns on investment rather than incomes and wages, promotion of regressive elements in the tax code (such as sales taxes), the imposition of user fees (now widespread in rural China), and the provision of a vast array of subsidies and tax breaks to corporations. The rate of corporate taxation in the US has steadily declined, and the Bush re-election was greeted with smiles by corporate leaders in anticipation of even further cuts in their tax obligations.

The corporate welfare programmes that now exist in the US at federal, state, and local levels amount to a vast redirection of public moneys for corporate benefit (directly as in the case of subsidies to agribusiness and indirectly as in the case of the military-industrial sector), in much the same way that the mortgage interest rate tax deduction operates in the US as a subsidy to upper-income homeowners and the construction industry. The rise of surveillance and policing and, in the case of the US, incarceration of recalcitrant elements in the population indicates a more sinister turn towards intense social control. The prison-industrial complex is a thriving sector (alongside personal security services) in the US economy. In the developing countries, where opposition to accumulation by dispossession can be stronger, the role of the neoliberal state quickly assumes that of active repression even to the point of low-level warfare against oppositional movements (many of which can now conveniently be designated as 'drug trafficking' or 'terrorist' so as to garner US military assistance and support, as in Colombia). Other movements, such as the Zapatistas in Mexico or the landless peasant movement in Brazil, are contained by state power through a mix of co-optation and marginalization.[16]

The Commodification of Everything

To presume that markets and market signals can best determine all allocative decisions is to presume that everything can in principle be treated as a commodity. Commodification presumes the existence of property rights over processes, things, and social relations, that a price can be put on them, and that they can be traded subject to legal contract. The market is presumed to work as an appropriate guide—an ethic—for all human action. In practice, of course, every society sets some bounds on where commodification begins and ends. Where the boundaries lie is a matter of contention. Certain drugs are deemed illegal. The buying and selling of sexual favours is outlawed in most US states, though elsewhere it may be legalized, decriminalized, and even state-regulated as an industry. Pornography is broadly protected as a form of free speech under

US law although here, too, there are certain forms (mainly concerning children) that are considered beyond the pale. In the US, conscience and honour are supposedly not for sale, and there exists a curious penchant to pursue 'corruption' as if it is easily distinguishable from the normal practices of influence-peddling and making money in the marketplace. The commodification of sexuality, culture, history, heritage; of nature as spectacle or as rest cure; the extraction of monopoly rents from originality, authenticity, and uniqueness (of works or art, for example)—these all amount to putting a price on things that were never actually produced as commodities.[17] There is often disagreement as to the appropriateness of commodification (of religious events and symbols, for example) or of who should exercise the property rights and derive the rents (over access to Aztec ruins or marketing of Aboriginal art, for example).

Neoliberalization has unquestionably rolled back the bounds of commodification and greatly extended the reach of legal contracts. It typically celebrates (as does much of postmodern theory) ephemerality and the short-term contract—marriage, for example, is understood as a short-term contractual arrangement rather than as a sacred and unbreakable bond. The divide between neoliberals and neoconservatives partially reflects a difference as to where the lines are drawn. The neoconservatives typically blame 'liberals', 'Hollywood', or even 'postmodernists' for what they see as the dissolution and immorality of the social order, rather than the corporate capitalists (like Rupert Murdoch) who actually do most of the damage by foisting all manner of sexually charged if not salacious material upon the world and who continually flaunt their pervasive preference for short-term over long-term commitments in their endless pursuit of profit.

But there are far more serious issues here than merely trying to protect some treasured object, some particular ritual or a preferred corner of social life from the monetary calculus and the short-term contract. For at the heart of liberal and neoliberal theory lies the necessity of constructing coherent markets for land, labour, and money, and these, as Karl Polanyi pointed out, 'are obviously not commodities . . . the commodity description of labour, land, and money is entirely fictitious'. While capitalism cannot function without such fictions, it does untold damage if it fails to acknowledge the complex realities behind them. Polanyi, in one of his more famous passages, puts it this way:

To allow the market mechanism to be sole director of the fate of human beings and their natural environment, indeed, even of the amount and use of purchasing power, would result in the demolition of society. For the alleged commodity 'labour power' cannot be shoved about, used indiscriminately, or even left unused, without affecting also the human individual who happens to be the bearer of this peculiar commodity. In disposing of man's labour power the system would, incidentally, dispose of the physical, psychological, and moral entity 'man' attached to that tag. Robbed of the protective covering of cultural institutions, human beings would perish from the effects of social exposure; they would die as victims of acute social dislocation through vice, perversion, crime and starvation. Nature would be reduced to its elements, neighborhoods and landscapes defiled, rivers polluted, military safety jeopardized, the power to produce food and raw materials destroyed. Finally, the market administration of purchasing power would periodically liquidate business enterprise, for shortages and surfeits of money would prove as disastrous to business as floods and droughts in primitive society.[18]

The damage wrought through the 'floods and droughts' of fictitious capitals within the global credit system, be it in Indonesia, Argentina, Mexico, or even within the US, testifies all too well to Polanyi's final point. But his theses on labour and land deserve further elaboration.

Individuals enter the labour market as persons of character, as individuals embedded in networks of social relations and socialized in various ways, as physical beings identifiable by certain characteristics (such as phenotype and gender), as individuals who have accumulated various skills (sometimes referred to as 'human capital') and tastes (sometime referred to as 'cultural capital'), and as living beings endowed with dreams, desires, ambitions, hopes, doubts, and fears. For capitalists, however, such individuals are a mere factor of production, though not an undifferentiated factor since employers require labour of certain qualities, such as physical strength, skills, flexibility, docility, and the like, appropriate to certain tasks. Workers are hired on contract, and in the neoliberal scheme of things short-term contracts are preferred in order to maximize flexibility. Employers have historically used differentiations within the labour pool to divide and rule. Segmented labour markets then arise and distinctions of race, ethnicity, gender, and religion are frequently used, blatantly or covertly, in ways that redound to the employers' advantage. Conversely, workers may use the social networks in which they are embedded to gain privileged access to certain lines of employment. They typically seek to monopolize skills and, through collective action and the creation of appropriate institutions, seek to regulate the labour market to protect their interests. In this they are merely constructing that 'protective covering of cultural institutions' of which Polanyi speaks.

Neoliberalization seeks to strip away the protective coverings that embedded liberalism allowed and occasionally nurtured. The general attack against labour has been two-pronged. The powers of trade unions and other working-class institutions are curbed or dismantled within a particular state (by violence if necessary). Flexible labour markets are established. State withdrawal from social welfare provision and technologically induced shifts in job structures that render large segments of the labour force redundant complete the domination of capital over labour in the marketplace. The individualized and relatively powerless worker then confronts a labour market in which only short-term contracts are offered on a customized basis. Security of tenure becomes a thing of the past (Thatcher abolished it in universities, for example). A 'personal responsibility system' (how apt Deng's language was!) is substituted for social protections (pensions, health care, protections against injury) that were formerly an obligation of employers and the state. Individuals buy products in the markets that sell social protections instead. Individual security is therefore a matter of individual choice tied to the affordability of financial products embedded in risky financial markets.

The second prong of attack entails transformations in the spatial and temporal co-ordinates of the labour market. While too much can be made of the 'race to the bottom' to find the cheapest and most docile labour supplies, the geographical mobility of capital permits it to dominate a global labour force whose own geographical mobility is constrained. Captive labour forces abound because immigration is restricted. These barriers can be evaded only by illegal immigration (which creates an easily exploitable labour force) or through short-term contracts that permit, for example, Mexican labourers to work in Californian agribusiness only to be shamelessly shipped back to Mexico when they get sick and even die from the pesticides to which they are exposed.

Under neoliberalization, the figure of 'the disposable worker' emerges as prototypical upon the world stage.[19] Accounts of the appalling conditions of labour and the despotic conditions under which labourers work in the sweatshops of the world abound. In China, the conditions under which migrant young women from rural areas work are nothing short of appalling: 'unbearably long hours, substandard food, cramped dorms, sadistic managers who beat and sexually abuse them, and pay that arrives months late, or sometimes not at all'.[20] In Indonesia, two young women recounted their experiences working for a Singapore-based Levi-Strauss subcontractor as follows:

We are regularly insulted, as a matter of course. When the boss gets angry he calls the women dogs, pigs, sluts, all of which we have to endure patiently without reacting. We work officially from seven in the morning until three (salary less than $2 a day), but there is often compulsory overtime, sometimes—especially if there is an urgent order to be delivered—until nine. However tired we are, we are not allowed to go home. We may get an extra 200 rupiah (10 US cents) . . . We go on foot to the factory from where we live. Inside it is very hot. The building has a metal roof, and there is not much space for all the workers. It is very cramped. There are over 200 people working there, mostly women, but there is only one toilet for the whole factory . . . when we come home from work, we have no energy left to do anything but eat and sleep . . .[21]

Similar tales come from the Mexican maquila factories, the Taiwanese- and Korean-operated manufacturing plants in Honduras, South Africa, Malaysia, and Thailand. The health hazards, the exposure to a wide range of toxic substances, and death on the job pass by unregulated and unremarked. In Shanghai, the Taiwanese businessman who ran a textile warehouse 'in which 61 workers, locked in the building, died in a fire' received a 'lenient' two-year suspended sentence because he had 'showed repentance' and 'cooperated in the aftermath of the fire'.[22]

Women, for the most part, and sometimes children, bear the brunt of this sort of degrading, debilitating, and dangerous toil.[23] The social consequences of neoliberalization are in fact extreme. Accumulation by dispossession typically undermines whatever powers women may have had within household production/ marketing systems and within traditional social structures and relocates everything in male-dominated commodity and credit markets. The paths of women's liberation from traditional patriarchal controls in developing countries lie either through degrading factory labour or through trading on sexuality, which varies from respectable work as hostesses and waitresses to the sex trade (one of the most lucrative of all contemporary industries in which a good deal of slavery is involved). The loss of social protections in advanced capitalist countries has had particularly negative effects on lower-class women, and in many of the ex-communist countries of the Soviet bloc the loss of women's rights through neoliberalization has been nothing short of catastrophic.

So how, then, do disposable workers—women in particular— survive both socially and affectively in a world of flexible labour markets and short-term contracts, chronic job insecurities, lost social protections, and often debilitating labour, amongst the wreckage of collective institutions that once gave them a modicum of dignity and support? For some the increased flexibility in labour markets is a boon, and even when it does not lead to material gains the simple right to change jobs relatively easily and free of the traditional social constraints of patriarchy and family has intangible benefits. For those who successfully negotiate the labour market there are seemingly abundant rewards in the world of a capitalist consumer culture. Unfortunately, that culture, however spectacular, glamorous, and beguiling, perpetually plays with desires without ever conferring satisfactions beyond the limited identity of the shopping mall and the anxieties of status by way of good looks (in the case of women) or of material possessions. 'I shop therefore I am' and possessive individualism together construct a world of pseudo-satisfactions that is superficially exciting but hollow at its core.

But for those who have lost their jobs or who have never managed to move out of the extensive informal economies that now provide a parlous refuge for most of the world's disposable workers, the story is entirely different. With some 2 billion people condemned to live on less than $2 a day, the taunting world of capitalist consumer culture, the huge bonuses earned in financial services, and the self-congratulatory polemics as to the emancipatory potential of neoliberalization, privatization, and personal responsibility must seem like a cruel joke. From impoverished rural China to the affluent US, the loss of health-care protections and the increasing imposition of all manner of user fees adds considerably to the financial burdens of the poor.[24]

Neoliberalization has transformed the positionality of labour, of women, and of indigenous groups in the social order by emphasizing that labour is a commodity like any other. Stripped of the protective cover of lively democratic institutions and threatened with all manner of social dislocations, a disposable workforce inevitably turns to other institutional forms through which to construct social solidarities and express a collective will. Everything from gangs and criminal cartels, narco-trafficking networks, mini-mafias and favela bosses, through community, grassroots and non-governmental organizations, to secular cults and religious sects proliferate. These are the alternative social forms that fill the void left behind as state powers, political parties, and other institutional forms are actively dismantled or simply wither away as centres of collective endeavour and of social bonding. The marked turn to religion is in this regard of interest. Accounts of the sudden appearance and proliferation of religious sects in the derelict rural regions of China, to say nothing of the emergence of Fulan Gong, are illustrative of this trend.[25] The rapid progress of evangelical proselytizing in the chaotic informal economies that have burgeoned under neoliberalization in Latin America, and the revived and in some instances newly constructed religious tribalism and fundamentalism that structure politics in much of Africa and the Middle East, testify to the need to construct meaningful mechanisms of social solidarity. The progress of fundamentalist evangelical Christianity in the US has some connection with proliferating job insecurities, the loss of other forms of social

171

solidarity, and the hollowness of capitalist consumer culture. In Thomas Frank's account, the religious right took off in Kansas only at the end of the 1980s, after a decade or more of neoliberal restructuring and deindustrialization.[26] Such connections may seem far-fetched. But if Polanyi is right and the treatment of labour as a commodity leads to social dislocation, then moves to rebuild different social networks to defend against such a threat become increasingly likely.

Environmental Degradations

The imposition of short-term contractual logic on environmental uses has disastrous consequences. Fortunately, views within the neoliberal camp are somewhat divided on this issue. While Reagan cared nothing for the environment, at one point characterizing trees as a major source of air pollution, Thatcher took the problem seriously. She played a major role in negotiating the Montreal Protocol to limit the use of the CFCs that were responsible for the growing ozone hole around Antarctica. She took the threat of global warming from rising carbon dioxide emissions seriously. Her environmental commitments were not entirely disinterested, of course, since the closure of the coalmines and the destruction of the miners' union could be partially legitimized on environmental grounds.

Neoliberal state policies with respect to the environment have therefore been geographically uneven and temporally unstable (depending on who holds the reins of state power, with the Reagan and George W. Bush administrations being particularly retrograde in the US). The environmental movement, furthermore, has grown in significance since the 1970s. It has often exerted a restraining influence, depending on time and place. And in some instances capitalist firms have discovered that increasing efficiency and improved environmental performance can go hand in hand. Nevertheless, the general balance sheet on the environmental consequences of neoliberalization is almost certainly negative. Serious though controversial efforts to create indices of human well-being including the costs of environmental degradations suggest an accelerating negative trend since 1970 or so. And there are enough specific examples of environmental losses resulting from the unrestrained application of neoliberal principles to give sustenance to such a general account. The accelerating destruction of tropical rain forests since 1970 is a well-known example that has serious implications for climate change and the loss of biodiversity. The era of neoliberalization also happens to be the era of the fastest mass extinction of species in the Earth's recent history.[27] If we are entering the danger zone of so transforming the global environment, particularly its climate, as to make the earth unfit for human habitation, then further embrace of the neoliberal ethic and of neoliberalizing practices will surely prove nothing short of deadly. The Bush administration's approach to environmental issues is usually to question the scientific evidence and do nothing (except cut back on the resources for relevant scientific research). But his own research team reports that the human contribution to global warming soared after 1970. The Pentagon also argues that global warming might well in the long run be a more serious threat to the security of the US than terrorism.[28] Interestingly, the two main culprits in the growth of carbon dioxide emissions these last few years have been the powerhouses of the global economy, the US and China (which increased its emissions by 45 per cent over the past decade). In the US, substantial progress has been made in increasing energy efficiency in industry and residential construction. The profligacy in this case largely derives from the kind of consumerism that continues to encourage high-energy-consuming suburban and ex-urban sprawl and a culture that opts to purchase gas-guzzling SUVs rather than the more energy-efficient cars that are available. Increasing US dependency on imported oil has obvious geopolitical ramifications. In the case of China, the rapidity of industrialization and of the growth of car ownership doubles the pressure on energy consumption. China has moved from self-sufficiency in oil production in the late 1980s to being the second largest global importer after the US. Here, too, the geopolitical implications are rife as China scrambles to gain a foothold in the Sudan, central Asia, and the Middle East to secure its oil supplies. But China also has vast rather low-grade coal supplies with a high sulphur content. The use of these for power generation is creating major environmental problems, particularly those that contribute to global warming. Furthermore, given the acute power shortages that now bedevil the Chinese economy, with brownouts and blackouts common, there is no incentive whatsoever for local government to follow central government mandates to close down inefficient and 'dirty' power stations. The astonishing increase in car ownership and use, largely replacing the bicycle in large cities like Beijing in ten years, has brought China the negative distinction of having sixteen of the twenty worst cities in the world with respect to air quality.[29] The cognate effects on global warming are obvious. As usually happens in phases of rapid industrialization, the failure to pay any mind to the environmental consequences is having deleterious effects everywhere. The rivers are highly polluted, water supplies are full of dangerous cancer-inducing chemicals, public health provision is weak (as illustrated by the problems of SARS and the avian flu), and the rapid conversion of land resources to urban uses or to create massive hydroelectric projects (as in the Yangtze valley) all add up to a significant bundle of environmental problems that the central government is only now beginning to address. China is not alone in this, for the rapid burst of growth in India is also being accompanied by stressful environmental changes deriving from the expansion of consumption as well as the increased pressure on natural resource exploitation.

Neoliberalization has a rather dismal record when it comes to the exploitation of natural resources. The reasons are not far to seek. The preference for short-term contractual relations puts pressure on all producers to extract everything they can while the contract lasts. Even though contracts and options may be renewed there is always uncertainty because other sources may be found. The longest possible time-horizon for natural resource exploitation is that of the discount rate (i.e. about twenty-five years) but most contracts are now far shorter. Depletion is usually assumed to be linear, when it is now evident that many ecological systems crash suddenly after they have hit some tipping point beyond which their natural reproduction capacity cannot function. Fish stocks—sardines off California, cod off Newfoundland, and Chilean sea bass—are classic examples of a resource exploited at an 'optimal' rate that suddenly crashes without any seeming warning.[30] Less dramatic but equally insidious is the case of forestry.

Neoliberal insistence upon privatization makes it hard to establish any global agreements on principles of forest management to protect valuable habitats and biodiversity, particularly in the tropical rain forests. In poorer countries with substantial forest resources, the pressure to increase exports and to allow foreign ownerships and concessions means that even minimal protections of forests break down. The over-exploitation of forestry resources after privatization in Chile is a good case in point. But structural adjustment programmes administered by the IMF have had even worse impacts. Imposed austerity means that poorer countries have less money to put into forest management. They are also pressurized to privatize the forests and to open up their exploitation to foreign lumber companies on short-term contracts. Under pressure to earn foreign exchange to pay off their debts, the temptation exists to concede a maximal rate of short-term exploitation. To make matters worse, when IMF-mandated austerity and unemployment strikes, redundant populations may seek sustenance on the land and engage in indiscriminate forest clearance. Since the favoured method is by burning, landless peasant populations together with the logging companies can massively destroy forest resources in very short order, as has happened in Brazil, Indonesia, and several African countries.[31] It was no accident that at the height of the fiscal crisis that displaced millions from the job market in Indonesia in 1997–8, forest fires raged out of control in Sumatra (associated with the logging operations of one of Suharto's richest ethnic Chinese businessmen), creating a massive smoke-pall that engulfed the whole of South-East Asia for several months. It is only when states and other interests are prepared to buck the neoliberal rules and the class interests that support them—and this has occurred on a significant number of occasions—that any modicum of balanced use of the environment is achieved.

On Rights

Neoliberalization has spawned within itself an extensive oppositional culture. The opposition tends, however, to accept many of the basic propositions of neoliberalism. It focuses on internal contradictions. It takes questions of individual rights and freedoms seriously, for example, and opposes them to the authoritarianism and frequent arbitrariness of political, economic, and class power. It takes the neoliberal rhetoric of improving the welfare of all and condemns neoliberalization for failing in its own terms. Consider, for example, the first substantive paragraph of that quintessential neoliberal document, the WTO agreement. The aim is:

raising standards of living, full employment and a large and steadily growing volume of real income and effective demand, and expanding the production of and trade in goods and services while allowing for the optimal use of the world's resources in accordance with the objective of sustainable development, seeking both to protect and preserve the environment and to enhance the means for doing so in a manner consistent with their respective needs and concerns at different levels of economic development.[32]

Similar pious hopes can be found in World Bank pronouncements ('the reduction of poverty is our chief aim'). None of this sits easily with the actual practices that underpin the restoration or creation of class power and the results in terms of impoverishment and environmental degradation.

The rise of opposition cast in terms of rights violations has been spectacular since 1980. Before then, Chandler reports, a prominent journal such as *Foreign Affairs* carried not a single article on human rights.[33] Human rights issues came to prominence after 1980 and positively boomed after the events in Tiananmen Square and the end of the Cold War in 1989. This corresponds exactly with the trajectory of neoliberalization, and the two movements are deeply implicated in each other. Undoubtedly, the neoliberal insistence upon the individual as the foundational element in political-economic life opens the door to individual rights activism. But by focusing on those rights rather than on the creation or re-creation of substantive and open democratic governance structures, the opposition cultivates methods that cannot escape the neoliberal frame. Neoliberal concern for the individual trumps any social democratic concern for equality, democracy, and social solidarities. The frequent appeal to legal action, furthermore, accepts the neoliberal preference for appeal to judicial and executive rather than parliamentary powers. But it is costly and time-consuming to go down legal paths, and the courts are in any case heavily biased towards ruling class interests, given the typical class allegiance of the judiciary. Legal decisions tend to favour rights of private property and the profit rate over rights of equality and social justice. It is, Chandler concludes, 'the liberal elite's disillusionment with ordinary people and the political process [that] leads them to focus more on the empowered individual, taking their case to the judge who will listen and decide'.[34]

Since most needy individuals lack the financial resources to pursue their own rights, the only way in which this ideal can be articulated is through the formation of advocacy groups. The rise of advocacy groups and NGOs has, like rights discourses more generally, accompanied the neoliberal turn and increased spectacularly since 1980 or so. The NGOs have in many instances stepped into the vacuum in social provision left by the withdrawal of the state from such activities. This amounts to privatization by NGO. In some instances this has helped accelerate further state withdrawal from social provision. NGOs thereby function as 'Trojan horses for global neoliberalism'.[35] Furthermore, NGOs are not inherently democratic institutions. They tend to be elitist, unaccountable (except to their donors), and by definition distant from those they seek to protect or help, no matter how well-meaning or progressive they may be. They frequently conceal their agendas, and prefer direct negotiation with or influence over state and class power. They often control their clientele rather than represent it. They claim and presume to speak on behalf of those who cannot speak for themselves, even define the interests of those they speak for (as if people are unable to do this for themselves). But the legitimacy of their status is always open to doubt. When, for example, organizations agitate successfully to ban child labour in production as a matter of universal human rights, they may undermine economies where that labour is fundamental to family survival. Without any viable economic alternative the children may be sold into prostitution instead (leaving yet another advocacy group to pursue the eradication of that). The universality presupposed in 'rights talk' and the dedication of the NGOs and advocacy groups to universal principles sits uneasily with the local particularities and daily practices of political and economic life under the pressures of commodification and neoliberalization.[36]

But there is another reason why this particular oppositional culture has gained so much traction in recent years. Accumulation by dispossession entails a very different set of practices from accumulation through the expansion of wage labour in industry and agriculture. The latter, which dominated processes of capital accumulation in the 1950s and 1960s, gave rise to an oppositional culture (such as that embedded in trade unions and working-class political parties) that produced embedded liberalism. Dispossession, on the other hand, is fragmented and particular—a privatization here, an environmental degradation there, a financial crisis of indebtedness somewhere else. It is hard to oppose all of this specificity and particularity without appeal to universal principles. Dispossession entails the loss of rights. Hence the turn to a universalistic rhetoric of human rights, dignity, sustainable ecological practices, environmental rights, and the like, as the basis for a unified oppositional politics.

This appeal to the universalism of rights is a double-edged sword. It may and can be used with progressive aims in mind. The tradition that is most spectacularly represented by Amnesty International, Médecins sans Frontières, and others cannot be dismissed as a mere adjunct of neoliberal thinking. The whole history of humanism (both of the Western—classically liberal—and various non-Western versions) is too complicated for that. But the limited objectives of many rights discourses (in Amnesty's case the exclusive focus, until recently, on civil and political as opposed to economic rights) makes it all too easy to absorb them within the neoliberal frame. Universalism seems to work particularly well with global issues such as climate change, the ozone hole, loss of biodiversity through habitat destruction, and the like. But its results in the human rights field are more problematic, given the diversity of political-economic circumstances and cultural practices to be found in the world. Furthermore, it has been all too easy to co-opt human rights issues as 'swords of empire' (to use Bartholomew and Breakspear's trenchant characterization[37]). So-called 'liberal hawks' in the US, for example, have appealed to them to justify imperialist interventions in Kosovo, East Timor,

Haiti, and, above all, in Afghanistan and Iraq. They justify military humanism 'in the name of protecting freedom, human rights and democracy even when it is pursued unilaterally by a self-appointed imperialist power' such as the US.[38] More broadly, it is hard not to conclude with Chandler that 'the roots of today's human rights-based humanitarianism lie in the growing consensus of support for Western involvement in the internal affairs of the developing world since the 1970s'. The key argument is that 'international institutions, international and domestic courts, NGOs or ethics committees are better representatives of the people's needs than are elected governments. Governments and elected representatives are seen as suspect precisely because they are held to account by their constituencies and, therefore, are perceived to have "particular" interest, as opposed to acting on ethical principle'.[39] Domestically, the effects are no less insidious. The effect is to narrow 'public political debate through legitimizing the developing decision-making role for the judiciary and unelected task forces and ethics committees'. The political effects can be debilitating. 'Far from challenging the individual isolation and passivity of our atomised societies, human rights regulation can only institutionalise these divisions.' Even worse, 'the degraded vision of the social world provided by the ethical discourse of human rights serves, like any elite theory, to sustain the self-belief of the governing class'.[40]

The temptation in the light of this critique is to eschew all appeal to universals as fatally flawed and to abandon all mention of rights as an untenable imposition of abstract, market-based ethics as a mask for the restoration of class power. While both propositions deserve to be seriously considered, I think it unfortunate to abandon the field of rights to neoliberal hegemony. There is a battle to be fought, not only over which universals and what rights should be invoked in particular situations but also over how universal principles and conceptions of rights should be constructed. The critical connection forged between neoliberalism as a particular set of political-economic practices and the increasing appeal to universal rights of a certain sort as an ethical foundation for moral and political legitimacy should alert us. The Bremer decrees impose a certain conception of rights upon Iraq. At the same time

179

they violate the Iraqi right to self-determination. 'Between two rights', Marx famously commented, 'force decides'.[41] If class restoration entails the imposition of a distinctive set of rights, then resistance to that imposition entails struggle for entirely different rights.

The positive sense of justice as a right has, for example, been a powerful provocateur in political movements: struggles against injustice have often animated movements for social change. The inspiring history of the civil rights movement in the US is a case in point. The problem, of course, is that there are innumerable concepts of justice to which we may appeal. But analysis shows that certain dominant social processes throw up and rest upon certain conceptions of justice and of rights. To challenge those particular rights is to challenge the social process in which they inhere. Conversely, it proves impossible to wean society away from some dominant social process (such as that of capital accumulation through market exchange) to another (such as political democracy and collective action) without simultaneously shifting allegiance from one dominant conception of rights and of justice to another. The difficulty with all idealist specifications of rights and of justice is that they hide this connection. Only when they come to earth in relation to some social process do they find social meaning.[42]

Consider the case of neoliberalism. Rights cluster around two dominant logics of power—that of the territorial state and that of capital.[43] However much we might wish rights to be universal, it is the state that has to enforce them. If political power is not willing, then notions of rights remain empty. Rights are, therefore, derivative of and conditional upon citizenship. The territoriality of jurisdiction then becomes an issue. This cuts both ways. Difficult questions arise because of stateless persons, illegal immigrants, and the like. Who is or is not a 'citizen' becomes a serious issue defining principles of inclusion and exclusion within the territorial specification of the state. How the state exercises sovereignty with respect to rights is itself a contested issue, but there are limits placed on that sovereignty (as China is discovering) by the global rules embedded in neoliberal capital accumulation. Nevertheless, the nation-state, with its monopoly over legitimate forms of violence, can in Hobbesian fashion define its own bundle of rights and be only loosely bound by international conventions. The US, for one, insists on its right not to be held accountable for crimes against humanity as defined in the international arena at the same time as it insists that war criminals from elsewhere must be brought to justice before the very same courts whose authority it denies in relation to its own citizens.

To live under neoliberalism also means to accept or submit to that bundle of rights necessary for capital accumulation. We live, therefore, in a society in which the inalienable rights of individuals (and, recall, corporations are defined as individuals before the law) to private property and the profit rate trump any other conception of inalienable rights you can think of. Defenders of this regime of rights plausibly argue that it encourages 'bourgeois virtues', without which everyone in the world would be far worse off. These include individual responsibility and liability; independence from state interference (which often places this regime of rights in severe opposition to those defined within the state); equality of opportunity in the market and before the law; rewards for initiative and entrepreneurial endeavour; care for oneself and one's own; and an open marketplace that allows for wide-ranging freedoms of choice of both contract and exchange. This system of rights appears even more persuasive when extended to the right of private property in one's own body (which underpins the right of the person to freely contract to sell his or her labour power as well as to be treated with dignity and respect and to be free from bodily coercions such as slavery) and the right to freedom of thought, expression, and speech. These derivative rights are appealing. Many of us rely heavily upon them. But we do so much as beggars live off the crumbs from the rich man's table.

I cannot convince anyone by philosophical argument that the neoliberal regime of rights is unjust. But the objection to this regime of rights is quite simple: to accept it is to accept that we have no alternative except to live under a regime of endless capital accumulation and economic growth no matter what the social, ecological, or political consequences. Reciprocally, endless capital accumulation implies that the neoliberal regime of rights must be geographically expanded across the globe by violence (as in Chile and Iraq), by imperialist practices (such as those of the World

Trade Organization, the IMF, and the World Bank) or through primitive accumulation (as in China and Russia) if necessary. By hook or by crook, the inalienable rights of private property and the profit rate will be universally established. This is precisely what Bush means when he says the US dedicates itself to extend the sphere of freedom across the globe.

But these are not the only rights available to us. Even within the liberal conception as laid out in the UN Charter there are derivative rights, such as freedoms of speech and expression, of education and economic security, rights to organize unions, and the like. Enforcing these rights would have posed a serious challenge to neoliberalism. Making these derivative rights primary and the primary rights of private property and the profit rate derivative would entail a revolution of great significance in political-economic practices. There are also entirely different conceptions of rights to which we may appeal—of access to the global commons or to basic food security, for example. 'Between equal rights force decides.' Political struggles over the proper conception of rights, and even of freedom itself, move centre-stage in the search for alternatives.

7

Freedom's Prospect

In his annual message to Congress in 1935, President Roosevelt made clear his view that excessive market freedoms lay at the root of the economic and social problems of the 1930s Depression. Americans, he said, 'must forswear that conception of the acquisition of wealth which, through excessive profits, creates undue private power'. Necessitous men are not free men. Everywhere, he argued, social justice had become a definite goal rather than a distant ideal. The primary obligation of the state and its civil society was to use its powers and allocate its resources to eradicate poverty and hunger and to assure security of livelihood, security against the major hazards and vicissitudes of life, and the security of decent homes.[1] Freedom from want was one of the cardinal four freedoms he later articulated as grounding his political vision for the future. These broad themes contrast with the far narrower neoliberal freedoms that President Bush places at the centre of his political rhetoric. The only way to confront our problems, Bush argues, is for the state to cease to regulate private enterprise, for the state to withdraw from social provision, and for the state to foster the universalization of market freedoms and of market ethics. This neoliberal debasement of the concept of freedom 'into a mere advocacy of free enterprise' can only mean, as Karl Polanyi points out, 'the fullness of freedom for those whose income, leisure and security need no enhancing, and a mere pittance of liberty for the people, who may in vain attempt to make use of their democratic rights to gain shelter from the power of the owners of property'.[2]

What is so astonishing about the impoverished condition of contemporary public discourse in the US, as well as elsewhere, is the lack of any serious debate as to which of several divergent concepts of freedom might be appropriate to our times. If it is indeed the case that the US public can be persuaded to support almost anything in the name of freedom, then surely the meaning of this word should be subjected to the deepest scrutiny. Unfortunately, contemporary contributions either take a purely neoliberal line (as does the political commentator Fareed Zakaria, who purports to demonstrate irrefutably that an excess of democracy is the main threat to individual liberty and freedom) or else trim their sails so closely to dominant neoliberal winds as to offer little in the way of counterpoint to the neoliberal logic. Such is, regrettably, the case with Amartya Sen (who finally, and deservedly, won a Nobel Prize in Economics but only after the neoliberal banker who had long chaired the Nobel committee was forced to step down). Sen's *Development as Freedom*, by far the most sensitive contribution to the discussion over recent years, unfortunately wraps up important social and political rights in the mantle of free market interactions.[3] Without a liberal–style market, Sen seems to say, none of the other freedoms can work. A substantial segment of the US public seems for its part to accept that the distinctively neoliberal freedoms that Bush and his fellow Republicans promote are all there is. These freedoms, we are told, are worth dying for in Iraq and the US 'as the greatest power on earth' has 'an obligation' to help spread them everywhere. The conferral of the prestigious Presidential Medal of Freedom on Paul Bremer, architect of the neoliberal reconstruction of the Iraqi state, says much about what this segment of the US public stands for.

Roosevelt's entirely reasonable conceptions sound positively radical by contemporary standards, which probably explains why they have not been articulated by the current Democratic Party as a counterpoint to the narrow entrepreneurial conceptions that Bush holds so dear. Roosevelt's vision does have an impressive genealogy in humanist thinking. Karl Marx, for example, also held the outrageously radical view that an empty stomach was not conducive to freedom. 'The realm of freedom', he wrote, 'actually begins only where labour which is determined by necessity and of mundane considerations ceases', adding, for good measure, that it therefore 'lies beyond the sphere of actual material production'.

Freedom's Prospect

He well understood that we could never free ourselves from our metabolic relations with nature or our social relations with each other, but we could at least aspire to build a social order in which the free exploration of our individual and species potential became a real possibility.[4] By Marx's standard of freedom, and almost certainly by that laid out by Adam Smith in his *Theory of Moral Sentiments*, neoliberalization would surely be regarded as a monumental failure. For those left or cast outside the market system—a vast reservoir of apparently disposable people bereft of social protections and supportive social structures—there is little to be expected from neoliberalization except poverty, hunger, disease, and despair. Their only hope is somehow to scramble aboard the market system either as petty commodity producers, as informal vendors (of things or labour power), as petty predators to beg, steal, or violently secure some crumbs from the rich man's table, or as participants in the vast illegal trade of trafficking in drugs, guns, women, or anything else illegal for which there is a demand. This is the Malthusian world blamed on its victims in works such as political journalist Robert Kaplan's influential essay on 'the coming anarchy'.[5] It never crosses Kaplan's mind that neoliberalization and accumulation by dispossession have anything to do with any of the conditions he describes. The incredible number of anti-IMF riots on record, to say nothing of the crime waves that swept through New York City, Mexico City, Johannesburg, Buenos Aires, and many other major cities in the wake of structural adjustment and neoliberal reform, should surely have alerted him.[6] At the other end of the wealth scale, those thoroughly incorporated within the inexorable logic of the market and its demands find that there is little time or space in which to explore emancipatory potentialities outside what is marketed as 'creative' adventure, leisure, and spectacle. Obliged to live as appendages of the market and of capital accumulation rather than as expressive beings, the realm of freedom shrinks before the awful logic and the hollow intensity of market involvements.

It is in this context that we can better understand the emergence of diverse oppositional cultures that from both within and without the market system either explicitly or tacitly reject the market ethic and the practices that neoliberalization imposes. Within the US, for example, there is a sprawling environmental movement hard at work promoting alternative visions of how to better connect political and ecological projects. There is also a burgeoning anarchist movement among the young, one wing of which—'the primitivists'—believes that the only hope for humanity is to return to that stage of hunter-gathering that preceded the rise of civilization and, in effect, start human history all over again. Others, influenced by movements like CrimeThink and authors such as Derrick Jensen, seek to purge themselves of all traces of incorporation into the capitalist market logic.[7] Others seek a world of mutual support through, for example, the formation of local economic trading systems (LETS) with their own 'local moneys' even in the very heart of a neoliberalizing capitalism. Religious variants of this secular trend are also flourishing, from the US through Brazil to rural China, where religious sects are reported to be forming at an astonishing rate.[8] And many sectors of organized religion, the evangelical Christians, Wahabi Islam, and some variants of Buddhism and Confucianism, preach an intensely anti-market and specifically anti-neoliberal stance. Then there are all those social movements struggling against specific aspects of neoliberal practices, particularly accumulation by dispossession, that either resist predatory neoliberalism (such as the Zapatista revolutionary movement in Mexico) or seek access to resources hitherto denied them (such as the landless peasant movement in Brazil or those leading the factory occupations in Argentina). Centre-left coalitions, openly critical of neoliberalization, have taken over political power, and seem poised to deepen and extend their influence all over Latin America. The surprise success of the Congress Party returning to power in India with a left-wing mandate is yet another case in point. The desire for an alternative to neoliberalization is abundantly in evidence.[9]

There are even signs of discontent within ruling policy circles as to the wisdom of neoliberal propositions and prescriptions. Some earlier enthusiasts (such as the economists Jeffrey Sachs, Joe Stiglitz, and Paul Krugman) and participants (such as George Soros) have now turned critical, even to the point of suggesting some sort of return to a modified Keynesianism or a more 'institutional' approach to the solution of global problems—everything from better regulatory structures of global governance to closer supervision of the reckless speculations of the financiers.[10] In recent years there have been not only insistent calls but also major blueprints for the reform of global governance.[11] A revival of academic and institutional interest in the cosmopolitan ethic ('an injury to one is an injury to all') as a basis for global governance has also occurred and, problematic though its overly simplistic universalisms may be, it is not entirely bereft of merit.[12] It is exactly in such a spirit that heads of states periodically assemble, as 189 of them did at the Millennium Summit in 2000, to sign pious declarations of their collective commitments to eradicate poverty, illiteracy, and disease in short order. But commitments to eradicate illiteracy, for example, sound hollow against the background of substantial and continuing declines in the proportion of national product going into public education almost everywhere in the neoliberal world.

Objectives of this sort cannot be realized without challenging the fundamental power bases upon which neoliberalism has been built and to which the processes of neoliberalization have so lavishly contributed. This means not only reversing the withdrawal of the state from social provision but also confronting the overwhelming powers of finance capital. Keynes held the 'coupon clippers', who parasitically lived off dividends and interest, in contempt and looked forward to what he called 'the euthanasia of the rentier' as a necessary condition for not only achieving some modicum of economic justice but also avoiding the devastation of those periodic crises to which capitalism was prone. The virtue of the Keynesian compromise and the embedded liberalism constructed after 1945 was that it went some way to realizing those goals. The advent of neoliberalization, by contrast, has celebrated the role of the rentier, cut taxes on the rich, privileged dividends and speculative gains over wages and salaries, and unleashed untold though geographically contained financial crises, with devastating effects on employment and life chances in country after country. The only way to realize the pious goals is to confront the powers of finance and to roll back the class privileges that have been built thereon. But there is no sign anywhere among the powers that be of doing anything of the sort.

With respect to the return to Keynesianism, however, the Bush administration, as I earlier pointed out, has beaten everyone to the gun, being prepared to countenance spiralling federal deficits stretching on endlessly into the future. Contrary to traditional Keynesian prescriptions, however, the redistributions in this case are upwards towards the large corporations, their wealthy CEOs, and their financial/legal advisers at the expense of the poor, the middle classes, and even ordinary shareholders (including the pension funds), to say nothing of future generations. But the fact that traditional Keynesianism can be bowdlerized and turned upside-down in this fashion should not surprise us. For, as I have also already shown, there is abundant evidence that neoliberal theory and rhetoric (particularly the political rhetoric concerning liberty and freedom) has also all along primarily functioned as a mask for practices that are all about the maintenance, reconstitution, and restoration of elite class power. The exploration of alternatives has, therefore, to move outside the frames of reference defined by this class power and market ethics while staying soberly anchored in the realities of our time and place. And these realities point to the possibility of a major crisis within the heartland of the neoliberal order itself.

The End of Neoliberalism?

The internal economic and political contradictions of neoliberalization are impossible to contain except through financial crises. So far these have proven locally damaging but globally manageable. The manageability depends, of course, upon departing substantially from neoliberal theory. The mere fact that the two main powerhouses of the global economy—the US and China—are deficit financing up to the hilt is, surely, a compelling sign that neoliberalism is in trouble if not actually dead as a viable theoretical guide to ensuring the future of capital accumulation. This will not prevent it from continuing to be deployed as a rhetoric to sustain the restoration/creation of elite class power. But when income and wealth inequalities reach a point—as they have today—close to that which preceded the crash of 1929, then the economic imbalances become so chronic as to be in danger of generating a structural crisis. Unfortunately, regimes of accumulation rarely if ever dissolve peacefully. Embedded liberalism arose out of the ashes of the Second World War and the Great Depression. Neoliberalization was born in the midst of the 1970s crisis of accumulation, emerging from the womb of a played-out embedded liberalism with enough violence to support Karl Marx's observation that violence is invariably the midwife of history. The authoritarian option of neoconservatism is now emerging in the US. The violent assault upon Iraq abroad and incarceration policies at home signal a new-found determination on the part of the US ruling elite to redefine the global and domestic order to its own advantage. It therefore behoves us to consider very carefully whether and how a crisis of the neoliberal regime might unfold.

The financial crises that have so frequently preceded the predatory raiding of whole state economies by superior financial powers have usually been characterized by chronic economic imbalances. The typical signs are soaring and uncontrollable internal budgetary deficits, a balance of payments crisis, rapid currency depreciation, unstable valuations of internal assets (for example in property and financial markets), rising inflation, rising unemployment with falling wages, and capital flight. Of these seven main indicators the US now has the distinction of scoring high on the first three and there are serious concerns with respect to the fourth. The current 'jobless recovery' and stagnant wages suggest incipient problems with the sixth. Such a mix of indicators elsewhere would almost certainly have necessitated IMF intervention (and IMF economists are on record, as are both former and current Federal Reserve chairs Volcker and Greenspan, complaining that the economic imbalances within the US are threatening global stability).[13] But since the US dominates the IMF this means nothing more than that the US should discipline itself, and that appears unlikely. The big questions are: will global markets do the disciplining (as according to neoliberal theory they should), and if so how and with what effects?

It is unthinkable but not impossible that the US will become like Argentina in 2001 overnight. The consequences would, however, be catastrophic not only internally but also for global capitalism. Since almost everyone who constitutes the capitalist class and its global managers everywhere is well aware of this fact, the rest of the world is currently willing (in some cases reluctantly) to continue to support the US economy with sufficient credits to sustain its profligate ways. Private capital flows into the US have, however, seriously diminished (except to buy up relatively cheap assets given the fall in the value of the dollar) and so it is the world's central bankers—particularly in Japan and China—that now increasingly own America Inc. For them to withdraw support from the US would be devastating for their own economies since the US is still a major market for their exports. But there is a limit to which this system can progress. Already nearly one-third of stock assets on Wall Street and nearly half of US Treasury bonds are owned by foreigners, and the dividends and interest flowing out to foreign owners are now roughly equivalent to, if not more than, the tribute that US corporations and financial operations are extracting from abroad (Figure 7.1). This balance of benefits will turn more strongly negative the more the US borrows, and it is now borrowing from abroad at a rate approaching $2 billion per day. Furthermore, if US interest rates rise (as at some point they must) then what happened to Mexico after the Volcker interest rate increase in 1979 starts to loom as a real problem. The US will soon be paying out far more to service its debt to the rest of the world than it brings in.[14] This extraction of wealth from the US will not be welcome domestically. The perpetual increases in debt-financed consumerism that have been the foundation of social peace in the US since 1945 would have to stop.

The imbalances seem not to trouble the Bush administration, judging by cavalier statements to the effect that the current account deficit, if it is a problem, can easily be dealt with by people buying US-made goods (as if such goods are readily available and cheap enough and as if nominally US-made goods do not have a high foreign-input component). If this really happened then Wal-Mart would be put out of business. The budget deficit, Bush says, can easily be dealt with without raising taxes by curbing domestic programmes (as if there are any large discretionary programmes left to dismantle). Vice-President Cheney's remark that 'Reagan taught us that budget deficits do not matter' is alarming, because what Reagan also taught is that running up deficits is a way to force

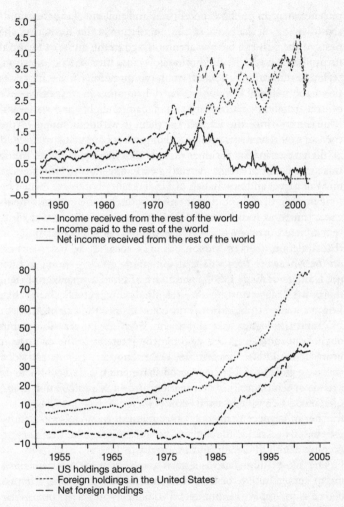

Figure 7.1 The deteriorating position of the US in global capital and ownership flows, 1960–2002: inflow and outflow of US investments (above) and change in foreign ownership shares (below)

Source: Duménil and Lévy, 'The Economics of US Imperialism'.

retrenchment in public expenditures and that attacking the standard of living of the mass of the population while feathering the nests of the rich can best be accomplished in the midst of financial turmoil and crisis. If, furthermore, we ask the general question, 'Who has actually benefited from the numerous financial crises that have cascaded from one country to another in wave after wave of catastrophic deflations, inflations, capital flights and structural adjustments since the late 1970s?', the weak commitment of the current US administration to fending off a fiscal crisis in spite of all the warning signs becomes more readily understandable. In the wake of a financial crash, the ruling elite may hope to emerge even more empowered than before.

It may be that the US economy can finesse the current imbalances (much as it did after 1945) and grow its own way out of its self-inflicted problems. There are some weak signs that point in that direction. Current policy, however, seems to be based at best on the Micawber principle that something good is bound to turn up. Leaders of many US corporations, after all, managed to live in their own fantasy world before seemingly invulnerable entities like Enron came crashing down. This could also be the fate of America Inc., and the fantasy-like statements from the current leadership ought to trouble everyone who has the interests of the country at heart. It could also be that the US ruling elite calculates it can survive a global fiscal crisis in good shape and use it to complete its agenda of total domestic domination. But such a calculation could turn out to be a monumental error. The result may be to hasten the transfer of hegemony to some other regional economy (most probably based in Asia) while undercutting the ruling elite's capacity to dominate both internally and externally.

The most immediate question concerns what sort of crisis might serve the US best in resolving its own situation, for that choice is indeed within the realm of policy options. In presenting these options it is important to recall that the US has not been immune to financial difficulties over the last twenty years. The stock market crash of 1987 deleted nearly 30 per cent of asset values, and at the trough of the crash that followed the bursting of the new economy bubble in the late 1990s more that $8 trillion in paper assets was lost, before the recovery to former levels. The bank and savings and loan failures of 1987 cost nearly $200 billion to remedy, and in that year matters became so bad that William Isaacs, chairman of the Federal Deposit Insurance Corporation, warned that 'the US may be headed towards the nationalization of banking'. And the huge bankruptcies of Long Term Capital Management, Orange County, and others who speculated and lost, followed by the collapse of several major companies in 2001–2 in the midst of astonishing accounting lapses, not only cost the public dear but also demonstrated how fragile and fictitious much of neoliberal financialization has become. The fragility is by no means confined to the US, of course. Most countries, including China, face financial volatility and uncertainty. The debt of the developing world, for example, rose 'from $580 billion in 1980 to $2.4 trillion in 2002 and much of it is unrepayable. In 2002 there was a net outflow of $340 billion in servicing this debt, compared to overseas development aid of $37 billion.'[15] In some cases the debt service exceeds foreign earnings and, understandably, some countries, such as Argentina, are exhibiting considerable recalcitrance in the face of their creditors.

Consider, then, the two worst-case scenarios from the standpoint of the US. A short burst of hyper-inflation would provide one way to delete the outstanding international and consumer debt. The US would in effect pay off its debts to Japan, China, and the others in grossly depreciated dollars. Such inflationary confiscation would not be well received in the rest of the world (though it could do little about it since sending gunboats up the Potomac is not a feasible option). Hyper-inflation would also destroy savings, pensions, and much else internally within the US. It would entail reversing the monetarist course that Volcker and Greenspan have generally followed. At the least hint of such a switch away from monetarism (in effect declaring neoliberalism dead), however, central bankers everywhere would almost certainly create a run on the dollar and thus prematurely precipitate a crisis of capital flight that would be unmanageable by US financial institutions alone. The US dollar would lose all credibility as a global reserve currency and lose all the future benefits (for example of seignorage—the power to print money) of being the dominant financial power. That mantle would then be assumed either by Europe or East Asia or both (the world's central bankers are already exhibiting a preference to hold more of their balances in euros). A more modest return to inflation may also be on the cards, for there is abundant evidence that inflation is by no means the inherent evil that monetarists describe, and that some modest relaxation of monetary targets (as Thatcher showed in the more pragmatic phases of her drive towards neoliberalization) is workable.

The other option is for the US to accept a long-drawn-out period of deflation of the sort that Japan has been experiencing since 1989. This would create serious global problems unless other economies—with China, perhaps coupled with India, obviously in the vanguard—can pick up the slack of lagging dynamism. But, as we have seen, the China option is deeply problematic for both economic and political reasons. The internal imbalances in China are serious, and mainly take the form of excess capacity— everything from too many airports to too many car plants. This overcapacity would become even more palpable in the event of any prolonged stagnation in US consumer markets. The outstanding debt in China (in the form of non-performing bank loans), on the other hand, is by no means as monumental as that in the US. The dangers in the Chinese case are as much political as economic. But the extraordinary dynamism within the Asian complex of econ-omies may be sufficient to propel capital accumulation well into the future, though almost certainly with remarkably deleterious effects on the quality of the environment as well as on the trad-itional US position as top dog in the global order. Whether or not the US will meekly surrender its hegemonic position is an open question. It will almost certainly maintain military domination even as its dominant position in almost every other significant realm of political-economic power diminishes. Whether or not the US will seek to use its military superiority, as it has done in Iraq, for political and economic purposes will then depend crucially upon the internal dynamics within the US itself.

Long-drawn-out deflation will be extremely hard for the US to absorb internally. If the debt problems of the federal government and of financial institutions are to be resolved without threatening the wealth of elite classes, then 'confiscatory deflation' (deeply inconsistent with neoliberalism) of the sort Argentina experienced (hints of which could be found in the US savings and loan crisis of the late 1980s when many depositors could not get access to their moneys) will be the only option. The substantial public programmes that still exist (Social Security and Medicare), pension rights, and asset values (property and savings in particular) will likely be the first victims, and under such conditions popular consent will almost certainly begin to fray at the seams. The big question would then be how extensive and expressive the discontent is, and how it might be handled.

The consolidation of neoconservative authoritarianism then emerges as one potential answer. Neoconservatism, I argued in Chapter 3, sustains the neoliberal drive towards the construction of asymmetric market freedoms but makes the anti-democratic tendencies of neoliberalism explicit through a turn into authoritarian, hierarchical, and even militaristic means of maintaining law and order. In *The New Imperialism* I explored Hannah Arendt's thesis that militarization abroad and at home inevitably go hand in hand, and concluded that the international adventurism of the neoconservatives, long planned and legitimized after the 9/11 attacks, had as much to do with asserting domestic control over a fractious and much-divided body politic in the US as it did with a geopolitical strategy of maintaining global hegemony through control over oil resources. Fear and insecurity both internally and externally were all too easily—and in this case successfully when it came to re-election time—manipulated for political purposes.[16]

But the neoconservatives also assert a higher moral purpose, at the core of which lies an appeal to a nationalism that has long had, as we saw in Chapter 3, a fraught relationship with neoliberalization. US nationalism has, however, a dual character. On the one hand it presumes that it is the God-given (and the religious invocation is deliberate) manifest destiny of the US to be the greatest power on earth (if not number one in everything from baseball to the Olympics) and that, as a beacon of freedom, liberty, and progress, it has been and continues to be universally admired and considered worthy of emulation. Everyone, it is said, wants to either live in or be like the US. The US therefore benevolently and generously gives freely of its resources and its values and culture to the rest of the world, in the cause of conferring the privilege of

Americanization and American values on all and sundry. But US nationalism also has a darker side in which paranoia about fearful threats from enemies and evil forces from outside take over. The fear is of foreigners and of immigrants, of outside agitators, and now, of course, of 'terrorists'. This leads to the internal circling of wagons and the closing down of civil liberties and freedoms in episodes like the persecution of anarchists in the 1920s, the McCarthyism of the 1950s directed against communists and their sympathizers, the paranoid style of Richard Nixon towards opponents of the Vietnam War and, since 9/11, the tendency to characterize all critics of administration policies as aiding and abetting the enemy. This kind of nationalism easily fuses with racism (most particularly now towards Arabs), the restriction of civil liberties (the Patriot Act), the curbing of press freedoms (the gaoling of journalists for not revealing their sources), and the embrace of incarceration and the death penalty to deal with malfeasance. Externally this nationalism leads to covert action and now to preemptive wars to eradicate anything that seems like the remotest threat to the hegemony of US values and the dominance of US interests. Historically, these two strains of nationalism have always coexisted.[17] They have sometimes been in open conflict with each other (in the divisions over how to deal with the revolutions in Central America in the 1980s, for example).

After 1945, the US was in a position to project the first assumption, always self-interestedly and sometimes benevolently (as in the Marshall Plan, which helped revive war-torn European economies after 1945), onto the world, at the same time as it was engaging with McCarthyism at home. But the end of the Cold War has changed everything. The rest of the world no longer looks to the US for military protection and has broken free from US domination in almost everything. The US has never been so isolated from the rest of the world politically, culturally, and even militarily as now. And this isolation is not, as it was in the past, the product of a US withdrawal from world affairs but a consequence of its excessive and unilateralist interventionism. It also comes at a time when the US economy is more interwoven into global production and financial networks than ever before. The result has been a dangerous fusion of the two forms of nationalism. Through the formulation of the doctrine of 'pre-emptive strike' against foreign nations in the midst of a supposedly all-threatening global war on terror, the US public can imagine that it is struggling benevolently to bring freedom and democracy everywhere (particularly in Iraq) while playing out its darkest fears regarding some unknown and hidden enemy that is threatening its very existence. The rhetoric of the Bush administration and of the neoconservatives plays indefatigably upon both themes. This served Bush well in his successful re-election campaign.

In *The New Imperialism*, I argued that there are many signs that US hegemony is crumbling. It lost its dominance in global production during the 1970s and its power in global finance began to erode in the 1990s. Its technological leadership role is being challenged and its hegemony with respect to culture and moral leadership is waning fast, leaving its military strength as its only clear weapon of global domination. Even its military might is confined to what can be done with high-tech destructive power wielded from thirty thousand feet up. Iraq has demonstrated its limits on the ground. The transition to some new hegemonic structure in global capitalism poses a choice for the US: to manage the transition peacefully or through catastrophe.[18] The current stance of US ruling elites points more towards the latter rather than to the former course. Nationalism within the US can all too easily be rallied to the idea that the economic difficulties of either hyper-inflation or long-drawn-out deflation are attributable to others, such as China and East Asia or to OPEC and Arab states that fail to respond to its profligate demands for energy in an appropriate way. The doctrine of pre-emptive strike is already in place and the destructive capacities are readily at hand. A beleaguered and plainly threatened US state has, the argument goes, an obligation to defend itself, its values, and its way of life by military means if necessary. Such a catastrophic and in my judgement suicidal calculation is not beyond the capacity of the current US leadership. That leadership has already demonstrated its penchant to suppress internal dissent and in this it has garnered considerable popular support. A substantial proportion of the US populace, after all, views the US Bill of Rights as a communist-inspired document, while others, a minority to be sure, welcomes anything that smacks of Armageddon. The anti-terrorism laws, the abandonment of the Geneva Conventions in Guantánamo Bay, and the readiness to depict any oppositional force as 'terrorist' are warning signs.

Fortunately, there is a substantial opposition that can be and to some degree already is mobilized within the US against such catastrophic and suicidal tendencies. Unfortunately, as it is currently constituted this opposition is fragmented, rudderless, and lacking coherent organization. To some degree this is the consequence of self-inflicted wounds within the labour movement, within the movements that have broadly embraced identity politics, and within all those postmodern intellectual currents that accord, without knowing it, with the White House line that truth is both socially constructed and a mere effect of discourse. Terry Eagleton's critique of Lyotard's *Postmodern Condition*, in which 'there can be no difference between truth, authority and rhetorical seductiveness; he who has the smoothest tongue or the raciest story has the power', bears repeating. It is, I would argue, even more relevant to our times than when I cited it back in 1989.[19] The story-telling from the White House and the spin-meistering from Downing Street have to be rebutted then stopped if we are to find any kind of exit from our current impasse. There is a reality out there and it is catching up with us fast. But where should we strive to go? If we were able to mount that wondrous horse of freedom, where would we seek to ride it?

Alternatives

There is a tendency to take up the issue of alternatives as if it is about describing some blueprint for a future society and an outline of the way to get there. Much can be gained from such exercises. But we first need to initiate a political process that can lead us to a point where feasible alternatives, real possibilities, become identifiable. There are two main paths to take. We can engage with the plethora of oppositional movements actually existing and seek to distil from and through their activism the essence of a broad-based oppositional programme. Or we can resort to theoretical and practical enquiries into our existing condition (of the sort I have engaged in here) and seek to derive alternatives through critical analysis. To take the latter path in no way presumes that existing oppositional movements are wrong or somehow defective in their understandings. By the same token, oppositional movements cannot presume that analytical findings are irrelevant to their cause. The task is to initiate dialogue between those taking each path and thereby to deepen collective understandings and define more adequate lines of action.

Neoliberalization has spawned a swath of oppositional movements both within and outside its compass. Many of these movements are radically different from the worker-based movements that dominated before 1980.[20] I say 'many', but not 'all'. Traditional worker-based movements are by no means dead even in the advanced capitalist countries where they have been much weakened by the neoliberal onslaught on their power. In South Korea and South Africa vigorous labour movements arose during the 1980s and in much of Latin America working-class parties are flourishing if not in power. In Indonesia a fledgling labour movement of great potential importance is struggling to be heard. The potential for labour unrest in China is immense though unpredictable. And it is not clear either that the mass of the working people in the US, who have over this last generation often willingly voted against their own material interests for reasons of cultural nationalism, religion, and moral values, will for ever stay locked into such a politics by the machinations of Republicans and Democrats alike. Given the volatility, there is no reason to rule out the resurgence of popular social democratic or even populist anti-neoliberal politics within the US in future years.

But struggles against accumulation by dispossession are fomenting quite different lines of social and political struggle.[21] Partly because of the distinctive conditions that give rise to such movements, their political orientation and modes of organization depart markedly from those typical of social democratic politics. The Zapatista rebellion in Chiapas, Mexico, for example, did not seek to take over state power or accomplish a political revolution; it sought instead a more inclusionary politics. The idea is to work through the whole of civil society in a more open and fluid search for alternatives that would look to the specific needs of the different social groups and allow them to improve their lot.

Organizationally, it tended to avoid avant-gardism and refused to take on the form of a political party. It preferred instead to remain a social movement within the state, attempting to form a political power bloc in which indigenous cultures would be central rather than peripheral. Many environmental movements—such as those for environmental justice—proceed in the same way.

The effect of such movements has been to shift the terrain of political organization away from traditional political parties and labour organizing into a less focused political dynamic of social action across the whole spectrum of civil society. What such movements lose in focus they gain in terms of direct relevance to particular issues and constituencies. They draw strength from being embedded in the nitty-gritty of daily life and struggle, but in so doing they often find it hard to extract themselves from the local and the particular to understand the macro-politics of what neoliberal accumulation by dispossession and its relation to the restoration of class power was and is all about.

The variety of these struggles is simply stunning, so much so that it is hard sometimes to even imagine connections between them. They are all part of a volatile mix of protest movements that have swept the world and increasingly grabbed the headlines during and since the 1980s. These movements and revolts have sometimes been crushed with ferocious violence, for the most part by state powers acting in the name of 'order and stability'. Elsewhere they have degenerated into inter-ethnic violence and civil war as accumulation by dispossession produced intense social and political rivalries. The divide-and-rule tactics of ruling elites or competition between rival factions (for example French versus US interests in some African countries) have more often than not been central to these struggles. Client states, supported militarily or in some instances with special forces trained by the major military apparatuses (led by the US, with Britain and France playing a minor role) often take the lead in a system of repressions and liquidations to ruthlessly check activist movements challenging accumulation by dispossession in many parts of the developing world.

The movements themselves have produced a plethora of ideas regarding alternatives. Some seek to de-link wholly or partially from the overwhelming powers of neoliberal globalization. Others (such as the 'Fifty Years Is Enough' movement) seek global social and environmental justice by reform or dissolution of powerful institutions such as the IMF, the WTO, and the World Bank (though, interestingly, the core power of the US Treasury is rarely mentioned). Still others (particularly environmentalists such as Greenpeace) emphasize the theme of 'reclaiming the commons', thereby signalling deep continuities with struggles of long ago as well as with struggles waged throughout the bitter history of colonialism and imperialism. Some (such as Hardt and Negri) envisage a multitude in motion, or a movement within global civil society, to confront the dispersed and decentred powers of the neoliberal order (construed as 'Empire'), while others more modestly look to local experiments with new production and consumption systems (such as the LETS) animated by completely different kinds of social relations and ecological practices. There are also those who put their faith in more conventional political party structures (for example the Workers Party in Brazil or the Congress Party in India in alliance with communists) with the aim of gaining state power as one step towards global reform of the economic order. Many of these diverse currents now come together at the World Social Forum in an attempt to define their commonalities and to build an organizational power capable of confronting the many variants of neoliberalism and of neoconservatism. A flurry of literature suggesting that 'another world is possible' has emerged. This summarizes and on occasion attempts to synthesize the diverse ideas arising from the various social movements occurring in all parts of the world. There is much here to admire and to inspire.

But what sorts of conclusions can be derived from an analytical exercise of the sort here constructed? To begin with, the whole history of embedded liberalism and the subsequent turn to neoliberalization indicates the crucial role played by class struggle in either checking or restoring elite class power. Though it has been effectively disguised, we have lived through a whole generation of sophisticated strategizing on the part of ruling elites to restore, enhance, or, as in China and Russia, to construct an overwhelming class power. The further turn to neoconservatism is illustrative of the lengths to which economic elites will go and the authoritarian strategies they are prepared to deploy in order to sustain their power. And all of this occurred in decades when working-class institutions were in decline and when many progressives were increasingly persuaded that class was a meaningless or at least long defunct category. In this, progressives of all stripes seem to have caved in to neoliberal thinking since it is one of the primary fictions of neoliberalism that class is a fictional category that exists only in the imagination of socialists and crypto-communists. In the US in particular, the phrase 'class warfare' is now confined to the right-wing media (for example the *Wall Street Journal*) to denigrate all forms of criticism that threaten to undermine a supposedly unified and coherent national purpose (i.e. the restoration of upper-class power!). The first lesson we must learn, therefore, is that if it looks like class struggle and acts like class war then we have to name it unashamedly for what it is. The mass of the population has either to resign itself to the historical and geographical trajectory defined by overwhelming and ever-increasing upper-class power, or respond to it in class terms.

To put it this way is not to wax nostalgic for some lost golden age when some fictional category like 'the proletariat' was in motion. Nor does it necessarily mean (if it ever should have) that there is some simple conception of class to which we can appeal as the primary (let alone exclusive) agent of historical transformation. There is no proletarian field of utopian Marxian fantasy to which we can retire. To point to the necessity and inevitability of class struggle is not to say that the way class is constituted is determined or even determinable in advance. Popular as well as elite class movements make themselves, though never under conditions of their own choosing. And those conditions are full of the complexities that arise out of race, gender, and ethnic distinctions that are closely interwoven with class identities. The lower classes are highly racialized and the increasing feminization of poverty has been a notable feature of neoliberalization. The neoconservative assault on women's and reproductive rights, which, interestingly, got into high gear at the end of the 1970s when neoliberalism first came to prominence, is a key element in its notion of a proper moral order built upon a very particular conception of the family.

Analysis also shows how and why popular movements are

currently bifurcated. On the one hand there are movements around what I call 'expanded reproduction' in which the exploitation of wage labour and conditions defining the social wage are the central issues. On the other hand there are movements against accumulation by dispossession. These include resistance to classic forms of primitive accumulation (such as displacement of peasant populations from the land); to the brutal withdrawal of the state from all social obligations (except surveillance and policing); to practices destructive of cultures, histories, and environments; and to the 'confiscatory' deflations and inflations wrought by the contemporary forms of finance capital in alliance with the state. Finding the organic link between these different movements is an urgent theoretical and practical task. But our analysis has also shown that this can only be done by tracking the dynamics of a capital accumulation process that is marked by volatile as well as deepening uneven geographical developments. This unevenness, as we saw in Chapter 4, actively promotes the spread of neoliberalization through inter-state competition. Part of the task of a rejuvenated class politics is to turn this uneven geographical development into an asset rather than a liability. The divide-and-rule politics of ruling-class elites must be confronted with alliance politics on the left sympathetic to the recuperation of local powers of self-determination.

But analysis also points up exploitable contradictions within the neoliberal and neoconservative agendas. The widening gap between rhetoric (for the benefit of all) and realization (the benefit of a small ruling class) is now all too visible. The idea that the market is about competition and fairness is increasingly negated by the fact of the extraordinary monopolization, centralization, and internationalization of corporate and financial power. The startling increase in class and regional inequalities, both within states (such as China, Russia, India, and Southern Africa) and internationally between states, poses a serious political problem that can no longer be swept under the rug as something 'transitional' on the way to a perfected neoliberal world. The more neoliberalism is recognized as a failed utopian rhetoric masking a successful project for the restoration of ruling-class power, the more the basis is laid for a resurgence of mass movements voicing egalitarian political demands and seeking economic justice, fair trade, and greater economic security.

The rise of rights discourses, of the sort considered in the previous chapter, presents opportunities as well as problems. Even appeal to the conventional liberal notions of rights can form a powerful 'sword of resistance' from which to critique neoconservative authoritarianism, particularly given the way in which 'the war on terror' has everywhere (from the US to China and Chechnya) been deployed as an excuse to diminish civil and political liberties. The rising call to acknowledge Iraqi rights to self-determination and sovereignty is a powerful weapon with which to check US imperial designs there. But alternative rights can also be defined. The critique of endless capital accumulation as the dominant process that shapes our lives entails critique of those specific rights— the right to individual private property and the profit rate—that ground neoliberalism and vice versa. I have argued elsewhere for an entirely different bundle of rights, to include the right to life chances, to political association and 'good' governance, for control over production by the direct producers, to the inviolability and integrity of the human body, to engage in critique without fear of retaliation, to a decent and healthy living environment, to collective control of common property resources, to the production of space, to difference, as well as rights inherent in our status as species beings.[22] To propose different rights to those held sacrosanct by neoliberalism carries with it, however, the obligation to specify an alternative social process within which such alternative rights can inhere.

A similar argument can be made against the neoconservative assertion of a moral high ground for its authority and legitimacy. Ideals of moral community and of a moral economy are not foreign to progressive movements historically. Many of those, like the Zapatistas, now struggling against accumulation by dispossession are actively articulating the desire for alternative social relations in moral economy terms. Morality is not a field to be defined solely by a reactionary religious right mobilized under the hegemony of media and articulated through a political process dominated by corporate money power. The restoration of ruling-class power under a welter of confusing moral arguments has to be confronted.

The so-called 'culture wars'—however misguided some of them may have been—cannot be sloughed off as some unwelcome distraction (as some on the traditional left argue) from class politics. Indeed, the rise of moral argument among the neoconservatives attests not only to the fear of social dissolution under an individualizing neoliberalism but also to the broad swaths of moral repugnance already in motion against the alienations, anomie, exclusions, marginalizations, and environmental degradations produced through the practices of neoliberalization. The transformation of that moral repugnance towards a pure market ethic into cultural and then political resistance is one of the signs of our times that needs to be read correctly rather than shunted aside. The organic link between such cultural struggles and the struggle to roll back the overwhelming consolidation of ruling-class power calls for theoretical and practical exploration.

But it is the profoundly anti-democratic nature of neoliberalism backed by the authoritarianism of the neoconservatives that should surely be the main focus of political struggle. The democratic deficit in nominally 'democratic' countries such as the US is now enormous.[23] Political representation is there compromised and corrupted by money power, to say nothing of an all too easily manipulated and corrupted electoral system. Basic institutional arrangements are seriously biased. Senators from twenty-six states with less than 20 per cent of the population have more than half the votes to determine the Congressional legislative agenda. The blatant gerrymandering of congressional districts to advantage whoever is in power is, furthermore, deemed constitutional by a judicial system increasingly packed with political appointees of a neoconservative persuasion. Institutions with enormous power, like the Federal Reserve, are outside any democratic control whatsoever. Internationally the situation is even worse since there is no accountability, let alone democratic influence, over institutions such as the IMF, the WTO, and the World Bank, while NGOs can also operate without democratic input or oversight no matter how well-intentioned their actions. This is not to say that there is nothing unproblematic about democratic institutions. Neoliberal theoretical fears of the undue influence of special-interest groups on legislative processes are all too well illustrated by the corporate lobbyists and the revolving door between the state and corporations that ensure that the US Congress (as well as state legislatures in the US) does the bidding of moneyed interests and moneyed interests alone.

To bring back the demands for democratic governance and for economic, political, and cultural equality and justice is not to suggest a return to some golden age. The meanings in each instance have to be reinvented to deal with contemporary conditions and potentialities. Democracy in ancient Athens has little to do with the meanings we must invest that term with today in circumstances as diverse as São Paulo, Johannesburg, Shanghai, Manila, San Francisco, Leeds, Stockholm, and Lagos. But the stunning point here is that right across the globe, from China, Brazil, Argentina, Taiwan, and Korea to South Africa, Iran, India, and Egypt, in the struggling nations of eastern Europe as well as the heartlands of contemporary capitalism, there are groups and social movements in motion that are rallying to reforms expressive of some version of democratic values.[24]

US leaders have, with considerable domestic public support, projected upon the world the idea that American neoliberal values of freedom are universal and supreme, and that such values are to die for. The world is in a position to reject that imperialist gesture and refract back into the heartland of neoliberal and neoconservative capitalism a completely different set of values: those of an open democracy dedicated to the achievement of social equality coupled with economic, political, and cultural justice. Roosevelt's arguments are one place to start. Within the US an alliance has to be built to regain popular control of the state apparatus and to thereby advance the deepening rather than the evisceration of democratic practices and values under the juggernaut of market power.

There is a far, far nobler prospect of freedom to be won than that which neoliberalism preaches. There is a far, far worthier system of governance to be constructed than that which neoconservatism allows.

Notes

Introduction

1. S. George, 'A Short History of Neoliberalism: Twenty Years of Elite Economics and Emerging Opportunities for Structural Change', in W. Bello, N. Bullard, and K. Malhotra (eds.), *Global Finance: New Thinking on Regulating Capital Markets* (London: Zed Books, 2000) 27–35; G. Duménil and D. Lévy, *Capital Resurgent: Roots of the Neoliberal Revolution*, trans. D. Jeffers (Cambridge, Mass.: Harvard University Press, 2004); J. Peck, 'Geography and Public Policy: Constructions of Neoliberalism', *Progress in Human Geography*, 28/3 (2004), 392–405; J. Peck and A. Tickell, 'Neoliberalizing Space', *Antipode*, 34/3 (2002), 380–404; P. Treanor, 'Neoliberalism: Origins, Theory, Definition', http://web.inter.nl.net/users/Paul.Treanor/neoliberalism.html.
2. Treanor, 'Neoliberalism'.
3. D. Harvey, *The Condition of Postmodernity* (Oxford: Basil Blackwell, 1989); J.-F. Lyotard, *The Postmodern Condition* (Manchester: Manchester University Press, 1984), 66.

1. Freedom's Just Another Word . . .

1. G. W. Bush, 'President Addresses the Nation in Prime Time Press Conference', 13 Apr. 2004; http://www.whitehouse.gov/news/releases/2004/0420040413-20.html.
2. Matthew Arnold is cited in R. Williams, *Culture and Society, 1780–1850* (London: Chatto & Windus, 1958), 118.
3. A. Juhasz, 'Ambitions of Empire: The Bush Administration Economic Plan for Iraq (and Beyond)', *Left Turn Magazine*, 12 (Feb./Mar. 2004), 27–32.
4. N. Klein, 'Of Course the White House Fears Free Elections in Iraq', *Guardian*, 24 Jan. 2004, 18.
5. T. Crampton, 'Iraqi Official Urges Caution on Imposing Free Market', *New York Times*, 14 Oct. 2003, C5.
6. Juhasz, 'Ambitions of Empire', 29.

7. G. W. Bush, 'Securing Freedom's Triumph', *New York Times*, 11 Sept. 2002, A33. *The National Security Strategy of the United State of America* can be found on the website: www.whitehouse.gov/nsc/nss.

8. M. Fourcade-Gourinchas and S. Babb, 'The Rebirth of the Liberal Creed: Paths to Neoliberalism in Four Countries', *American Journal of Sociology*, 108 (2002), 542–9; J. Valdez, *Pinochet's Economists: The Chicago School in Chile* (New York: Cambridge University Press, 1995); R. Luders, 'The Success and Failure of the State-Owned Enterprise Divestitures in a Developing Country: The Case of Chile', *Journal of World Business* (1993), 98–121.

9. R. Dahl and C. Lindblom, *Politics, Economy and Welfare: Planning and Politico-Economic Systems Resolved into Basic Social Processes* (New York: Harper, 1953).

10. S. Krasner (ed.), *International Regimes* (Ithaca, NY: Cornell University Press, 1983); M. Blyth, *Great Transformations: Economic Ideas and Institutional Change in the Twentieth Century* (Cambridge: Cambridge University Press, 2002).

11. P. Armstrong, A. Glynn, and J. Harrison, *Capitalism Since World War II: The Making and Breaking of the Long Boom* (Oxford: Basil Blackwell, 1991).

12. G. Eley, *Forging Democracy: The History of the Left in Europe, 1850–2000* (Oxford: Oxford University Press, 2000).

13. G. Duménil and D. Lévy, 'Neoliberal Dynamics: Towards A New Phase?', in K. van der Pijl, L. Assassi, and D. Wigan (eds.), *Global Regulation: Managing Crises after the Imperial Turn* (New York: Palgrave Macmillan, 2004) 41–63. See also Task Force on Inequality and American Democracy, *American Democracy in an Age of Rising Inequality* (American Political Science Association, 2004); T. Piketty and E. Saez, 'Income Inequality in the United States, 1913–1998', *Quarterly Journal of Economics*, 118 (2003), 1–39.

14. United Nations Development Program, *Human Development Report, 1999* (New York: Oxford University Press, 1999), 3.

15. See the website http://www.montpelerin.org/aboutmps.html.

16. A judicious review can be found in H.-J. Chang, *Globalisation, Economic Development and the Role of the State* (London: Zed Books, 2003). But as Peck, 'Geography and Public Policy', points out, neoliberalism has often absorbed other elements within its frame so that it is hard to conceive of it as a 'pure' theory.

17. The story of Thatcher's path to neoliberalism is outlined in D. Yergin and J. Stanislaw, *The Commanding Heights: The Battle Between Government and Market Place that is Remaking the Modern World* (New York: Simon & Schuster, 1999).

18. L. Panitch and S. Gindin, 'Finance and American Empire', in *The Empire Reloaded: Socialist Register 2005* (London: Merlin Press, 2005) 46–81.

19. D. Henwood, *After the New Economy* (New York: New Press, 2003), 208.

20. L. Alvarez, 'Britain Says U.S. Planned to Seize Oil in '73 Crisis', *New York Times*, 4 Jan. 2004, A6. On the Saudi agreement to recycle petro-dollars through the US see P. Gowan, *The Global Gamble: Washington's Faustian Bid for World Dominance* (London: Verso, 1999), 20.

21. D. Harvey, *The New Imperialism* (Oxford: Oxford University Press, 2003); N. Smith, *American Empire, Roosevelt's Geographer and the Prelude to Globalization* (Berkeley: University of California Press, 2003); N. Smith, *The Endgame of Globalization* (New York: Routledge, 2005).

22. Panitch and Gindin, 'Finance and American Empire'.

23. The many debt crises of the 1980s are covered extensively in Gowan, *The Global Gamble*.

24. J. Stiglitz, *Globalization and its Discontents* (New York: Norton, 2002).

25. G. Duménil and D. Lévy, 'The Economics of U.S. Imperialism at the Turn of the 21st Century', *Review of International Political Economy*, 11/4 (2004), 657–76.

26. A. Chua, *World on Fire: How Exporting Free Market Democracy Breeds Ethnic Hatred and Global Instability* (New York: Doubleday, 2003), provides examples.

27. Cited in Harvey, *Condition of Postmodernity*, 158.

28. R. Martin, *The Financialization of Daily Life* (Philadelphia: Temple University Press, 2002).

29. This is the exclusive definition favoured in the works of Duménil and Lévy for example.

30. Chua, *World on Fire*.

31. United Nations Development Program, *Human Development Report, 1996* (New York: Oxford University Press, 1996), 2, and United Nations Development Program, *Human Development Report, 1999*, 3.

32. W. Robinson, *A Theory of Global Capitalism: Production, Class, and State in a Transnational World* (Baltimore: Johns Hopkins University Press, 2004), makes an outstanding case for this argument.

33. K. Polanyi, *The Great Transformation* (Boston: Beacon Press, 1954 edn.).

34. Ibid. 256–8.

35. Ibid.

36. Ibid.

37. Bush, 'Securing Freedom's Triumph'; see also F. Zakaria, *The Future of Freedom: Illiberal Democracy at Home and Abroad* (New York: Norton, 2003).

2. The Construction of Consent

1. A. Gramsci, *Selections from the Prison Notebooks*, trans. Q. Hoare and G. Nowell Smith (London: Lawrence & Wishart, 1971), 321–43.

2. J. Rapley, *Globalization and Inequality: Neoliberalism's Downward Spiral* (Boulder, Col.: Lynne Reiner, 2004), 55.

3. Gramsci, *Selections from the Prison Notebooks*, 149.

4. J. Court, *Corporateering: How Corporate Power Steals your Personal Freedom* (New York: J. P. Tarcher/Putnam, 2003), 33–8.

5. Blyth, *Great Transformations*, 155. The information in the preceding paragraph comes from chs. 5 and 6 of Blyth's account, supported by T. Edsall, *The New Politics of Inequality* (New York: Norton, 1985), chs, 2 and 3.

6. Court, *Corporateering*, 34.

7. W. Tabb, *The Long Default: New York City and the Urban Fiscal Crisis* (New York: Monthly Review Press, 1982); J. Freeman, *Working Class New York: Life and Labor Since World War II* (New York: New Press, 2001).

8. R. Zevin, 'New York City Crisis: First Act in a New Age of Reaction', in R. Alcalay and D. Mermelstein (eds.), *The Fiscal Crisis of American Cities: Essays on the Political Economy of Urban America with Special Reference to New York* (New York: Vintage Books, 1977), 11–29.

9. Tabb, *The Long Default*, 28. For Walter Wriston see T. Frank, *One Market Under God: Extreme Capitalism, Market Populism and the End of Economic Democracy* (New York: Doubleday, 2000), 53–6.

10. Freeman, *Working Class New York*.

11. R. Koolhaas, *Delirious New York* (New York: Monacelli Press, 1994); M. Greenberg, 'The Limits of Branding: The World Trade Center, Fiscal Crisis and the Marketing of Recovery', *International Journal of Urban and Regional Research*, 27 (2003), 386–416.

12. Tabb, *The Long Default*; On the subsequent 'selling' of New York see Greenberg, 'The Limits of Branding'; on urban entrepreneurialism more generally see D. Harvey, 'From Managerialism to Entrepreneurialism: The Transformation of Urban Governance in Late Capitalism', in id., *Spaces of Capital* (Edinburgh: Edinburgh University Press, 2001), ch. 16.

13. Tabb, *The Long Default*, 15.

14. Edsall, *The New Politics of Inequality*, 128.

15. Court, *Corporateering*, 29–31, lists all the relevant legal decisions of the 1970s.

16. The accounts of Edsall, *The New Politics of Inequality*, followed by Blyth, *Great Transformations*, are compelling.

17. Edsall, *The New Politics of Inequality*, 235.

18. T. Frank, *What's the Matter with Kansas: How Conservatives Won the Hearts of America* (New York: Metropolitan Books, 2004).

19. D. Kirkpatrick, 'Club of the Most Powerful Gathers in Strictest Privacy', *New York Times*, 28 Aug. 2004, A10.

20. See J. Stiglitz, *The Roaring Nineties* (New York: Norton, 2003).

21. Yergin and Stanislaw, *Commanding Heights*, 337; Stiglitz, *The Roaring Nineties*, 108.

22. Edsall, *The New Politics of Inequality*, 217.

23. Again, the account here rests heavily on Blyth, *Great Transformations*, and Edsall, *The New Politics of Inequality*.

24. M. Angell, *The Truth About the Drug Companies: How They Deceive Us and What To Do About It* (New York: Random House, 2004).

25. Blyth, *Great Transformations*; see also Frank, *One Market Under God*, particularly on the role of Gilder.

26. Edsall, *The New Politics of Inequality*, 107.

27. S. Hall, *Hard Road to Renewal: Thatcherism and the Crisis of the Left* (New York: Norton, 1988).

28. Yergin and Stanislaw, *Commanding Heights*, 92.

29. T. Benn, *The Benn Diaries, 1940–1990*, ed. R. Winstone (London: Arrow, 1996).

30. Yergin and Stanislaw, *Commanding Heights*, 104.

31. R. Brooks, 'Maggie's Man: We Were Wrong', *Observer*, 21 June 1992, 15; P. Hall, *Governing the Economy: The Politics of State Intervention in Britain and France* (Oxford: Oxford University Press, 1986); Fourcade-Gourinchas and Babb, 'The Rebirth of the Liberal Creed'.

32. T. Hayter and D. Harvey (eds.), *The Factory in the City* (Brighton: Mansell, 1995).

33. G. Rees and J. Lambert, *Cities in Crisis: The Political Economy of Urban Development in Post-War Britain* (London: Edward Arnold, 1985); M. Harloe, C. Pickvance, and J. Urry (eds.), *Place, Policy and Politics: Do Localities Matter?* (London: Unwin Hyman, 1990); M. Boddy and C. Fudge (eds.), *Local Socialism? Labour Councils and New Left Alternatives* (London: Macmillan, 1984).

34. Thatcher's failure to reach several of her macro-economic policy goals is well documented in P. Hall, *Governing the Economy*.

3. The Neoliberal State

1. Chang, *Globalisation*; B. Jessop, 'Liberalism, Neoliberalism, and Urban Governance: A State-Theoretical Perspective', *Antipode*, 34/3 (2002), 452–72; N. Poulantzas, *State Power Socialism*, trans. P. Camiller (London: Verso, 1978); S. Clarke (ed.), *The State Debate* (London: Macmillan, 1991); S. Haggard and R. Kaufman (eds.), *The Politics of Economic Adjustment: International Constraints, Distributive Conflicts and the State* (Princeton: Princeton University Press, 1992); M. Nozick, *Anarchy, State and Utopia* (New York: Basic Books, 1977).

2. Stiglitz, *The Roaring Nineties* won his Nobel Prize for his studies on how asymmetries of information affected market behaviours and outcomes.

3. See Harvey, *Condition of Postmodernity*; Harvey, *The Limits to Capital* (Oxford: Basil Blackwell, 1982).

4. P. Evans, *Embedded Autonomy: States and Industrial Transformation* (Princeton: Princeton University Press, 1995); R. Wade, *Governing the Market* (Princeton: Princeton University Press, 1992); M. Woo-Cummings (ed.), *The Developmental State* (Ithaca, NY: Cornell University Press, 1999).

5. J. Henderson, 'Uneven Crises: Institutional Foundation of East Asian Turmoil, *Economy and Society*, 28/3 (1999), 327–68.

6. Stiglitz, *The Roaring Nineties*, 227; P. Hall, *Governing the Economy*; Fourcade-Gourinchas and Babb, 'The Rebirth of the Liberal Creed'.

7. I. Vasquez, 'The Brady Plan and Market-Based Solutions to Debt Crises', *The Cato Journal*, 16/2 (online).

8. M. Piore and C. Sable, *The Second Industrial Divide: Possibilities for Prosperity* (New York: Basic Books, 1986).

9. See Harvey, *Condition of Postmodernity*.

10. V. Navarro (ed.), *The Political Economy of Social Inequalities: Consequences for Health and the Quality of Life* (Amityville, NY: Baywood, 2002).

11. P. McCarney and R. Stren, *Governance on the Ground: Innovations and Discontinuities in the Cities of the Developing World* (Princeton: Woodrow Wilson Center Press, 2003); A. Dixit, *Lawlessness and Economics: Alternative Modes of Governance* (Princeton: Princeton University Press, 2004).

12. R. Miliband, *The State in Capitalist Society* (New York: Basic Books, 1969).

13. N. Rosenblum and R. Post (eds.), *Civil Society and Government* (Princeton: Princeton University Press, 2001); S. Chambers and W. Kymlicka (eds.), *Alternative Conceptions of Civil Society* (Princeton: Princeton University Press, 2001).

14. K. Ohmae, *The End of the Nation State: The Rise of the Regional Economies* (New York: Touchstone Press, 1996).

15. Court, *Corporateering*.

16. D. Healy, *Let Them Eat Prozac: The Unhealthy Relationship Between the Pharmaceutical Industry and Depression* (New York: New York University Press, 2004).

17. W. Bello, N. Bullard, and K. Malhotra (eds.), *Global Finance: New Thinking on Regulating Speculative Markets* (London: Zed Books, 2000).

18. K. Schwab and C. Smadja, cited in D. Harvey, *Spaces of Hope* (Edinburgh: Edinburgh University Press, 2000), 70.

19. H. Wang, *China's New Order: Society, Politics and Economy in Transition* (Cambridge, Mass.: Harvard University Press, 2003), 44.

20. J. Mann, *The Rise of the Vulcans: The History of Bush's War Cabinet* (New

York: Viking Books, 2004); S. Drury, *Leo Strauss and the American Right* (New York: Palgrave Macmillan, 1999).

21. R. Hofstadter, *The Paranoid Style in American Politics and Other Essays* (Cambridge, Mass.: Harvard University Press, 1996 edn.).
22. Harvey, *The New Imperialism*, ch. 4.
23. Chang, *Globalisation*, 31.
24. M. Kaldor, *New and Old Wars: Organized Violence in a Global Era* (Cambridge: Polity, 1999), 130.
25. Frank, *What's the Matter with Kansas.*
26. Lee Kuan Yew, *From Third World to First: The Singapore Story, 1965–2000* (New York: HarperCollins, 2000).

4. Uneven Geographical Developments

1. Peck, 'Geography and Public Policy'.
2. World Bank, *World Development Report 2005: A Better Investment Climate for Everyone* (New York: Oxford University Press, 2004).
3. Gowan, *The Global Gamble.*
4. Duménil and Lévy, 'The Economics of US Imperialism'.
5. Stiglitz, *The Roaring Nineties.*
6. R. Brenner, *The Boom and the Bubble: The US in the World Economy* (London: Verso, 2002).
7. S. Corbridge, *Debt and Development* (Oxford: Blackwell, 1993).
8. Stiglitz, *Globalization and its Discontents*, 57.
9. Chua, *World on Fire.*
10. Henderson, 'Uneven Crises'; Stiglitz, *Globalization and its Discontents*, 99, concurs with this view: 'capital account liberalization was the single most important factor leading to the crisis'.
11. Stiglitz, *Globalization and its Discontents*, 129–30.
12. Ibid.
13. Vasquez, 'The Brady Plan'.
14. D. MacLeod, *Downsizing the State: Privatization and the Limits of Neoliberal Reform in Mexico* (University Park: Pennsylvania University Press, 2004).
15. C. Lomnitz-Adler, 'The Depreciation of Life During Mexico City's Transition into "The Crisis" ', in J. Schneider and I. Susser (eds.), *Wounded Cities* (New York: Berg, 2004) 47–70.
16. D. Davis, *Urban Leviathan: Mexico City in the Twentieth Century* (Philadelphia: Temple University Press, 1994).
17. MacLeod, *Downsizing the State*, 90–4.
18. Ibid. 71.
19. J. Nash, *Mayan Visions: The Quest for Autonomy in an Age of Globalization* (New York: Routledge, 2001).

20. J. Forero, 'As China Gallops, Mexico Sees Factory Jobs Slip Away', *New York Times*, 3 Sept. 2003, A3. 'Mexico, long the king of the low-cost plants and exporter to the United States . . . is fast being supplanted by China and its hundreds of millions of low wage workers . . . In all, 500 of Mexico's 3,700 maquiladoras have shut down since 2001, at a cost of 218,000 jobs, the Mexican government says.' Recent reports suggest that maquila employment has been recovering as industries have become more efficient and more flexible, able to use proximity to the US to ensure a steady flow of deliveries that permits retailers to minimize inventories. See E. Malkin, 'A Boom Along the Border', *New York Times*, 26 Aug. 2004, W1 and W7.

21. MacLeod, *Downsizing the State*, 99–100; Chua, *World on Fire*, 61–3, provides a brief account of the activities of Carlos Slim.

22. S. Sharapura, 'What Happened in Argentina?', *Chicago Business Online*, 28 May 2002, http://www.chibus.com/news/2002/05/28/ Worldview.

23. J. Petras and H. Veltmeyer, *System in Crisis: The Dynamics of Free Market Capitalism* (London: Zed Books, 2003), 87–110.

24. S. Soederberg, *Contesting Global Governance in the South: Debt, Class, and the New Common Sense in Managing Globalisation* (London: Pluto Press, 2005).

25. J. Salerno, 'Confiscatory Deflation: The Case of Argentina', Ludwig von Mise Institute, http://www.mises.org?fullstory.aspx?control=890.

26. Petras and Veltmeyer, *System in Crisis*, 86.

27. V. Chibber, *Locked in Place: State-Building and Late Industrialization in India* (Princeton: Princeton University Press, 2003).

28. Ibid. 245.

29. R. Wade and F. Veneroso, 'The Asian Crisis: The High Debt Model versus the Wall Street–Treasury–IMF Complex', *New Left Review*, 228 (1998), 3–23.

30. M. Woo-Cummings, *South Korean Anti-Americanism*, Japan Policy Research Institute Working Paper 93 (July 2003).

31. Ibid. 5.

32. Stiglitz, *Globalization and its Discontents*.

33. Ibid. 130.

34. Woo-Cummings, *South Korean Anti-Americanism*, 4.

35. Stiglitz, *Globalization and its Discontents*, 130, 206–7.

36. Blyth, *Great Transformations*, 205.

37. Ibid. 238–42.

38. Ibid. 229–30.

39. Ibid. 231–3.

40. P. Bond, *Elite Transition: From Apartheid to Neoliberalism in South Africa* (London: Pluto Press, 2000); id., *Against Global Apartheid: South Africa*

Meets the World Bank, the IMF and International Finance (London: Zed Books, 2003)

41. World Bank, *World Development Report 2005*.

42. Stiglitz, *Globalization and its Discontents*, frequently returns to this point.

43. J. Mittelman, *The Globalization Syndrome: Transformation and Resistance* (Princeton: Princeton University Press, 2000), 90–106.

5. Neoliberalism 'with Chinese Characteristics'

1. N. Lardy, *China's Unfinished Economic Revolution* (Wasington, DC: Brookings Institution, 1998); S.-M. Li and W.-S. Tang, *China's Regions, Polity and Economy* (Hong Kong: Chinese University Press, 2000),

2. I lean somewhat to the latter interpretation, though not quite as strongly as Hart-Landsberg and Burkett, whose work I rely on here quite extensively. See M. Hart-Landsberg and P. Burkett, *China and Socialism: Market Reforms and Class Struggle* (New York, 2004; = *Monthly Review*, 56/3).

3. L. Cao, 'Chinese Privatization: Between Plan and Market', *Law and Contemporary Problems*, 63/13 (2000), 13–62.

4. This point is emphatically made in Y. Huang, 'Is China Playing by the Rules?', *Congressional-Executive Commission on China*, http://www.cecc.gov/pages/hearings/092403/huang.php.

5. Wang, *China's New Order*, 66.

6. D. Hale and L. Hale, 'China Takes Off', *Foreign Affairs*, 82/6 (2003), 36–53.

7. J. Kahn and J. Yardley, 'Amid China's Boom, No Helping Hand for Young Qingming, *New York Times*, 1 Aug. 2004, A1 and A6.

8. J. Yardley, 'In a Tidal Wave, China's Masses Pour from Farm to City', *New York Times*, Sept. 12, 2004, Week in Review, 6.

9. Kahn and Yardley, 'Amid China's Boom'.

10. C. Stevenson, *Reforming State-Owned Enterprises: Past Lessons for Current Problems* (Washington, DC: George Washington University), http:www.gwu.edu/~ylowrey/stevensonc.html.

11. Hart-Landsberg and Burkett, *China and Socialism*, 35; Li and Tang, *China's Regions*.

12. Hart-Landsberg and Burkett, *China and Socialism*, 38.

13. See ibid., and Global Policy Forum, *Newsletter* 'China's Privatization', http:www.globalpolicy.org.socecon/ffd/fdi/2003/1112chinaprivatization.

14. Li and Tang, *China's Regions*, ch. 6.

15. Ibid. 82.

16. China Labor Watch, 'Mainland China Jobless Situation Grim, Minister Says', http://www.chinalaborwatch.org/en/web/article.php?article_id=50043, 18 Nov. 2004.

17. J. Kahn, 'China Gambles on Big Projects for its Stability', *New York Times*, 13 Jan. 2003, A1 and A8; K. Bradsher, 'Chinese Builders Buy Abroad', *New York Times*, 2 Dec. 2003, W1 and W7; T. Fishman, 'The Chinese Century', *New York Times Magazine*, 4 July 2004, 24–51.

18. H. French, 'New Boomtowns Change Path of China's Growth', *New York Times*, 28 July 2004, A1 and A8.

19. K. Bradsher, 'Big China Trade Brings Port War', *International Herald Tribune*, 27 Jan. 2003, 12.

20. S. Sharma, 'Stability Amidst Turmoil: China and the Asian Financial Crisis', *Asia Quarterly* (Winter 2000), www.fas.harvard.edu/~asiactr/haq/2000001/0001a006.htm.

21. Hale and Hale, 'China Takes Off', 40.

22. H. Liu, 'China: Banking on Bank Reform', *Asia Times Online*, atimes.com, 1 June 2002.

23. K. Bradsher, 'A Heated Chinese Economy Piles up Debt', *New York Times*, 4 Sept. 2003, A1 and C4; K. Bradsher, 'China Announces New Bailout of Big Banks', *New York Times*, 7 Jan. 2004, C1.

24. Liu, 'China: Banking on Bank Reform'.

25. C. Buckley, 'Let a Thousand Ideas Flower: China Is a New Hotbed of Research', *New York Times*, 13 Sept. 2004, C1 and C4.

26. J. Warner, 'Why the World's Economy is Stuck on a Fast Boat to China', *The Independent*, Jan. 24, 2004, 23.

27. C. Buckley, 'Rapid Growth of China's Huawei Has its High-Tech Rivals on Guard', *New York Times*, 6 Oct. 2003, C1 and C3.

28. K. Bradsher, 'GM To Speed Up Expansion in China: An Annual Goal of 1.3 Million Cars', *New York Times*, 8 June 2004, W1 and W7.

29. Z. Zhang, *Whither China? Intellectual Politics in Contemporary China* (Durham, NC: Duke University Press, 2001).

30. K. Bradsher, 'China's Factories Aim to Fill Garages Around the World', *New York Times*, 2 Nov. 2003, International Section, 8; id., 'GM To Speed Up Expansion in China'; id., 'Is China The Next Bubble?', *New York Times*, 18 Jan. 2004, sect. 3, 1 and 4.

31. K. Bradsher, 'Chinese Provinces Form Regional Power Bloc', *New York Times*, 2 June 2004, W1 and W7.

32. H. Yasheng and T. Khanna 'Can India Overtake China?', *China Now Magazine*, 3 Apr. 2004, www.chinanowmag.com/business/business.htm.

33. P. Dicken, *Global Shift: Reshaping the Global Economic Map in the 21st Century*, 4th edn. (New York: Guilford Press, 2003), 332.

34. T. Hout and J. Lebretton, 'The Real Contest Between America and China', *The Wall Street Journal on Line*, 16 Sept. 2003; interestingly, this is exactly the point that Marx makes about the differential application of technology between the US and Britain in the nineteenth century: see *Capital* (New York: International Publishers, 1967), i. 371–2.

35. See Hart-Landsberg and Burkett, *China and Socialism*, 94–5; K. Brooke, 'Korea Feeling Pressure as China Grows', *New York Times*, 8 Jan. 2003, W1 and W7.

36. J. Belson, 'Japanese Capital and Jobs Flowing to China', *New York Times*, 17 Feb. 2004, C1 and C4.

37. See Forero, 'As China Gallops'.

38. K. Bradsher, 'China Reports Economic Growth of 9.1% in 2003', *New York Times*, 20 Feb. 2004, W1 and W7.

39. K. Bradsher, 'Taiwan Watches its Economy Slip to China', *New York Times*, 13 Dec. 2004, C7.

40. W. Arnold, 'BHP Billiton Remains Upbeat Over Bet on China's Growth', *New York Times*, 8 June 2004, W1 and W7.

41. M. Landler, 'Hungary Eager and Uneasy Over New Status', *New York Times*, 5 Mar. 2004, W1 and W7; K. Bradsher, 'Chinese Automaker Plans Assembly Line in Malaysia', *New York Times*, 19 Oct. 2004, W1 and W7.

42. K. Bradsher, 'China's Strange Hybrid Economy', *New York Times*, 21 Dec. 2003, C5.

43. Volcker's remarks are cited in P. Bond, 'US and Global Economic Volatility: Theoretical, Empirical and Political Considerations', paper presented to the Empire Seminar, York University, Nov. 2004.

44. Wang, *China's New Order*; T. Fishman, *China Inc.: How the Rise of the Next Superpower Challenges America and the World* (New York: Scribner, 2005).

45. K. Bradsher, 'Now, a Great Leap Forward in Luxury', *New York Times*, 10 June 2004, C1 and C6.

46. X. Wu and J. Perloff, *China's Income Distribution Over Time: Reasons for Rising Inequality*, CUDARE Working Papers 977 (Berkeley: University of California at Berkeley, 2004).

47. Wang, *China's New Order*.

48. L. Wei, *Regional Development in China* (New York: Routledge/Curzon, 2000).

49. L. Shi, 'Current Conditions of China's Working Class', *China Study Group*, 3 Nov. 2003, http://www.chinastudygroup.org/index.php?action=article&type.

50. China Labor Watch, 'Mainland China Jobless Situation Grim'.

51. Shi, 'Current Conditions of China's Working Class'.

52. D. Barboza, 'An Unknown Giant Flexes its Muscles', *New York Times*, 4 Dec. 2004, C1 and C3; S. Lohr, 'IBM's Sale of PC Unit Is a Bridge Between Companies and Cultures', *New York Times*, 8 Dec. 2004, A1 and C4; S. Lohr, 'IBM Sought a China Partnership, Not Just a Sale', *New York Times*, 13 Dec. 2004, C1 and C6.

53. Wang, *China's New Order*; J. Yardley, 'Farmers Being Moved Aside by China's Real Estate Boom', *New York Times*, 8 Dec. 2004, A1 and A16.

54. C. Cartier, 'Zone Fever. The Arable Land Debate and Real Estate Speculation: China's Evolving Land Use Regime and its Geographical Contradictions', *Journal of Contemporary China*, 10 (2001), 455–69; Z. Zhang,
*Strangers in the City: Reconfigurations of Space, Power, and Social Net-
works within China's Floating Population* (Stanford: Stanford University
Press, 2001).

55. C. Cartier, 'Symbolic City/Regions and Gendered Identity Formation in
South China', *Provincial China*, 8/1 (2003), 60–77; Z. Zhang, 'Mediating
Time: The "Rice Bowl of Youth" in Fin-de-Siècle Urban China', *Public
Culture*, 12/1 (2000), 93–113.

56. S. K. Lee, 'Made In China: Labor as a Political Force?', panel statement,
2004 Mansfield conference, University of Montana, Missoula, 18–20
Apr. 2004.

57. Ibid.; J. Yardley, 'Chinese Appeal to Beijing to Resolve Local
Complaints', *New York Times*, 8 Mar. 2004, A3.

58. E. Rosenthal, 'Workers Plight Brings New Militancy in China', *New
York Times*, 10 Mar. 2003, A8.

59. E. Cody, 'Workers in China Shed Passivity: Spate of Walkouts Shakes
Factories', *Washington Post*, 27 Nov. 2004, A01; A.Cheng 'Labor Unrest
is Growing in China', *International Herald Tribune Online*, Oct. 27, 2004;
Yardley, 'Farmers Being Moved Aside'.

60. Lee, 'Made In China'.

61. Cited in Cody, 'Workers in China Shed Passivity'; see also various issues
of the *China Labor Bulletin*.

62. Cody, 'Workers in China'.

6. Neoliberalism on Trial

1. Marx, *Theories of Surplus Value*, pt. 2, (London: Lawrence & Wishart,
1969), 200.

2. J. Gray, *False Dawn: The Illusions of Global Capitalism* (London: Granta
Press, 1998).

3. Bond, 'US and Global Economic Volatility'.

4. The two best official assessments can be found in World Commission on
the Social Dimension of Globalization, *A Fair Globalization: Creating
Opportunities for All* (Geneva, International Labour Office, 2004); United
Nations Development Program, *Human Development Report, 1999;
Human Development Report, 2003*.

5. M. Weisbrot, D. Baker, E. Kraev, and J. Chen, 'The Scorecard on
Globalization 1980–2000: Its Consequences for Economic and Social
Well-Being', in V. Navarro and C. Muntaner, *Political and Economic
Determinants of Population Health and Well-Being* (Amityville, NY:
Baywood, 2004) 91–114.

6. G. Monbiot, 'Punitive—and It Works', *Guardian*, 11 Jan. 2005, online edition.

7. Henwood, *After the New Economy*; Duménil and Lévy, *Capital Resurgent*, fig. 17.1.

8. The literature on globalization is immense. My own views were spelled out in Harvey, *Spaces of Hope*.

9. Ibid., ch. 4.

10. M. Derthick and P. Quirk, *The Politics of Deregulation* (Washington, DC: Brookings Institution Press, 1985); W. Megginson and J. Netter, 'From State to Market: A Survey of Empirical Studies of Privatization', *Journal of Economic Lite*rature (2001), online.

11. Dicken, *Global Shift*, ch. 13.

12. The importance of spreading risks and assuming leadership through financial derivatives is stressed in Panitch and Gindin, 'Finance and American Empire'; S. Soederberg, 'The New International Financial Architecture: Imposed Leadership and "Emerging Markets" ', *Socialist Register* (2002), 175–92.

13. Corbridge, *Debt and Development*; S. George, *A Fate Worse Than Debt* (New York: Grove Press, 1988).

14. E. Toussaint, *Your Money or Your Life: The Tyranny of Global Finance* (London: Pluto Press, 2003); Stiglitz, *Globalization and its Discontents*, 225; Wade and Veneroso, 'The Asian Crisis', 21.

15. J. Farah, 'Brute Tyranny in China', WorldNetDaily.com, posted 15 Mar. 2004; I. Peterson, 'As Land Goes To Revitalization, There Go the Old Neighbors', *New York Times*, 30 Jan. 2005, 29 and 32.

16. J. Holloway and E. Pelaez, *Zapatista: Reinventing Revolution* (London: Pluto, 1998); J. Stedile, 'Brazil's Landless Battalions', in T. Mertes (ed.), *A Movement of Movements* (London: Verso, 2004).

17. D. Harvey, 'The Art of Rent: Globalization, Monopoly and the Commodification of Culture', *Socialist Register* (2002), 93–110.

18. Polanyi, *The Great Transformation*, 73.

19. K. Bales, *Disposable People: New Slavery in the Global Economy* (Berkeley: University of California Press, 2000); M. Wright, 'The Dialectics of Still Life: Murder, Women and the Maquiladoras', *Public Culture*, 11 (1999), 453–74.

20. A. Ross, *Low Pay High Profile: The Global Push for Fair Labor* (New York: The New Press, 2004), 124.

21. J. Seabrook, *In the Cities of the South: Scenes from a Developing World* (London: Verso, 1996), 103.

22. J. Sommer, 'A Dragon Let Loose on the Land: And Shanghai is at the Epicenter of China's Economic Boom', *Japan Times*, 26 Oct. 1994, 3.

23. C. K. Lee, *Gender and the South China Miracle* (Berkeley: University of

California Press, 1998); C. Cartier, *Globalizing South China* (Oxford: Basil Blackwell, 2001), particularly ch. 6.

24. The global impacts are discussed in detail in Navarro, *The Political Economy of Social Inequalities*; Navarro and Muntaner, *Political and Economic Determinants*.

25. J. Kahn, 'Violence Taints Religion's Solace for China's Poor', *New York Times*, 25 Nov. 2004, A1 and A24.

26. Frank, *What's the Matter with Kansas*.

27. N. Myers, *Ultimate Security: The Environmental Basis of Political Stability* (New York: Norton, 1993); id., *The Primary Resource: Tropical Forests and Our Future/Updated for the 1990s* (New York: Norton, 1993); M. Novacek (ed.), *The Biodiversity Crisis: Losing What Counts* (New York: American Museum of Natural History, 2001).

28. Climate Change Science Program, 'Our Changing Planet: The US Climate Change Science Program for Fiscal Years 2004 and 2005', http://www.usgcrp.gov/usgcrp/Library/ocp2004–5; M. Townsend and P. Harris, 'Now the Pentagon Tells Bush: Climate Change Will Destroy Us', *Observer*, 22 Feb. 2004, online.

29. K. Bradsher, 'China's Boom Adds to Global Warming', *New York Times*, 22 Oct. 2003, A1 and A8; J. Yardley, 'Rivers Run Black, and Chinese Die of Cancer', *New York Times*, 12 Sept. 2004, A1 and A17; D. Murphy, 'Chinese Province: Stinking, Filthy, Rich', *Wall Street Journal*, 27 Oct. 2004, B2H.

30. Petras and Veltmeyer, *System in Crisis*, ch. 6.

31. American Lands Alliance, 'IMF Policies Lead to Global Deforestation', http://americanlands.org/imfreport.htm.

32. D. Rodrik, *The Global Governance of Trade: As If Development Really Mattered* (New York, United Nations Development Program, 2001), 9.

33. D. Chandler, *From Kosovo to Kabul: Human Rights and International Intervention* (London: Pluto Press, 2002), 89.

34. Ibid. 230.

35. T. Wallace, 'NGO Dilemmas: Trojan Horses for Global Neoliberalism?', *Socialist Register* (2003), 202–19. For a general survey of the role of NGOs see M. Edwards and D. Hulme (eds.), *Non-Governmental Organisations: Performance and Accountability* (London: Earthscan, 1995).

36. L. Gill, *Teetering on the Rim* (New York: Columbia University Press, 2000); J. Cowan, M.-B. Dembour, and R. Wilson (eds.), *Culture and Rights: Anthropological Perspectives* (Cambridge: Cambridge University Press, 2001).

37. A. Bartholomew and J. Breakspear, 'Human Rights as Swords of Empire', *Socialist Register* (London: Merlin Press, 2003), 124–45.

38. Ibid. 126.

39. Chandler, *From Kosovo to Kabul*, 27, 218.

40. Ibid. 235.
41. Marx, *Capital*, i. 225.
42. D. Harvey, 'The Right to the City', in R. Scholar (ed.), *Divided Cities: Oxford Amnesty Lectures 2003* (Oxford, Oxford University Press, forthcoming).
43. Harvey, *The New Imperialism*, ch. 2.

7. Freedom's Prospect

1. Cited in Vicente Navarro's insightful critique of Sen: 'Development as Quality of Life: A Critique of Amartya Sen's *Development as Freedom*', in Navarro (ed.), *The Political Economy of Social Inequalities* 13–26.
2. Polanyi, *The Great Transformation*, 257.
3. Zakaria, *The Future of Freedom*; A. Sen, *Development as Freedom* (New York: Knopf, 1999).
4. Marx, *Capital*, iii. 820.
5. R. Kaplan, *The Coming Anarchy: Shattering the Dreams of the Post Cold War* (New York: Vintage, 2001).
6. J. Walton, 'Urban Protest and the Global Political Economy: The IMF Riots', in M. Smith and J. Feagin (eds.), *The Capitalist City* (Oxford: Blackwell, 1987) 354–86.
7. D. Jensen, *The Culture of Make Believe* (New York: Context Books, 2002); J. Zergan, *Future Primitive and Other Essays* (Brooklyn, NY: Autonomedia, 1994).
8. Kahn, 'Violence Taints Religion's Solace for China's Poor'.
9. B. Gills (ed.), *Globalization and the Politics of Resistance* (New York: Palgrave, 2001); T. Mertes (ed.), *A Movement of Movements* (London: Verso, 2004); P. Wignaraja (ed.), *New Social Movements in the South: Empowering the People* (London: Zed Books, 1993); J. Brecher, T. Costello, and B. Smith, *Globalization from Below: The Power of Solidarity* (Cambridge, Mass.: South End Press, 2000).
10. Stiglitz, *Globalization and its Discontents*, and *The Roaring Nineties*; P. Krugman, *The Great Unravelling: Losing Our Way in the Twentieth Century* (New York: Norton, 2003). G. Soros, *George Soros on Globalization* (New York: Public Affairs, 2002); id., *The Bubble of American Supremacy: Correcting the Misuse of American Power* (New York: Public Affairs, 2003); J. Sachs, 'New Global Consensus on Helping the Poorest of the Poor', *Global Policy Forum Newsletter*, 18 Apr. 2000. Says Sachs, for example, 'I do not believe in global governance by the rich countries, or international voting weighted by money as in the IMF and the World Bank today, or permanent government by entrenched bureaucracies unencumbered by external review as has been true of the IMF, or governance by conditionality set by rich countries and imposed on the desperately poor.'

11. I cite just two: United Nations Development Program, *Human Development Report 1999*; World Commission on the Social Dimension of Globalization, *A Fair Globalization*.

12. D. Held, *Global Covenant: The Social Democratic Alternative to the Washington Consensus* (Cambridge: Polity, 2004); I reviewed some of the dilemmas of application of the cosmopolitan ethic in D. Harvey, 'Cosmopolitanism and the Banality of Geographical Evils', in J. Comaroff and J. Comaroff, *Millennial Capitalism and the Culture of Neoliberalism* (Durham, NC: Duke University Press, 2000) 271–310.

13. For Volcker see Bond, 'US and Global Economic Volatility'; M. Muhleisen and C. Towe (eds.), *US Fiscal Policies and Priorities for Long-Run Sustainability*, Occasional Paper 227 (Washington, DC: International Monetary Fund, 2004).

14. Duménil and Lévy, 'Neoliberal Dynamics'.

15. Harvey, *Condition of Postmodernity*, 169.

16. H. Arendt, *Imperialism* (New York: Harcourt Brace Janovich, 1968 edn.); Harvey, *The New Imperialism*, 12–17.

17. D. King, *The Liberty of Strangers: Making the American Nation* (New York: Oxford University Press, 2004).

18. G. Arrighi and B. Silver, *Chaos and Governance in the Modern World System* (Minneapolis: Minnesota University Press, 1999); see also the Afterword to the paperback edition of Harvey, *The New Imperialism* (Oxford: Oxford University Press, 2005).

19. Cited in Harvey, *Condition of Postmodernity*, 168–70.

20. S. Amin, 'Social Movements at the Periphery', in Wignaraja (ed.), *New Social Movements in the South*, 76–100.

21. W. Bello, *Deglobalization: Ideas for a New World Economy* (London: Zed Books, 2002); Bello, Bullard, and Malhotra (eds.), *Global Finance*; S. George, *Another World is Possible IF . . .* (London: Verso, 2003); W. Fisher and T. Ponniah (eds.), *Another World is Possible: Popular Alternatives to Globalization at the World Social Forum* (London: Zed Books, 2003); P. Bond, *Talk Left Walk Right: South Africa's Frustrated Global Reforms* (Scottsville, South Africa: University of KwaZulu-Natal Press, 2004); Mertes, *A Movement of Movements*; Gill, *Teetering on the Rim*; Brecher, Costello, and Smith, *Globalization from Below*.

22. Harvey, *Spaces of Hope*, 248–52.

23. Task Force on Inequality and American Democracy, *American Democracy in an Age of Rising Inequality*, paints a disturbing picture.

24. This is the argument to which Wang, *China's New Order*, frequently returns in the case of China, for example.

Bibliography

Press Comment and Web Sources

Alvarez, L., 'Britain Says U.S. Planned to Seize Oil in '73 Crisis', *New York Times*, 4 Jan. 2004, A6.

American Lands Alliance, 'IMF Policies Lead to Global Deforestation', http://americanlands.org/imfreport.htm.

Arnold, W., 'BHP Billiton Remains Upbeat Over Bet on China's Growth', *New York Times*, 8 June 2004, W1 and W7.

Barboza, D., 'An Unknown Giant Flexes its Muscles', *New York Times*, 4 Dec. 2004, C1 and C3.

Belson, J., 'Japanese Capital and Jobs Flowing to China', *New York Times*, 17 Feb. 2004, C1 and C4.

Bradsher, K., 'Big China Trade Brings Port War', *International Herald Tribune*, 27 Jan. 2003, 12.

—— 'China Announces New Bailout of Big Banks', *New York Times*, 7 Jan. 2004, C1.

—— 'China Reports Economic Growth of 9.1% in 2003', *New York Times*, 20 Feb. 2004, W1 and W7.

—— 'China's Boom Adds to Global Warming', *New York Times*, 22 Oct. 2003, A1 and A8.

—— 'China's Factories Aim to Fill Garages Around the World', *New York Times*, 2 Nov. 2003, International Section, 8.

—— 'China's Strange Hybrid Economy', *New York Times*, 21 Dec. 2003, C5.

—— 'Chinese Automaker Plans Assembly Line in Malaysia', *New York Times*, 19 Oct. 2004, W1 and W7.

—— 'Chinese Builders Buy Abroad', *New York Times*, 2 Dec. 2003, W1 and W7.

—— 'Chinese Provinces Form Regional Power Bloc', *New York Times*, 2 June 2004, W1 and W7.

—— 'GM To Speed Up Expansion in China: An Annual Goal of 1.3 Million Cars', *New York Times*, 8 June 2004, W1 and W7.

—— 'A Heated Chinese Economy Piles up Debt', *New York Times*, 4 Sept. 2003, A1 and C4.

Bibliography

Bradsher, K., 'Is China the Next Bubble?' *New York Times*, 18 Jan. 2004, sect. 3, 1 and 4.

—— 'Now, a Great Leap Forward in Luxury', *New York Times*, 10 June 2004, C1 and C6.

—— 'Taiwan Watches its Economy Slip to China', *New York Times*, 13 Dec. 2004, C7.

Brooke, K., 'Korea Feeling Pressure as China Grows', *New York Times*, 8 Jan 2003, W1 and W7.

Brooks, R., 'Maggie's Man: We Were Wrong', *Observer*, 21 June 1992, 15.

Buckley, C., 'Let a Thousand Ideas Flower: China Is a New Hotbed of Research', *New York Times*, 13 Sept. 2004, C1 and C4.

—— 'Rapid Growth of China's Huawei Has its High-Tech Rivals on Guard,' *New York Times*, 6 Oct. 2003, C1 and C3.

Bush, G. W., 'President Addresses the Nation in Prime Time Press Conference', 13 Apr. 2004, http://www.whitehouse.gov/news/releases/2004/0420040413–20.html.

—— 'Securing Freedom's Triumph', *New York Times*, 11 Sept. 2002, A33.

Cheng, A., 'Labor Unrest is Growing in China', *International Herald Tribune Online*, 27 Oct. 2004.

China Labor Watch, 'Mainland China Jobless Situation Grim, Minister Says', http://www.chinalaborwatch.org/en/web/article.php?article_id=50043 (18 Nov. 2004).

Climate Change Science Program, 'Our Changing Planet: The US Climate Change Science Program for Fiscal Years 2004 and 2005', http://www.usgcrp.gov/usgcrp/Library/ocp2004–5.

Cody, E., 'Workers in China Shed Passivity: Spate of Walkouts Shakes Factories', *Washington Post*, 27 Nov. 2004, A01.

Crampton, T., 'Iraqi Official Urges Caution on Imposing Free Market', *New York Times*, 14 Oct. 2003, C5.

Farah, J., 'Brute Tyranny in China' WorldNetDaily.com, posted 15 Mar. 2004.

Fishman, T., 'The Chinese Century', *New York Times Magazine*, 4 July 2004, 24–51.

Forero, J., 'As China Gallops, Mexico Sees Factory Jobs Slip Away', *New York Times*, 3 Sept. 2003, A3.

French, H., 'New Boomtowns Change Path of China's Growth', *New York Times*, 28 July 2004, A1 and A8.

Global Policy Forum, *Newsletter* 'China's Privatization', http:www.globalpolicy.org.socecon/ffd/fdi/2003/1112chinaprivatization.

Hout, T., and Lebretton, J., 'The Real Contest Between America and China', *The Wall Street Journal on Line*, 16 Sept. 2003.

Huang, Y. 'Is China Playing by the Rules?', *Congressional-Executive Commission on China*, http://www.cecc.gov/pages/hearings/092403/huang.php.

Bibliography

Kahn, J., and Yardley, J., 'Amid China's Boom, No Helping Hand for Young Qingming, *New York Times*, 1 Aug. 2004, A1 and A6.

—— 'China Gambles on Big Projects for its Stability, *New York Times*, 13 Jan. 2003, A1 and A8.

—— 'Violence Taints Religion's Solace for China's Poor', *New York Times*, 25 Nov. 2004, A1 and A24.

Kirkpatrick, D., 'Club of the Most Powerful Gathers in Strictest Privacy', *New York Times*, 28 Aug. 2004, A10.

Klein, N., 'Of Course the White House Fears Free Elections in Iraq', *Guardian*, 24 Jan. 2004, 18.

Landler, M., 'Hungary Eager and Uneasy Over New Status', *New York Times*, 5 Mar. 2004, W1 and W7.

Liu, H., 'China: Banking on Bank Reform, *Asia Times Online*, atimes.com, 1 June 2002.

Liu Shi, 'Current Conditions of China's Working Class', *China Study Group*, 3 Nov. 2003, http://www.chinastudygroup.org/index.php?action=article&type.

Lohr, S., 'IBM Sought a China Partnership, Not Just a Sale', *New York Times*, 13 Dec. 2004, C1 and C6.

—— 'IBM's Sale of PC Unit Is a Bridge Between Companies and Cultures', *New York Times*, 8 Dec. 2004, A1 and C4.

Malkin, E., 'A Boom Along the Border', *New York Times*, 26 Aug. 2004, W1 and W7.

Monbiot, G., 'Punitive—and It Works', *Guardian*, 11 Jan. 2005, online edition.

Montpelerin website, http://www.montpelerin.org/aboutmps.html.

Murphy, D., 'Chinese Province: Stinking, Filthy, Rich', *Wall Street Journal*, 27 Oct. 2004, B2H.

National Security Strategy of the United State of America website: www.whitehouse.gov/nsc/nss.

Peterson, I., 'As Land Goes To Revitalization, There Go the Old Neighbors', *New York Times*, 30 Jan. 2005, 29 and 32.

Rosenthal, E., 'Workers Plight Brings New Militancy in China', *New York Times*, 10 Mar. 2003, A8.

Salerno, J., 'Confiscatory Deflation: The Case of Argentina', Ludwig von Mise Institute, http://www.mises.org?fullstory.aspx?control=890.

Sharapura, S., 'What Happened in Argentina?', *Chicago Business Online*, 28 May 2002, http://www.chibus.com/news/2002/05/28/Worldview.

Sharma, S., 'Stability Amidst Turmoil: China and the Asian Financial Crisis, *Asia Quarterly* (Winter 2000), www.fas.harvard.edu/~asiactr/haq/2000001/0001a006.htm.

Shi, L., 'Current Conditions of China's Working Class', *China Study Group*, 3 Nov. 2003, http://www.chinastudygroup.org/index.php?action=article&type.

Bibliography

Sommer, J., 'A Dragon Let Loose on the Land: And Shanghai is at the Epicenter of China's Economic Boom', *Japan Times*, 26 Oct. 1994, 3.

Stevenson, C., *Reforming State-Owned Enterprises: Past Lessons for Current Problems* (Washington, DC: George Washington University), http:www.gwu.edu/~ylowrey/stevensonc.httml.

Townsend, M., and Harris, P., 'Now the Pentagon Tells Bush: Climate Change Will Destroy Us', *Observer*, 22 Feb. 2004, online.

Treanor, P., 'Neoliberalism: Origins, Theory, Definition', http://web.inter.nl.net/users/Paul.Treanor/neoliberalism.html.

Warner, J., 'Why the World's Economy Is Stuck on a Fast Boat to China', *Independent*, 24 Jan. 2004, 23.

Yardley, J., 'Chinese Appeal to Beijing to Resolve Local Complaints', *New York Times*, 8 Mar. 2004, A3.

—— 'Farmers Being Moved Aside by China's Real Estate Boom', *New York Times*, 8 Dec. 2004, A1 and A16.

—— 'In a Tidal Wave, China's Masses Pour from Farm to City', *New York Times*, 12 Sept. 2004, 'Week in Review', 6.

—— 'Rivers Run Black, and Chinese Die of Cancer', *New York Times*, 12 Sept. 2004, A1 and A17.

Yasheng, H., and Khanna, T., 'Can India Overtake China?', *China Now Magazine*, 3 Apr. 2004, www.chinanowmag.com/business/business.htm.

Books and Journal Articles

Amin, S., 'Social Movements at the Periphery', in P. Wignaraja (ed.), *New Social Movements in the South: Empowering the People* (London: Zed Books, 1993), 76–100.

Angell, M., *The Truth About the Drug Companies: How They Deceive Us and What To Do About It* (New York: Random House, 2004).

Arendt, H., *Imperialism* (New York: Harcourt Brace Janovich, 1968).

Armstrong, A., Glynn, A., and Harrison, J., *Capitalism Since World War II: The Making and Breaking of the Long Boom* (Oxford: Basil Blackwell, 1991).

Arrighi, G., and Silver, B., *Chaos and Governance in the Modern World System* (Minneapolis: Minnesota University Press, 1999).

Bales, K., *Disposable People: New Slavery in the Global Economy* (Berkeley: University of California Press, 2000).

Bartholomew, A., and Breakspear, J., 'Human Rights as Swords of Empire', *Socialist Register* (London: Merlin Press, 2003), 124–45.

Bello, W., *Deglobalization: Ideas for a New World Economy* (London: Zed Books, 2002).

—— Bullard, N., and Malhotra, K. (eds.), *Global Finance: New Thinking on Regulating Speculative Markets* (London: Zed Books, 2000).

Bibliography

Benn, T., *The Benn Diaries, 1940–1990*, ed. R. Winstone (London: Arrow, 1996).

Blyth, M., *Great Transformations: Economic Ideas and Institutional Change in the Twentieth Century* (Cambridge: Cambridge University Press, 2002).

Boddy, M., and Fudge, C. (eds.), *Local Socialism? Labour Councils and New Left Alternatives* (London: Macmillan, 1984).

Bond, P., *Against Global Apartheid: South Africa Meets the World Bank, the IMF and International Finance* (London: Zed Books, 2003)

—— *Elite Transition: From Apartheid to Neoliberalism in South Africa* (London: Pluto Press, 2000).

—— *Talk Left Walk Right: South Africa's Frustrated Global Reforms* (Scottsville, South Africa: University of KwaZulu-Natal Press, 2004).

—— 'US and Global Economic Volatility: Theoretical, Empirical and Political Considerations', paper presented to the Empire Seminar, York University, November 2004.

Brecher, J., Costello, T., and Smith, B., *Globalization from Below: The Power of Solidarity* (Cambridge, Mass.: South End Press, 2000).

Brenner, R., *The Boom and the Bubble: The US in the World Economy* (London: Verso, 2002).

Cao, L., 'Chinese Privatization: Between Plan and Market', *Law and Contemporary Problems*, 63/13 (2000), 13–62.

Cartier, C., *Globalizing South China* (Oxford: Basil Blackwell, 2001).

—— 'Symbolic City/Regions and Gendered Identity Formation in South China', *Provincial China*, 8/1 (2003), 60–77.

—— 'Zone Fever. The Arable Land Debate and Real Estate Speculation: China's Evolving Land Use Regime and its Geographical Contradictions', *Journal of Contemporary China*, 10 (2001), 455–69.

Chambers, S., and Kymlicka, W. (eds.), *Alternative Conceptions of Civil Society* (Princeton: Princeton University Press, 2001).

Chandler, D., *From Kosovo to Kabul: Human Rights and International Intervention* (London: Pluto Press, 2002).

Chang, H.-J., *Globalisation, Economic Development and the Role of the State* (London: Zed Books, 2003).

Chibber, V., *Locked in Place: State-Building and Late Industrialization in India* (Princeton: Princeton University Press, 2003).

Chua, A., *World on Fire: How Exporting Free Market Democracy Breeds Ethnic Hatred and Global Instability* (New York: Doubleday, 2003).

Clarke, S. (ed.), *The State Debate* (London: Macmillan, 1991).

Corbridge, S., *Debt and Development* (Oxford: Blackwell, 1993).

Court, J., *Corporateering: How Corporate Power Steals your Personal Freedom* (New York: J. P. Tarcher/Putnam, 2003).

Cowan, J., Dembour, M.-B., and Wilson, R. (eds.), *Culture and Rights:*

Bibliography

Anthropological Perspectives (Cambridge: Cambridge University Press, 2001).

Dahl, R., and Lindblom, C., *Politics, Economy and Welfare: Planning and Politico-Economic Systems Resolved into Basic Social Processes* (New York: Harper, 1953).

Davis, D., *Urban Leviathan: Mexico City in the Twentieth Century* (Philadelphia: Temple University Press, 1994).

Derthick, M., and Quirk, P., *The Politics of Deregulation* (Washington, DC: Brookings Institution Press, 1985).

Dicken, P., *Global Shift: Reshaping the Global Economic Map in the 21st Century*, 4th edn. (New York: Guilford Press, 2003).

Dixit, A., *Lawlessness and Economics: Alternative Modes of Governance* (Princeton: Princeton University Press, 2004).

Drury, S., *Leo Strauss and the American Right* (New York: Palgrave Macmillan, 1999).

Duménil, G., and Lévy, D., *Capital Resurgent: Roots of the Neoliberal Revolution*, trans. D. Jeffers (Cambridge, Mass.: Harvard University Press, 2004).

—— —— 'The Economics of US Imperialism at the Turn of the 21st Century', *Review of International Political Economy*, 11/4 (2004), 657–76.

—— —— 'Neoliberal Dynamics: Towards A New Phase?', in K. van der Pijl, L. Assassi, and D. Wigan (eds.), *Global Regulation: Managing Crises after the Imperial Turn* (New York: Palgrave Macmillan, 2004) 41–63.

—— —— 'Neoliberal Income Trends: Wealth, Class and Ownership in the USA', *New Left Review*, 30 (2004), 105–33.

Edsall, T., *The New Politics of Inequality* (New York: Norton, 1985).

Edwards, M., and Hulme, D. (eds.), *Non-Governmental Organisations: Performance and Accountability* (London: Earthscan, 1995).

Eley, G., *Forging Democracy: The History of the Left in Europe, 1850–2000* (Oxford: Oxford University Press, 2000).

Evans, P., *Embedded Autonomy: States and Industrial Transformation* (Princeton: Princeton University Press, 1995).

Fisher, W., and Ponniah, T. (eds.), *Another World is Possible: Popular Alternatives to Globalization at the World Social Forum* (London: Zed Books, 2003).

Fishman, T., *China Inc.: How the Rise of the Next Superpower Challenges America and the World* (New York: Scribner, 2005).

Fourcade-Gourinchas, M., and Babb, S., 'The Rebirth of the Liberal Creed: Paths to Neoliberalism in Four Countries', *American Journal of Sociology*, 108 (2002), 533–79.

Frank, T., *One Market Under God: Extreme Capitalism, Market Populism and the End of Economic Democracy* (New York: Doubleday, 2000).

—— *What's the Matter with Kansas: How Conservatives Won the Hearts of America* (New York: Metropolitan Books, 2004).

Bibliography

Freeman, J., *Working Class New York: Life and Labor Since World War II* (New York: New Press, 2001).

George, S., *Another World is Possible IF . . .* (London: Verso, 2003).

—— *A Fate Worse Than Debt* (New York: Grove Press, 1988).

—— 'A Short History of Neoliberalism: Twenty Years of Elite Economics and Emerging Opportunities for Structural Change', in W. Bello, N. Bullard, and K. Malhotra (eds.), *Global Finance: New Thinking on Regulating Capital Markets* (London: Zed Books, 2000) 27–35.

Gill, L., *Teetering on the Rim* (New York: Columbia University Press, 2000).

Gills, B. (ed.), *Globalization and the Politics of Resistance* (New York: Palgrave, 2001).

Gowan, P., *The Global Gamble: Washington's Faustian Bid for World Dominance* (London: Verso, 1999).

Gramsci, A., *Selections from the Prison Notebooks*, trans Q. Hoare and G. Nowell Smith (London: Lawrence & Wishart, 1971).

Gray, J. *False Dawn: The Illusions of Global Capitalism* (London: Granta Press, 1998).

Greenberg, M., 'The Limits of Branding: The World Trade Center, Fiscal Crisis and the Marketing of Recovery', *International Journal of Urban and Regional Research*, 27 (2003), 386–416.

Haggard, S., and Kaufman, R. (eds.), *The Politics of Economic Adjustment: International Constraints, Distributive Conflicts and the State* (Princeton: Princeton University Press, 1992).

Hale, D., and Hale, L., 'China Takes Off', *Foreign Affairs*, 82/6 (2003), 36–53.

Hall, P., *Governing the Economy: The Politics of State Intervention in Britain and France* (Oxford: Oxford University Press, 1986).

Hall, S., *Hard Road to Renewal: Thatcherism and the Crisis of the Left* (New York: Norton, 1988).

Harloe, M., Pickvance, C., and Urry, J. (eds.), *Place, Policy and Politics: Do Localities Matter?* (London: Unwin Hyman, 1990).

Hart-Landsberg, M., and Burkett, P., *China and Socialism: Market Reforms and Class Struggle* (New York, 2004; = *Monthly Review*, 56/3).

Harvey, D., 'The Art of Rent: Globalization, Monopoly and the Commodification of Culture', *Socialist Register* (2002), 93–110.

—— *The Condition of Postmodernity* (Oxford: Basil Blackwell, 1989).

—— 'Cosmopolitanism and the Banality of Geographical Evils', in J. Comaroff and J. Comaroff, *Millennial Capitalism and the Culture of Neoliberalism* (Durham, NC: Duke University Press, 2000) 271–310.

—— 'From Managerialism to Entrepreneurialism: The Transformation of Urban Governance in Late Capitalism', in id., *Spaces of Capital* (Edinburgh: Edinburgh University Press, 2001), ch.16.

—— *The Limits to Capital* (Oxford: Basil Blackwell, 1982).

Bibliography

Harvey, D., *The New Imperialism* (Oxford: Oxford University Press, 2003).

—— 'The Right to the City', in R. Scholar (ed.), *Divided Cities: Oxford Amnesty Lectures 2003* (Oxford, Oxford University Press, forthcoming).

—— *Spaces of Hope* (Edinburgh: Edinburgh University Press, 2000).

Hayter, T., and Harvey, D. (eds.), *The Factory in the City* (Brighton: Mansell, 1995).

Healy, D., *Let Them Eat Prozac: The Unhealthy Relationship Between the Pharmaceutical Industry and Depression* (New York: New York University Press, 2004).

Held, D., *Global Covenant: The Social Democratic Alternative to the Washington Consensus* (Cambridge: Polity, 2004).

Henderson, J., 'Uneven Crises: Institutional Foundation of East Asian Turmoil', *Economy and Society*, 28/3 (1999), 327–68.

Henwood, D., *After the New Economy* (New York: New Press, 2003).

Hofstadter, R., *The Paranoid Style in American Politics and Other Essays* (Cambridge, Mass.: Harvard University Press, 1996).

Holloway, J., and Pelaez, E., *Zapatista: Reinventing Revolution* (London: Pluto, 1998).

Jensen, D., *The Culture of Make Believe* (New York: Context Books, 2002).

Jessop, B., 'Liberalism, Neoliberalism, and Urban Governance: A State-Theoretical Perspective', *Antipode*, 34/3 (2002), 452–72.

Juhasz, A., 'Ambitions of Empire: The Bush Administration Economic Plan for Iraq (and Beyond)', *Left Turn Magazine*, 12 (Feb./Mar. 2004), 27–32.

Kaldor, M., *New and Old Wars: Organized Violence in a Global Era* (Cambridge: Polity, 1999).

Kaplan, R., *The Coming Anarchy: Shattering the Dreams of the Post Cold War* (New York: Vintage, 2001).

King, D., *The Liberty of Strangers: Making the American Nation* (New York: Oxford University Press, 2004).

Koolhaas, R., *Delirious New York* (New York: Monacelli Press, 1994).

Krasner, S. (ed.), *International Regimes* (Ithaca, NY: Cornell University Press, 1983).

Krugman, P., *The Great Unravelling: Losing Our Way in the Twentieth Century* (New York: Norton, 2003).

Lardy, N., *China's Unfinished Economic Revolution* (Washington, DC: Brookings Institution, 1998).

Lee, C. K., *Gender and the South China Miracle* (Berkeley: University of California Press, 1998).

Lee, S. K., 'Made In China: Labor as a Political Force?', panel statement, 2004 Mansfield conference, University of Montana, Missoula, 18–2 Apr. 2004.

Li, S.-M., and Tang, W.-S., *China's Regions, Polity and Economy* (Hong Kong: Chinese University Press, 2000).

Bibliography

Lomnitz-Adler, C., 'The Depreciation of Life During Mexico City's Transition into "The Crisis"', in J. Schneider and I. Susser (eds.), *Wounded Cities* (New York: Berg, 2004) 47–70.

Lu, M., Fan, J., Liu, S., and Yan, Y., 'Employment Restructuring During China's Economic Transition', *Monthly Labor Review*, 128/8 (2002), 25–31.

Luders, R., 'The Success and Failure of the State-Owned Enterprise Divestitures in a Developing Country: The Case of Chile', *Journal of World Business* (1993), 98–121.

Lyotard, J.-F., *The Postmodern Condition* (Manchester: Manchester University Press, 1984).

McCartney, P., and Stren, R., *Governance on the Ground: Innovations and Discontinuities in the Cities of the Developing World* (Princeton: Woodrow Wilson Center Press, 2003).

MacLeod, D., *Downsizing the State: Privatization and the Limits of Neoliberal Reform in Mexico* (University Park: Pennsylvania University Press, 2004).

Mann, J., *The Rise of the Vulcans: The History of Bush's War Cabinet* (New York: Viking Books, 2004).

Martin, R., *The Financialization of Daily Life* (Philadelphia: Temple University Press, 2002).

Marx, K., *Capital*, vols. i and iii (New York: International Publishers, 1967).
—— *Theories of Surplus Value*, pt. 2 (London: Lawrence & Wishart, 1969).

Megginson, W., and Netter, J., 'From State to Market: A Survey of Empirical Studies of Privatization', *Journal of Economic Literature* (2001), online.

Mertes, T. (ed.), *A Movement of Movements* (London: Verso, 2004).

Miliband, R., *The State in Capitalist Society* (New York: Basic Books, 1969).

Mittelman, J., *The Globalization Syndrome: Transformation and Resistance* (Princeton: Princeton University Press, 2000).

Muhleisen, M., and Towe, C. (eds.), *US Fiscal Policies and Priorities for Long-Run Sustainability*, Occasional Paper 227 (Washington, DC: International Monetary Fund, 2004).

Myers, N., *The Primary Resource: Tropical Forests and Our Future/Updated for the 1990s* (New York: Norton, 1993).
—— *Ultimate Security: The Environmental Basis of Political Stability* (New York: Norton, 1993).

Nash, J., *Mayan Visions: The Quest for Autonomy in an Age of Globalization* (New York: Routledge, 2001).

Navarro, V. (ed.), 'Development as Quality of Life: A Critique of Amartya Sen's *Development as Freedom*', in id. (ed.), *The Political Economy of Social Inequalities* 13–26.
—— *The Political Economy of Social Inequalities: Consequences for Health and the Quality of Life* (Amityville, NY: Baywood, 2002).
—— and Muntaner, C., *Political and Economic Determinants of Population Health and Well-Being* (Amityville, NY: Baywood, 2004).

Bibliography

Novacek, M. (ed.), *The Biodiversity Crisis: Losing What Counts* (New York: American Museum of Natural History, 2001).

Nozick, M., *Anarchy, State and Utopia* (New York: Basic Books, 1977).

Ohmae, K., *The End of the Nation State: The Rise of the Regional Economies* (New York: Touchstone Press, 1996).

Panitch, L., and Gindin, S., 'Finance and American Empire', in *The Empire Reloaded: Socialist Register 2005* (London: Merlin Press, 2005) 46–81.

Peck, J., 'Geography and Public Policy: Constructions of Neoliberalism', *Progress in Human Geography*, 28/3 (2004), 392–405.

—— and Tickell, A., 'Neoliberalizing Space', *Antipode*, 34/3 (2002), 380–404.

Petras, J., and Veltmeyer, H., *System in Crisis: The Dynamics of Free Market Capitalism* (London: Zed Books, 2003).

Piketty, T., and Saez, E., 'Income Inequality in the United States, 1913–1998', *Quarterly Journal of Economics*, 118 (2003), 1–39.

Piore, M., and Sable, C., *The Second Industrial Divide: Possibilities for Prosperity* (New York: Basic Books, 1986).

Polanyi, K., *The Great Transformation* (Boston: Beacon Press, 1954).

Pollin, R., *Contours of Descent* (London: Verso, 2003).

Poulantzas, N., *State Power Socialism*, trans. P. Camiller (London: Verso, 1978).

Prasad, E. (ed.), *China's Growth and Integration into the World Economy: Prospects and Challenges*, Occasional Paper 232 (Washington, DC: International Monetary Fund, 2004).

Rapley, J., *Globalization and Inequality: Neoliberalism's Downward Spiral* (Boulder, Col.: Lynne Reiner, 2004).

Rees, G., and Lambert, J., *Cities in Crisis: The Political Economy of Urban Development in Post-War Britain* (London: Edward Arnold, 1985).

Robinson, W., *A Theory of Global Capitalism: Production, Class, and State in a Transnational World* (Baltimore: Johns Hopkins University Press, 2004).

Rodrik, D., *The Global Governance of Trade: As If Development Really Mattered* (New York: United Nations Development Program, 2001).

Rosenblum, N., and Post, R. (eds.), *Civil Society and Government* (Princeton: Princeton University Press, 2001).

Ross, A., *Low Pay High Profile: The Global Push for Fair Labor* (New York: The New Press, 2004).

Roy, A., *Power Politics* (Cambridge, Mass.: South End Press, 2001).

Sachs, J., 'New Global Consensus on Helping the Poorest of the Poor', *Global Policy Forum Newsletter*, 18 Apr. 2000.

Seabrook, J., *In the Cities of the South: Scenes from a Developing World* (London: Verso, 1996).

Sen, A., *Development as Freedom* (New York: Knopf, 1999).

Bibliography

Smith, N., *American Empire, Roosevelt's Geographer and the Prelude to Global-ization* (Berkeley: University of California Press, 2003).

—— *The Endgame of Globalization* (New York: Routledge, 2005).

Soederberg, S., *Contesting Global Governance in the South: Debt, Class, and the New Common Sense in Managing Globalisation* (London: Pluto Press, 2005).

—— 'The New International Financial Architecture: Imposed Leadership and "Emerging Markets",' *Socialist Register* (2002), 175–92.

Soros, G., *The Bubble of American Supremacy: Correcting the Misuse of American Power* (New York: Public Affairs, 2003).

—— *George Soros on Globalization* (New York: Public Affairs, 2002).

Stedile, J., 'Brazil's Landless Battalions', in T. Mertes (ed.), *A Movement of Movements* (London: Verso, 2004).

Stiglitz, J., *Globalization and its Discontents* (New York: Norton, 2002).

—— *The Roaring Nineties* (New York: Norton, 2003).

Tabb, W., *The Long Default: New York City and the Urban Fiscal Crisis* (New York: Monthly Review Press, 1982).

Task Force on Inequality and American Democracy, *American Democracy in an Age of Rising Inequality* (American Political Science Association, 2004).

Toussaint, E., *Your Money or Your Life: The Tyranny of Global Finance* (London: Pluto Press, 2003).

United Nations Development Program, *Human Development Report, 1996* (New York: Oxford University Press, 1996).

—— *Human Development Report, 1999* (New York: Oxford University Press, 1999).

—— *Human Development Report, 2003* (New York: Oxford University Press, 2003).

Valdez, J., *Pinochet's Economists: The Chicago School in Chile* (New York: Cambridge University Press, 1995).

Vasquez, I., 'The Brady Plan and Market-Based Solutions to Debt Crises', *The Cato Journal*, 16/2 (online).

Wade, R., *Governing the Market* (Princeton: Princeton University Press, 1992).

—— and Veneroso, F., 'The Asian Crisis: The High Debt Model versus the Wall Street–Treasury–IMF Complex', *New Left Review*, 228 (1998), 3–23.

Wallace, T., 'NGO Dilemmas: Trojan Horses for Global Neoliberalism?', *Socialist Register* (2003), 202–19.

Walton, J., 'Urban Protest and the Global Political Economy: The IMF Riots', in M. Smith and J. Feagin (eds.), *The Capitalist City* (Oxford: Blackwell, 1987) 354–86.

Wang, H., *China's New Order: Society, Politics and Economy in Transition* (Cambridge, Mass.: Harvard University Press, 2003).

Wei, L., *Regional Development in China* (New York: Routledge/Curzon, 2000).

Bibliography

Weisbrot, M., Baker, D., Kraev, E., and Chen, J., 'The Scorecard on Globalization 1980–2000: Its Consequences for Economic and Social Well-Being', in V. Navarro and C. Muntaner, *Political and Economic Determinants of Population Health and Well-Being* (Amityville, NY: Baywood, 2004) 91–114.

Wignaraja, P. (ed.), *New Social Movements in the South: Empowering the People* (London: Zed Books, 1993).

Williams, R., *Culture and Society, 1780–1850* (London: Chatto & Windus, 1958), 118.

Woo-Cummings, M. (ed.), *The Developmental State* (Ithaca, NY: Cornell University Press, 1999).

—— *South Korean Anti-Americanism*, Japan Policy Research Institute Working Paper 93 (July 2003).

World Bank, *World Development Report, 2005: A Better Investment Climate for Everyone* (New York: Oxford University Press, 2004).

World Commission on the Social Dimension of Globalization, *A Fair Globalization: Creating Opportunities for All* (Geneva: International Labour Office, 2004).

Wright, M., 'The Dialectics of Still Life: Murder, Women and the Maquiladoras', *Public Culture*, 11 (1999), 453–74.

Wu, X., and Perloff, J., *China's Income Distribution Over Time: Reasons for Rising Inequality*, CUDARE Working Papers 977 (Berkeley: University of California at Berkeley, 2004).

Yergin, D., and Stanislaw, J., *Commanding Heights: The Battle between Government and the Marketplace that is Remaking the Modern World* (New York: Simon & Schuster, 1998).

Yew, L. K., *From Third World to First: The Singapore Story, 1965–2000* (New York: HarperCollins, 1999).

Zakaria, F., *The Future of Freedom: Illiberal Democracy at Home and Abroad* (New York: Norton, 1998).

Zergan, J., *Future Primitive and Other Essays* (Brooklyn, NY: Autonomedia, 1994).

Zevin, R., 'New York City Crisis: First Act in a New Age of Reaction', in R. Alcalay and D. Mermelstein (eds.), *The Fiscal Crisis of American Cities: Essays on the Political Economy of Urban America with Special Reference to New York* (New York: Vintage Books, 1977), 11–29.

Zhang, Z. 'Mediating Time: The "Rice Bowl of Youth" in Fin-de-Siècle Urban China', *Public Culture*, 12/1 (2000), 93–113.

—— *Strangers in the City: Reconfigurations of Space, Power, and Social Networks within China's Floating Population* (Stanford: Stanford University Press, 2001).

—— *Whither China? Intellectual Politics in Contemporary China* (Durham, NC: Duke University Press, 2001).

Index

Index

236

Index

Index

238

Index

239

Index

Index

Index

Index

Index

Index

US comparison with 189, 193, 194
see also Argentina; Brazil; Chile
South East Asia 2
  ASEAN 79
  and China 120, 122, 130, 138–41 *passim*
  consent, construction of 40, 41, 53
  freedom concept 5, 19, 31–2
  neoliberal state 71, 76, 81, 85–6
  neoliberalism on trial 153, 154, 156, 163, 167–9, 175, 178
  uneven development 89, 91, 94, 96–7, 108–9, 116, 117, 118
  see also crisis *under* Asia; Indonesia; Malaysia; Singapore; Thailand
South Korea 2, 35, 169
  and China 120, 123, 134, 136, 138–40
  freedom's prospect 199, 206
  neoliberal state 72, 85
  uneven development 89–91 *passim*, 94, 96, 97, 106–12, 115, 116, 118
'sovereignty' 7
Soviet Union 117, 154
  collapse of 3, 32, 87
  freedom concept 5, 10, 22, 32
  see also Russia
Spain 12, 15
special economic zones (China) 130
sport 85, 132, 164
stagflation *see under* inflation
Stanislaw, J. 51, 208, 211
state
  authoritarianism and market economy combined *see* China
  'crony capitalism' 97
  monopoly 98
  -owned enterprises *see* SOEs
  uneven development 112, 115
  see also neoliberal state; welfare
Stevenson, C. 215
Stiglitz, J. 29, 51, 74, 152
  freedom's prospect 186, 221
  uneven development 93, 98, 111, 118, 211, 213, 214
Strauss, L. 92
Stren, R. 212
strikes *see* unions
structural adjustment 163, 188–9
student movements 99, 100
  consent, construction of 41, 42, 44
  Tiananmen Square 5, 123, 142, 176
Sudan 139, 173
Suez venture (UK) 55–6

Suharto, T. N. J. 34, 175
'supply-side' *see* monetarism
surplus, extraction of *see* FDI
surveillance 77, 105
Sweden 3, 71, 156, 206
  freedom concept 9, 15, 22
  uneven development 90, 112–15, 116

Tabb, W. 48, 210
Taiwan 2, 72, 169, 206
  and China 120, 130, 136, 138, 140, 141, 142, 146, 149
  uneven development 87, 89, 90, 94, 96, 97
Tang, W.-S. 215
tariffs 71, 100
tax 5, 60
  cuts 17, 23, 26, 54, 152
technology, new 68–9, 89, 92
  China 121, 134–5, 138
  information 3–4, 34, 157, 159
tensions *see* contradictions
terrorism, US fear of 198, 204
  '9/11' attack 5, 83, 195
Thailand 5, 41, 169
  and China 138, 139, 140
  uneven development 89, 94, 96, 97, 108, 118
Thatcher, M. 1–2, 88
  consent, construction of 39, 40, 57–63 *passim*
  freedom concept 9, 22–3, 31
  neoliberal state 71, 76, 79, 80, 82, 86
  neoliberalism on trial 164, 168, 172
think tanks 40, 44, 54, 115
Tickell, A. 207
'time-space compression' 4
Toussaint, E. 219
Townsend, M. 220
township and village enterprises *see* TVEs
trade, free and international 98
  see also export-led; imports; market economy; WTO
Trades Union Congress (UK) 59
traditions *see* values
transitional nature of neoliberal state 79–81
transnationals 7, 35–6, 80
transport 92, 131–2
Treanor, P. 207
Treasury (US) 74–5, 141, 162–3, 190, 201
  uneven development 92, 99, 111, 117
'trickle down' 64–5

245

Index

Index